BREAKFAST

BREA

KFAST

200 recipes to jump-start the day

BRIAN WILTON

Foreword by NICK NAIRN

Consultant Chef,
GEORGE McIVOR,
Baxters of Speyside

Black & White Publishing

Please note that, unless otherwise stated, the recipes in this book serve four people. Teaspoons (tsp) and tablespoons (tbsp) are proper measuring spoons and are level unless stated otherwise.

Cooking of any sort requires the application of practical and basic kitchen skills. Although every care has been taken to ensure that recipes are exact and instructions are clear and unambiguous, neither the Author, the Publisher, nor others featured will accept any claim for actual or consequential loss or damage resulting from following the recipes, instructions or advice printed in this book.

BRIAN WILTON is a globe-trotting enthusiast with a keen sense of humour and an abiding passion for wholesome and inspiring food. Despite failing his cooking badge at Scout camp, he has devised and delivered award-winning training seminars and food projects, and played a key role in the Perth Food Festival. He also organised the first 'Teaching Bairns to Cook' conference and founded one of Scotland's most prestigious dining events, the annual Scone Palace Grand Buffet. Consultant Chef, GEORGE McIVOR, is executive Chef at the world-famous Baxters of Speyside. He is a Master Chef of Great Britain, Chairman of the judges of the Federation of Chefs, Scotland, and led the team of chefs who designed Stakis breakfasts throughout the UK.

First published 2002
by Black & White Publishing Ltd
99 Giles Street, Edinburgh EH6 6BZ

ISBN 1 902927 38 9

A CIP catalogue record for this book is available from The British Library.

Book designed by Janene Reid
Additional Photoshop work by Simon Fleming

Printed and bound by RDC Group Ltd

contents

ACKNOWLEDGEMENTS

Like hand-me-down clothes which get altered, repaired or lose their labels as they go through life, it is sometimes difficult to tell where recipes originated. In this age of the Internet this is even more applicable. Wherever known, reference works used have been listed in the Further Reading section at the end of this book. Where they have not been credited it is that the source is unknown or obscure. Any inadvertent plagiarism is regretted and if brought to the Publisher's attention will be credited in subsequent printings. Thanks are due to the Home-grown Cereals Authority, Tate and Lyle, the Seafish Industry Authority and many other companies too numerous to mention.

Photographs in this book are reproduced by kind permission of the following: specially commissioned images by Steven Kearney, cover, pp. ii, x, 2, 7, 11, 14, 31, 38, 58, 66, 82, 92, 100, 112, 128, 136, 140, 152, 156, 161, 166 and 174; the Home-grown Cereals Authority, pp. vii, 19, 22, 23, 42, 47, 50, 55, 71, 74, 79, 89, 96, 105, 117, 121 and 125; British Egg Information Service, pp. viii, 97, 179 and 191; Kenwood, pp. 11 and 85; Lakeland Ltd, pp. 27, 49, 124 and 133; Sea Fish Industry Authority, p. 149.

foreword

Increasingly, research shows us that breakfast is the most important meal of the day; it is the replenishment of the body's reserves, depleted during sleep, that sets us up for the day. Faced with the choice of either an extra 20 minutes in bed or breakfast, unfortunately many of us opt for the extra 20 minutes' kip, thereby depriving ourselves of the energy to withstand the rigours of modern life.

Hopefully *Breakfast* will introduce more people to the benefits of starting the day with food in your belly. A wonderful variety of breakfast goodies are revealed to us in this hugely informative, well-written and humorous book. From the definitive recipe for porridge through a comprehensive tour of the traditional Scottish breakfast, to the full range of modern, healthy breakfast options, *Breakfast* gives you all the information you need to prepare your perfect start to the day.

The book is laid out in a clear and concise manner, peppered throughout with well-researched, vitally important health notes, to give you a better understanding of how to construct a nutritious, as well as tasty, breakfast. The handy 'cooks' notes' will make food preparation that bit easier and hopefully encourage you to get the best from the day's most important meal – your breakfast. As a relatively recent convert to breakfasting myself, I can honestly promise you that this book will be of much more use to you than that extra 20 minutes in bed.

Yours, replete with a good breakfast

NICK NAIRN
May 2002

introduction

Breakfast like a king

Lunch like a lord

Dine like a pauper

Over 200 years ago Dr Samuel Johnston insisted that the best meal in the whole of Britain was breakfast in Scotland. It was certainly the main meal of the day north of the border and the birthplace of many classic elements of the modern British breakfast – porridge, kippers, smoked haddock, marmalade, black pudding, white pudding and a host of other dishes that we managed to keep hidden from old Sam.

The fact that, nutritionally speaking, breakfast is the most important meal of the day certainly seems to have been proved beyond doubt as far as children are concerned and it is suggested that the same benefits apply to adults. What's not surprising – but rather frightening – is that a higher percentage of breakfast 'skippers' come from low-income families, giving an additional depressing meaning to the poverty trap.

The opening quote shows that even the ancients understood the importance of a good healthy meal in the morning and a much lighter one in the evening. These lessons seem to have been forgotten over recent decades, and breakfast in Britain has become the Cinderella of our nutritional intake. Book after book by culinary icons either totally ignore it or give it scant attention. It's also safe to say that many of our hotels totally fail to appreciate the art or the importance of breakfast, frequently leaving its unimaginative production to the lesser stars of their kitchens.

In a 1999 study of almost 37,000 UK youngsters, the stats on skippers were as follows:
- 10–11-year-olds: 8%
- 12–13-year-olds: 24%
- 14–15-year-olds: 29%.

The percentage of youngsters having just a drink were:
- 10–11-year-olds: 11%
- 12–13-year-olds: 23%
- 14–15-year-olds: 31%.

What this boils down to is that, of the 36,856 children questioned, 22% had just a drink or nothing at all for breakfast. Scaling that figure up, there are 2.6 million of our children going to school with nothing to eat. In the USA it's estimated that the figure is 12–14 million. (Schools Health Education Unit)

THE CASE FOR BREAKFAST

Breakfast 'skippers' have been found to have higher plasma cholesterol levels than 'eaters' and surprisingly, even those eaters who had bacon and eggs still had lower cholesterol levels than the skippers – but not as low as cereal eaters. Another study showed that, on average, skippers are heavier than eaters because they tend to gorge more when they do eat later in the day, and the establishment of such an eating regime can easily lead to obesity. Bearing in mind the dangers of obesity and high cholesterol (heart attacks, diabetes and some cancers), establishing good breakfast habits in children assumes great importance for their well-being in later life.

A significant proportion of teenage skippers have also been shown to fall short of the recommended daily intake of a range of key nutrients. In the case of iron, this is particularly important to teenage girls, in whom iron deficiency anaemia isn't uncommon. Indeed, girls also suffer from skipping breakfast when social pressures push them into the dieting mode just when they most need those vitamins and minerals.

Skippers also seem to suffer in the mental performance stakes as well. In numerous studies, eaters have been shown to score better than skippers on functions such as reaction time, problem-solving, memory, work rate and vocabulary testing, whilst their absenteeism is also lower than that of skippers.

The final piece of evidence in the case for breakfast is of social rather than nutritional benefit: it encourages families to sit down together and interrelate, an important but frequently unappreciated boon to the emotional well-being of school-age children.

All this is a bit difficult to remember when you're rushing around demented, grabbing a quick bite before you go to work, or chasing cereal-eating youngsters on the hoof searching for their shoes and bits of homework.

MAKE IT YOURSELF

Because of our modern hectic lifestyles, cooking is a lost art in many homes and we have a generation of youngsters growing up thinking that all food comes out of packets, cans, sachets and chilled meal containers. And yet, as George and I can testify, youngsters are incredibly receptive to the creative process of preparing and cooking food and so we have deliberately included a whole chapter aimed specifically at them.

Breakfast or brunch probably offers the best chance of the family eating together when the smell of home-made bread rather than the ping of the microwave rouses everyone from their beds. And don't laugh. Bread-making can be a viable option for those quieter moments when time unfolds slowly in front of you to reveal a day off, a holiday or a weekend when you can indulge your creative streak and eat together as a family.

Although we've concentrated on breakfasts rather then brunches, you needn't be restricted by convention or the clock. Unlike teenage boys, who wolf down colossal bowls of cereal regardless of earth time, we can be a little more sophisticated. In addition to the ever-popular bacon sarnie or buttie, you can enjoy many of the quick and easy breakfast dishes in the pages that follow at any time as they're great for all-day snacks or late-night munchies.

As you'll see, George and I are graduates of the make-it-yourself school, whether it be bread, blended tea and coffee, fruit juice, jams and marmalades, sausages, ketchups, baked beans, muesli or whatever. The satisfaction and sense of achievement to be gained is worth its weight in gold and if, in the process, we adults can persuade our children to follow in our culinary footsteps, then we will have left them and *their* children a very valuable legacy.

Enjoy your breakfasts!

BRIAN WILTON
Crieff, Perthshire

GEORGE McIVOR
Baxters of Speyside

Cereals (including porridge) are the simplest, most convenient and nutritious choice for young people, the study opposite finding that it is the most popular breakfast in the UK.

a liquid start

The most common jump-start to the day is a hastily made jolt of caffeine in the form of tea or coffee. With a bit of planning, though, we could be enjoying the deluxe versions of these and some sustaining home-made juices.

MILK

When you consider that a young calf feeding on milk alone will double its birth weight in 50 days, it's not surprising that milk is one of our most valuable foods.

Pasteurised whole milk With a fat content of about 4%, this is the traditional milk, although sales of semi-skimmed and skimmed milks combined have now overtaken those of whole milk. Storage life unopened and refrigerated is about five days; open and refrigerated, three to four days; frozen, about three months but it should then only be used for cooking.

Standardised milk With a fat content reduced to a minimum of 3.5%, this type of milk is commonly sold in other EC countries as 'whole' milk and is now being made available in Britain as part of the EC single market. Storage is as for pasteurised whole milk.

Pasteurised semi-skimmed milk This has a fat content of about 1.6% and is now the most popular milk in the UK.

Pasteurised skimmed milk This has nearly all the fat removed leaving only about 0.1%. With the removal of the fat, vitamins A and D are also removed.

Pasteurised homogenised milk This is whole milk in which the cream globules have been mechanically broken up into smaller and more uniform particles which can't rise to the top and thus stay evenly dispersed throughout the milk.

Pasteurised Channel Islands milk This comes, of course, from Jersey, Guernsey and South Devon dairy breeds and has a high fat content of about 5%.

Sterilised milk Using a more severe form of heat treatment than pasteurisation, this milk is heated to 115–30°C for 10–30 minutes, producing a slight change in colour and a caramelised flavour. Sterilised milk is available in whole, semi-skimmed and skimmed varieties and is packaged in long-necked glass bottles with crown caps or in plastic bottles with blue foil caps. It will keep unopened for several months, and once opened will keep for up to five days in the fridge.

Ultra Heat Treated (UHT) milk Heated up to 138°C for 1–2 seconds and then hermetically sealed, UHT milk and cream will last unrefrigerated for up to three months and opened and refrigerated for 4–5 days. The downside is that the process destroys almost all the natural taste of the milk and cream and replaces it

- Most cow's milk for direct human consumption has been pasteurised to destroy all disease-producing organisms by being heated up in one of many different combinations of temperature and time.
- All milk should be refrigerated and stored in opaque containers since even indirect light destroys the vitamin B content and produces unpleasant flavours in the milk.
- Always cover milk in a fridge since it picks up other flavours very easily.

CALCIUM
- Calcium is vital for growing bones and teeth.
- Children replace their skeletons every two years, while an adult's is replaced every 7–10 years.
- There is virtually no difference in the calcium content of whole, semi-skimmed and skimmed milk.
- To get the same amount of calcium as in the old 'pinta' you would need to eat 6 large slices of brown or white bread, 3 medium oranges or 3 cans of baked beans.
- *Daily calcium needs:* aged 1–3: 350g; aged 4–6: 450g; aged 7–10: 550g; aged 11–18: 800g (girls) and 1000g (boys); aged 19+: 700g; breast-feeding mums: about 1250g.

with a cooked flavour. Whilst it may be of benefit to some sections of the catering industry, its best use is in cooking rather than in tea and coffee where it effectively negates the subtle flavours that have taken blenders years to perfect.

Cow's milk substitutes The most common substitute for cow's milk is soy milk made from soya beans and water, but sheep's and goat's milk are sometimes used too, the latter becoming more widely available, especially for those with a cow's milk intolerance. It's similar in composition to cow's milk, tasting slightly richer but being lower in cholesterol and more easily digested. Contrary to some opinion, when fresh, neither milk is tainted by any underlying animal flavours.

TEA

When tea was first introduced in America the women of the day allegedly infused the tea, threw away the resulting liquid and served the tea leaves with sugar or syrup. Tea has been part of our staple breakfast diet since the 1800s when it supplanted beer – much to the disgust of the beer-lovers of the time – and we now drink an incredible 175 million cups a day in the UK. It used to be credited with great medicinal properties, giving rise to brand names such as PG (Pre-Gestive) and Typhoo (Chinese for doctor). That it is a pick-me-up can't be disputed and the breakfast cuppa is probably the most important one of the day. The pick-me-up component is, of course, caffeine – one of the most common drugs that we consume and present not only in tea, but in coffee, cocoa and all cola drinks.

Nowadays we have a huge selection of teas in our grocers and supermarkets and it's fun to kick over the traces and experiment a bit. The grand-sounding Academy of Food and Wine has discovered that, by pairing certain teas with specific foods, not only is the flavour of the food enhanced but the specific quality of the tea is highlighted. One expert recommends Darjeeling with both bacon and eggs and kippers – it's tolerant of fatty food – and Ceylon with sausages! We're not suggesting you go to those lengths but should you wish to become a bit of a tea expert then the table from the Tea Council on p. 6 may be interesting.

And tea blenders may cringe but, if you would like to experiment, there's no reason why you shouldn't mix various proportions of a favourite tea (loose or in teabags) with something a little more exotic, such as Lapsang Souchong or Earl Grey.

Most of us know how to make a good pot of tea but for visitors from outer space, here's how we Earthlings do it.

Next time you murmur, 'Ah . . . there's nothing like a nice cup of tea', you might be interested in what it's actually doing to you:

- stimulating the cortex of your brain
- improving your attention, concentration and co-ordination
- acting on your kidneys to increase water elimination
- stimulating your gastric secretions
- stimulating the action of your heart
- making some of your muscles less susceptible to fatigue.

Tea is also a major source of flavonoids, said to reduce the risk of cancer and cardiovascular disease.

Now you know! But don't overdo it since too much caffeine can result in excessive skin sensitivity, heartbeat irregularities and muscular trembling!

Type	Country of origin	Brewing time	Milk/black/ lemon	Characteristics
Darjeeling	India	3–5 mins	Black or milk	Delicate, slightly astringent flavour
Assam	India	3–5 mins	Black or milk	Full-bodied, with a rich smooth malty flavour
Ceylon blend	Sri Lanka	3–5 mins	Black or milk	Brisk full flavour with a bright colour
Kenyan	Kenya	2–4 mins	Black or milk	Strong with a brisk flavour
Earl Grey	China	3–5mins	Black or lemon	Flavoured with the natural oil of citrus bergamot fruit
Lapsang Souchong	China	3–5 mins	Black	Smoky aroma and flavour
China Oolong	China	5–7 mins	Black	Subtle, delicate and lightly flavoured

- Store tea in an airtight container at room temperature.
- Always use freshly drawn cold water. In order to extract the best flavour from tea, the water must contain oxygen, and this is reduced if the water is boiled more than once or if it comes from the hot tap.
- Ensure that kettles or water boilers are de-scaled regularly.
- Ensure that teapots are spotlessly clean. Contrary to a popular old wife's tale, teapots should not have a layer of brown tannin on the inside.
- Always warm the teapot so that the water poured on to the tea stays around boiling-point for as long as possible.
- Use one teabag or one rounded teaspoon of loose tea per cup.
- Allow the tea to brew for the recommended time before pouring. If that's too strong, use less tea rather than pouring it out before it's fully infused.
- Purists will suggest that you use a glazed earthenware, porcelain or glass teapot rather than stainless steel as they hold the heat better.

Pouring milk into the teacup first blends it more easily with the tea. If put in after, it precipitates the release of tannins that stain the cup.

COFFEE

After decades of producing tepid dishwater masquerading as coffee, it's a matter of great rejoicing that the UK has, over the past few years, shrugged off its reputation for serving some of the worst coffee in Europe. Now there are specialist coffee-houses springing up in cities just as there were in the 17th century when coffee was first introduced to Britain.

The interest in good coffee has burgeoned and there's now a marvellous range of original, blended and flavoured coffees. As with tea, they're available in a variety of packs – roasted beans, ground, vacuum-packed in foil, portioned sachets suitable for various sized cafetières – and as with tea, some original and single-source coffees lend themselves to breakfast use: Kenyan, Colombian and Colombian Decaffeinated.

Legend has it that coffee was discovered about 1200 years ago by a young goat herder in Arabia, who noticed that his goats became more lively after eating the berries and leaves of a certain bush. The word is said to come from the Arabic 'kahw' meaning 'strength and vigour'.

The world of coffee is full of mystique, and each type has its own characteristics.

Kenyan   Brisk and invigorating, with a unique sharp flavour
Colombian   Well rounded and mellow, with a slightly nutty flavour
Colombian Decaffeinated   Full roasted, with a smooth, full bodied flavour
Costa Rican   Smooth and rich, with a delicate full flavour
Old Java   Mature and full bodied, with a distinctive flavour
Mysore Rich   Made from pure South Indian arabica coffee for a full but subtle taste
Mocha   This rich heavy coffee from the highlands of Ethiopia has a pungent,
                            exotic aroma and unique flavour

However, if you really want to go back to basics then experiment until you find a coffee that you like and buy the roasted beans. Just as with tea, you can also blend beans to your own taste, but only grind what you need, when you need it.

Cafetières It is probably the introduction of cafetières from France that has brought the art of good coffee-making into so many more homes. Here are some tips for making the perfect cup.

- Just as in good tea-making, always use freshly drawn cold water.
- Warm the cafetière with hot water.
- Add the required amount of ground coffee. Don't be miserly with it!
- Unlike in tea-making, don't use boiling water. Boil it by all means but leave it for a couple of minutes until the temperature drops (usually to around 95°C) and then pour it over the ground coffee and stir thoroughly. At this temperature the water extracts the desired substances quickly. If it's boiling, some of the flavour disappears with the steam and the coffee becomes bitter.
- With the plunger up, put on the lid and leave to stand.
- After about two minutes, press the plunger down slowly and pour.
- A stronger drink is produced by using more ground coffee, not by letting it stand for longer.
- Once ground coffee is opened it begins to deteriorate so seal the packet and store it in the fridge.
- Don't reheat left-over coffee and never reuse spent coffee grounds. The result will be bitter and nasty.
- Don't let coffee stand for longer than 20 minutes: it will be bitter and unpleasant

Espresso As if converting to cafetières wasn't a large enough leap, the scene becomes even more complicated when we consider espresso coffees. Whilst it will be some time before most homes have an espresso machine, they're coming down in price so it's only a matter of time before we all have one!

Espresso is the Italian for 'pressed out'. The process involves a combination of steam and water being forced through finely ground espresso coffee beans at very high speed. The flavours and aromas released are intense, which is why espresso is always served in small cups. It is also the basis for many other speciality coffees such as cappuccino (add frothed milk and a sprinkling of chocolate), latte (add steamed milk) or mocha (add steamed milk and chocolate).

HOT CHOCOLATE

Youngsters often like hot chocolate for breakfast, especially on a cold winter's day. Use full-cream milk for a quality drink, but whether you stir the powder into hot milk or pour the hot milk over the powder makes little difference. However, mixing the chocolate into a paste with a tiny drop of milk beforehand makes for a frothier drink, as does whisking in the pan. And if you run out of chocolate powder, just grate up a good block of chocolate instead.

Microwave The simplest way of making hot chocolate – or any hot milk drink, for that matter – is just to heat your mug of milk in the microwave for 2–2$^1/_2$ minutes, depending on the wattage. Add your chocolate and hey presto . . . no dirty pan to scrub. For those of us with a sweet tooth, a $^1/_2$ teaspoon of sugar can be added, and a nice finishing touch is to top it off with a marshmallow. Another luxurious addition – probably more appropriate to adults – is a blob of double cream topped with either a sprinkling of chocolate powder or a few shavings of solid chocolate. Most kids also love a swirl of squirty UHT cream, particularly if you let them dispense it.

Remember: children can't handle such hot drinks as adults, so don't fill the cup or mug up to the brim. Leave some space for adding cold milk.

WATER

We've never been great water drinkers in this country but this is changing as more and more of us are being exposed to US-style water-coolers in our offices and leisure centres. We're told that we should drink a minimum of 2 litres a day but many of us don't consume anything approaching this. In fact, some of us don't drink a drop from one week to another, thinking that drinking any fluid gives us all the water we need. Sadly we're wrong, as neither beer and gin and tonics nor tea and coffee count so we should at least try to start the day with a glass of ice-cold water.

If you're worried about the quality of your tap water then you'll no doubt prefer bottled water. To the average consumer there is very little difference between mineral water and spring water, but broadly speaking:
- mineral water (forming 69% of UK consumption) must be bottled at source and can receive some minor treatment
- spring water need not be bottled at source and can receive more in-depth treatment to ensure consistent quality.
Additionally, bottled water can be still (56% of the market) or sparkling.

Water is said to increase concentration, reduce susceptibility to stress, improve skin texture and improve respiratory health and digestive and urinary function. If you're lucky enough to live in a hard water area then you're also 10–15% less likely to suffer heart attacks or strokes than if you live in a soft water area.

Diuretics are chemical substances that help rid the body of excess fluids: tea, coffee and alcohol act as diuretics by blocking the brain secretion of the anti-diuretic hormone. Too much of those drinks – especially alcohol – can make you very dehydrated.

FRUIT JUICE

Even the world of fruit juice has become a bit of a jungle over the past few years with a huge array of seemingly similar products on the market, very few of which tell us in layman's terms how they're made. Most exotic juices are made from concentrate in their country of origin and then reconstituted with water at this end and treated in various ways to produce 'long life' juices (shelf life of 6–9 months) and short life/chilled juices (shelf life of 20–60 days).

Freshly squeezed/unpasteurised Oranges and grapefruit are shipped here from around the world – a journey that can take up to three weeks – and stored under refrigeration for up to a further three months. After squeezing, most juices are lightly pasteurised, packed and delivered to retailers/wholesalers within 24 hours. They must be kept chilled. If pasteurised they should last (unopened) for about 2–3 weeks. If unpasteurised then they have a shelf life of just a few days. Generally speaking, the more you pay for a juice, the fresher it is. However, orange juice can be pepped up by adding a good few dashes of lemon or lime juice (bottled will be fine), as can tomato juice. Alternatively, add a few dashes of Worcester sauce to tomato juice or, if you're really brave, Tabasco.

Juice mixtures As UK juice consumption has increased, so too has the variety of single exotic juices and mixtures, both commercial and domestic: mango, cranberry, passion-fruit, carrot, mixed vegetable and blends of pineapple and passion-fruit, mango and orange, raspberry and orange, raspberry and apple, mango and carrot, cranberries and apple. Don't be taken in, however, by juice lookalikes stored on supermarket cool shelves next to real fruit juices. The latter are normally 100% pure juice whereas the lookalikes are only 17–18% pure juice and are chock-a-block with sugar and flavourings. For a much healthier alternative to conventional fizzy drinks and sickly squashes, try using a mixture of fruit juice and diet lemonade, soda or sparkling water. Even the cheapest long-life juices are transformed, and at least you know that the kids are getting some goodness fed to them in an enjoyable form.

Making your own After all that, the best fruit juice around is the juice you make yourself. You need never have any wastage since you only squeeze what you need, when you need it and, even buying on a domestic scale from the supermarket, there are frequent special offer bags of citrus fruits which give excellent value for money. On a larger scale, speaking to your nearest fruit and vegetable wholesaler or even visiting a fruit market yourself can produce significant savings. And if you get really serious about it you can buy an electric juice extractor – a miniature spin-dryer that sucks out the moisture from fruit and vegetables by centrifugal force – for no more than the cost of a bottle of blended whisky (what a difficult choice!).

The essence of juice extraction is to experiment. Apples produce the best and cheapest fruit juice which can be drunk on its own or used in a variety of combinations. Choose really flavoursome apples such as Cox's, or add a cooking apple to give more bite to a bland juice. The following fruits are also great juicing favourites, either on their own or mixed with one another: apricots, bananas, black currants, blueberries, brambles, cherries, cranberries, grapefruit, grapes, kiwi fruit, lemons, mangoes, melons, nectarines, oranges, peaches, pears, pineapple, strawberries, raspberries . . . on and on it goes! However, if using citrus fruit, pierce the skin a few times and microwave them on high for 5–10 seconds so as to extract the maximum juice, and always peel them before juicing or the bitter pith will spoil the resultant juice.

Freshly squeezed orange juice

You can also extract juice from any vegetable but the most common ones used in addition to carrot and celery (which both go well with apple juice) are beetroot, broccoli, cabbage, cucumber, peppers (capsicums), spinach, mild onions – shallots or red onions – and tomatoes. Some herbs and spices also make good additives – cinnamon, basil, mint, parsley, root ginger and sorrel, to name just a few. If you want your vegetable juices pepped up a bit, add some cayenne pepper or chilli powder.

Home-made fruit and vegetable juices must be used within one or two days, and of course, without any chemicals, many of them will discolour although that shouldn't affect the taste. If you have a glut of fruit or vegetables then you can make juice and freeze it in ice-cube trays or small plastic containers. This is especially useful for creating a collection of vegetable juices – a stockpile! – to add to gravies or soups in the winter months.

Juice extractor

To make good use of spare citrus fruit try the following.

- Squeeze it and freeze it, and if you're interested in making marmalade with it when you have a bit more time, freeze the skins as well. Frozen skins will last almost indefinitely and the freezer life of juice is about six months. (The frozen skins can be put to another very good use as containers in which to serve tinned grapefruit or both of the recipes in Chapter 2 (*see* p. 32).

- Cut it into thin slices and freeze it. It's very useful for brightening up and cooling down soft drinks and gin and tonics! To prevent the slices from sticking together when freezing, lay them out on a tray on a polythene bag or sheet of baking paper.

- Try drying the rinds very slowly in the oven, grating or grinding them up and adding them to stewed fruits or to sugar to give flavour. In an airtight container they'll last for many months.

HOT TODDY

On the flimsy pretext that if you have flu or a heavy cold, you can't enjoy your breakfast, here's a version of the hot toddy that Superman uses to combat Kryptonite sniffles (so I tell my children!). If this is for a youngster, use your discretion about the whisky.

Empty the sachet of cold cure into a mug • Add lemon juice and half-fill the mug with boiling water • Add at least 2 laden teaspoonfuls of honey to taste • Add the whisky • Stir well. • Drink as hot as bearable • Get relative to help you to bed.

Serves 1

1 sachet proprietary lemon cold cure powder
Juice of 1 lemon or equivalent amount of bottled lemon juice.
Boiling water
Honey to taste
Tot (or more) of whisky, rum, brandy or whatever spirit takes your fancy

NICK NAIRN'S EYE-OPENER

Whenever George stays with good friend and fellow chef Nick Nairn, he's always treated to Nick's favourite breakfast juice, which is brimful of healthy ingredients. For a really cool drink, either store the fruit in the fridge overnight or, as this fresh juice does not discolour, make it the night before and allow it to chill until breakfast.

Cut the carrots, oranges and apples into chunks • Process all the ingredients through a juice extractor or blender • Garnish with a twist of orange or lemon or a mint leaf.

VARIATION
Put half a cup of proprietary juice into the liquidiser and then gradually add the chopped ingredients, drizzling extra liquid in if necessary • Strain the juice through a fine sieve or mesh • As an optional extra, slice a small banana and fold it into the drink together with 1 tsp runny honey • Garnish as before.

Makes about 700ml (24^{1}/$_{2}$fl. oz, or enough for 3–4 glasses)

3 medium carrots, peeled
2 juicy oranges, peeled
2 Cox's Orange Pippin apples, peeled and cored
15g (^{1}/$_{2}$oz) root ginger, peeled
Mint leaves to garnish (optional)

SCOTTISH BREAKFAST SMOOTHIE

Mix together the milk, honey and yoghurt in a bowl • Soak the oats in the mixture for 15 minutes • Place in a food processor with the banana and purée until smooth, gradually adding the raspberry or cranberry juice • Chill and serve.

150ml (5^{1}/$_{4}$fl. oz) semi-skimmed milk
1 tbsp clear honey
150g (5oz) natural yoghurt
125g (4^{1}/$_{2}$oz) porridge oats
1 banana, peeled and sliced
450ml (^{3}/$_{4}$pt) raspberry or cranberry juice

FRESH TOMATO JUICE

Place the tomatoes, celery, onion, Tabasco and water into the food processor bowl and blitz until smooth • Taste and fine-tune the seasoning with sugar, salt, black pepper and lemon juice • Add extra water, whisking it in until the thickness is to your liking • Chill overnight before serving.

Makes about 500ml (17fl. oz)

8 ripe tomatoes, cored and peeled

5cm (2in) piece of celery, grated

1 tsp grated onion

3 drops of Tabasco

150ml (5^1/$_4$fl. oz) water

A pinch of sugar

Salt and freshly ground black pepper

A squeeze of lemon juice

COOKED TOMATO JUICE

Place the tomatoes, water, onion, celery, parsley and basil in a medium pan • Season with salt and pepper • Simmer for 30 minutes • Pass through a sieve, pressing down on the ingredients to extract maximum juice • Discard the residue • Taste and adjust the seasoning with Tabasco, lemon juice and ketchup if needed • Whisk in extra water if the juice seems too thick • Cool and store in the fridge.

Makes about 500ml (17fl. oz)

8 ripe fresh tomatoes, roughly chopped *or* 1 x 400g tin of chopped plum tomatoes

150ml (5^1/$_4$fl. oz) water

1 small onion, chopped

2 sticks of celery heart with leaves

4 basil leaves, torn

4 parsley stalks, chopped

Salt and freshly ground black pepper

3 drops of Tabasco

A squeeze of lemon juice

1 tbsp tomato ketchup for added sweetness (optional)

TOMATO, CUCUMBER AND YOGHURT JUICE

Blitz together all but the salt, pepper and lemon juice • Taste and adjust the seasoning with salt, pepper and lemon juice • Pass through a sieve, discarding the residue • Add extra water if the juice seems too thick • Chill and consume within 2 days.

Makes about 550ml (19fl. oz)

300ml (10^1/$_2$fl. oz) tomato juice

^{1}/$_2$ a small cucumber, peeled, seeded and chopped

^{1}/$_2$ a small clove of garlic, crushed with a

pinch of salt

4 drops of Tabasco

6 mint leaves

150ml (5^1/$_4$fl. oz) plain yoghurt

150ml (5^1/$_4$fl. oz) water *or* light chicken stock

Salt and black pepper

Lemon juice

cereals, yoghurt and fruit

If you aspire to be a centenarian then this is the chapter to devour – fresh fruit, yoghurt and simple oat-based cereals will most certainly increase your chances. If your sights aren't that high, this is still the outstanding breakfast health zone.

OATMEAL

We couldn't possibly start off this chapter with anything other than oatmeal – Scotland's most famous staple commodity that has achieved cult status amongst healthy eaters over the last few years.

Some interesting traditions and rituals are associated with eating porridge. For instance, in the old days in Scotland it was always served in individual wooden bowls, each of which was twinned with a separate, smaller, china or pottery bowl of cold milk or cream. The porridge would be served very hot and each horn spoonful would be dipped into that bowl of cream or milk before being eaten so that the porridge stayed hot, the milk stayed cool and, being made of horn, the spoon didn't burn your mouth. Cunning! Another habit that ensured good luck and the dispersal of evil spirits was stirring the porridge clockwise with a thin tapered stick known as a 'spurtle' or 'spirtle' during cooking – giving rise to insults such as 'spurtle-leggit' and 'spurtle shanks' – while in most Highland homes porridge was always referred to as 'they' and was, by custom, eaten standing up. Two reasons have been advanced for this: one is that this allowed the diners to leap into action quickly if attacked, and the other is that you could eat much more if you stood up – 'a staunin sack fills the fu'est' ('a standing sack fills the fullest').

Grades Oatmeal is produced in five main grades: fine, medium, coarse, pinhead and rolled. 'Fine' grade is floury and good for some kinds of baking as well as for thickening stews and soups. It can be used to make porridge, although the more usual grade for this is 'medium' and sometimes 'coarse' – depending upon personal preference. 'Pinhead' is the thickest grade and, like 'coarse', is used in haggis. 'Rolled' oats were first marketed in 1877 by the American Quaker Oat Company and are usually the whole oat kernels, steamed and rolled to make them flat. Larger, jumbo-sized rolled oats are also available.

Sweet or salty And so to that old chestnut regarding porridge and salt. There are two separate processes here that are frequently misunderstood: one involves putting salt *in* the porridge and the other involves putting salt *on* the porridge. Just as boiled potatoes need salt in the cooking water, so too does porridge. Adding it too soon, however, hardens the meal and prevents it from swelling, so don't add it until the porridge has cooked for about ten minutes (or after it's cooked, if you're using the microwave). As for salt on your porridge, many Scots would have you believe that you're a sissy if you don't sprinkle copious amounts of artery-hardening salt all over their national dish before you eat it. Don't believe them! For generations perfectly true Scots have been topping their porridge with all sorts of goodies – most of them sweet! Indeed, on bitterly cold mornings with a three-mile

Oatmeal is a rich source of soluble and insoluble fibre and is good for maintaining unmentionable bodily functions. Even more important is the ability of the soluble fibre to lower blood cholesterol and thus reduce the risk of heart disease and strokes. A US study indicated that eating five or more portions a week of cereals such as oatmeal reduces the risk of heart disease by 19%: oatmeal fibre considered alone reduces it by 29%. Oats are also a valuable source of carbohydrates – essential fuel for everyone, especially growing children and those leading an active lifestyle – and porridge made and served with that great calcium source, milk, is undoubtedly one of the healthiest breakfast dishes in existence.

walk to school ahead of them, Skye youngsters would even have a spoonful or two of whisky added. (Lots of tales also abound about Scottish workers taking a slice of porridge with them for their lunch. Treat this with scepticism and, if you don't believe us, try cutting a slice of porridge for yourself!)

TRADITIONAL PORRIDGE

Obviously the most important ingredient here is the oatmeal. Whilst commercially available rolled oats are fine for a quick breakfast, you should give thought to ringing the changes and sourcing real stone-ground oatmeal either from one of the few remaining working water-mills around the country, or from your local super-market or health food shop.

Steep the oatmeal in water overnight or for at least 2 hours • Drain and add to the simmering water • Heat until the mixture bubbles, stirring continuously with a spurtle (porridge stick) or wooden spoon • Add the salt after about 10 minutes and then cook for about another 5 minutes until it spits and belches or, as an old saying instructs, it says 'Gargunnock and Perth' • Pour the porridge into cold dishes to set • If it can't be poured and you have to lever it out in glutinous dollops, it's too thick and you should stir in some more water.

Note: The first two steps can be replaced by the old method which has you letting the oatmeal fall from your left hand in a steady rain into the boiling water whilst you stir with the spurtle in your right hand. For a creamier porridge, replace some or all of the water with milk.

Serves 2 or 3
100g (3^1/$_2$oz) medium or
  pinhead oatmeal
600ml (21fl. oz) water
1 tsp salt

MICROWAVE PORRIDGE 1

For those of us who have neither the time nor the inclination to deal with the conventional dirty porridge pot, there's always the microwave.

Place the oatmeal in a microwave-proof bowl • Stir in the water/milk ensuring that all the oatmeal is thoroughly mixed • Cover with pierced clingfilm and microwave on low for 10–12 minutes, stirring twice • Add the salt after the second stir • When cooked, leave to stand for at least 2 minutes, remove the clingfilm and serve.

Serves 1
30g (1oz) medium oatmeal
175ml (6fl. oz) water or milk or
  combination of both
^{1}/$_4$ tsp salt

MICROWAVE PORRIDGE 2

Place the porridge oats in a microwave-proof bowl • Stir the water/milk ensuring that all the oatmeal is thoroughly mixed and leaving the bowl uncovered • Cook on full power for 5 minutes (based on a 750W microwave), stirring at half-time and adding the salt • Leave to stand for 1 minute when finished • Stir well and serve • For two servings, double the ingredients and cook for 6–8 minutes.

Serves 1

45g (1^1/$_2$oz or half a cup)
  porridge oats
175ml (6^1/$_4$fl. oz) milk or water
  or combination of both
^{1}/$_4$ tsp salt

SPEEDY PORRIDGE

Our grannies would never have dreamt of porridge entering the realms of fast food but most manufacturers now give a microwave recipe. Quaker's Oatso Simple™ is one of the handiest around in which the product is packed in single-portion sachets. You just empty one into a suitable cereal bowl, mix in 180ml (6fl.oz) milk, microwave for either 2^1/$_2$ minutes (800W) or 3 minutes (650W), stir and leave to stand for one minute. Even porridge aficionados have to admit that this is real progress – and no dirty pan!

PRIZE-WINNING PORRIDGE

Those same aficionados would also insist that there's nothing quite like the taste of porridge made with real oatmeal and here's a recipe from Scott Chance, a former winner of the World Porridge Making Competition.

In a large mixing bowl, make a paste from the oatmeal and milk • Bring the water to the boil in a suitably sized saucepan • Add the water slowly to the oatmeal, stirring rapidly with a porridge spurtle • Return the mixture to the saucepan • Gently bring back to the boil, stirring all the time – use a spurtle but only in a clockwise direction so as not to provoke the devil! • Gently simmer for about 15 minutes, stirring frequently • At this point add the salt and stir for another two minutes before serving.

110g (4oz) fine oatmeal
4 tbsp milk
600ml (21fl. oz) freshly drawn
  water
1 tsp salt

Try a topping of brown sugar, soured cream and nutmeg

PORRIDGE TOPPINGS

Here's a selection that can be used singly or in combination to produce a really decadent dish:

- *sweeteners:* honey, golden syrup, maple syrup, any of a variety of brown sugars, jam
- *dried/moist fruits:* sultanas, raisins, apricots, banana, pineapple, apple, pear, prunes, mango, pawpaw, dates, fruit pureé
- *fresh fruits:* whatever is in season, fresh, poached or puréed
- *dairy products:* fresh, clotted and soured cream, crème fraîche, natural yoghurt
- *chocolate:* plain or milk chocolate chips, grated chocolate, chocolate-covered raisins, chocolate sauce
- *alcohol:* whisky, Drambuie, Cointreau, Kahlua
- *others:* muesli, chopped nuts (almonds, hazelnuts, walnuts), black treacle, spices (cinnamon, nutmeg etc.)

APPLE PORRIDGE

Cook the porridge in the usual way (either in a pan or in the microwave) but with apple juice instead of the normal milk and/or water • Stir in the apple and sultanas • Serve topped with a spoonful of crème fraîche and a sprinkling of nutmeg.

Serves 2
60g (2oz) porridge oats
450ml (16fl. oz) apple juice
1 apple, quartered, cored and grated
2 tbsp sultanas
2 tbsp low-fat crème fraîche
Sprinkling of nutmeg

RASPBERRY PORRIDGE 1

Blitz the raspberries (retaining 12 for the garnish), orange juice and honey into a purée • Put the oatmeal and milk in a heavy-based pan and bring to the boil, stirring continuously • Add the salt and simmer for about 3 minutes • Transfer to 4 bowls and stir in the cream • When cold, stir in the yoghurt • Top with the purée and decorate with a few raspberries.

25g (8oz) fresh or frozen Scottish raspberries
Juice of 1 orange
1 tsp honey
40g (1½oz) medium oatmeal
425ml (15fl. oz) milk
150ml (5¼fl. oz) single cream
4 tbsp Greek yoghurt
½ tsp salt

RASPBERRY PORRIDGE 2

Soak the oatmeal in the water or milk overnight in the fridge • Place in a pan and bring the mixture to the boil, stirring constantly to avoid lumps • When it is of pouring consistency, add the salt, honey and raspberries, retaining several for a garnish • Serve with double cream.

Serves 2 or 3
120g (4oz) medium oatmeal
1200ml (42fl. oz) water or water and milk
1 tsp salt
2 tsp heather honey
1 punnet Scottish raspberries
Double cream to garnish

PEASE BROSE

Brose is a dish of oat- or pease-meal mixed with boiling water or milk, with salt and butter added. It is the archetypal fast food but differs from that genre in that it is 100% natural and highly nutritious – being especially rich in protein as it contains twice as much (24%) as other grains.

Like porridge, pease brose is a fascinating heritage food that has always been associated with poverty. In Scotland it was a regional dish and itinerant workmen in the last century were often fed porridge for six days a week and then given pease brose as a treat on Sunday. It's still a favourite with many elderly people

Serves 1
2 dsp pease-meal
A pinch of salt
A knob of butter
100ml (3½fl. oz) water or milk or a mixture of both

who find it easy to eat and digest and it provides a reassuring link with their younger days. Try your local health food shop who should stock it.

Put the pease-meal and salt in a bowl and add the butter • In a pan, bring the water/milk to the boil • Quickly pour on to the pease-meal and whisk the mixture vigorously • It's a matter of personal choice what you add to it after that: possibly more salt and then pepper and make it a savoury dish, or go to the other end of the spectrum and sweeten it with sugar, golden syrup or honey and add optional extras such as sultanas or other dried fruit.

Note: Don't be tempted to dispense with the butter – it's essential to emulsify the mixture.

MUESLI

Health fanatic Dr Bircher Muesli didn't invent the Swiss army knife but in 1887 he did invent the breakfast cereal. Originally it was called 'raw fruit porridge' but that wasn't quite catchy enough and it became known as 'muesli'. It's difficult to imagine a healthier and more versatile start to the day and there's always the hope that – like eating celery – the energy you put into chewing it might actually burn up more calories than you're consuming!

Joking aside, it is a very adaptable option since you can experiment with a host of ingredients until you come up with a recipe that pleases everyone. Ideally, muesli should contain nothing but natural ingredients, but cutting the odd corner by using processed breakfast cereals doesn't detract too much from the original concept.

We've got used to muesli being dry – and therefore easy to store and with a long shelf life – but in fact the original was made with a variety of liquids. If you want something with a bit more kick, soak the oatmeal overnight in whisky (or whiskey, if you prefer Irish or North American types more than Scotch!).

Nuts are a valuable functional food, with walnuts and almonds leading the field. A US study showed a 35% reduction in the risk of heart disease with the consumption of 140g (5oz) a week. So, if nut loaf is not your thing, muesli is a simple way of incorporating nuts into your daily diet.

MUESLI INGREDIENTS

There's a huge selection of ingredients that you can incorporate into your home-made muesli:

- *seeds:* poppy, sesame, sunflower
- *cereals:* puffed rice, rice flakes, rolled oats, crushed Weetabix, bran flakes, rice crispies
- *dried fruits:* sultanas, raisins, apricots, banana, pineapple, apple, pear, prunes, mango, pawpaw, dates
- *fresh fruit:* whatever is in season
- *sweeteners:* honey, golden syrup, maple syrup, any of a variety of brown sugars
- *nuts:* chopped or grated walnuts, hazelnuts, pecans, flaked almonds, filberts, Brazils, grated coconut
- *liquids:* single or double cream, milk, yoghurt, orange juice, lemon juice, pineapple juice

Muesli

ORIGINAL MUESLI

Soak the oatmeal or rolled oats overnight in the water • Mix the yoghurt, lemon juice and honey in a bowl and add to the oatmeal • Wash and dry the unpeeled apples and coarsely grate them in, stirring well to prevent discolouring • Sprinkle with the chopped nuts and serve.

Serves 6
3 tbsp medium oatmeal
  or 4 tbsp rolled oats
135ml (4¹/₂fl. oz) water
170ml (6fl. oz) yoghurt
  (low-fat and natural if
  possible)
4 tsp lemon juice

4 tsp runny honey
900g (2lb) eating
  apples (red if
  possible)
4 tbsp unblanched
  almonds or hazelnuts,
  chopped

MUESLI 1

Stir together the yoghurt, oats, milk, sugar and lemon juice • Add the remaining ingredients to your own taste • Leave overnight • Add some nuts, raisins or whipped cream (optional!) and serve.

Serves 4–6
2 cups natural yoghurt
2 cups rolled oats
1 cup milk
3–4 tbsp demerara
  sugar
Juice of ¹/₂ a lemon
2 apples, cored and
  chopped
2 bananas, sliced

1 orange, cut into
  segments
Grapes, strawberries,
  or any other fruit such
  as pears, pineapple,
  blueberries, raspberry,
  kiwi to taste
Nuts, raisins or
  whipped cream
  (optional) to serve

Opposite: Granola

MUESLI 2

Here's another one that cocks a snook at metrication and uses good old-fashioned units of biscuit tin, cup and handful! Mix well with your hands and enjoy!

Makes up to 20 portions

$1/2$ a biscuit tin of porridge oats or 1 x 500g packet

$1/2$ x 250g packet of bran flakes or 8 crushed Weetabix

4 cups demerara sugar

3 handfuls of sultanas

2 handfuls of dried apple flakes

1 handful of dried apricots, cut into small pieces

2 handfuls of broken walnuts

1 handful of hazelnuts, chopped

GRANOLA

The famous W. K. Kellogg's brother, John Harvey Kellogg, came up with granola in 1877 when he was seeking an interesting meat substitute for his sanatorium patients. Basically, it consists of various combinations of grains, nuts and dried fruits, often toasted with oil and honey giving a crisp and crunchy texture.

Preheat the oven to 180°C/350°F (gas mark 4) • Mix together the bran, oats, seeds, nuts and sugar in a bowl • Spread out on to a large baking sheet and bake for 40 minutes, stirring once halfway through • Allow to cool slightly • Stir in the cinnamon and fruit • Store in an airtight container until required • To serve, spoon into a bowl and add milk.

Serves 6–8

100g ($3^1/2$oz) bran

150g ($5^1/2$oz jumbo porridge oats (Scots Old-fashioned Porridge Oats)

1 tbsp poppy seeds

25g (1oz) pumpkin seeds

100g ($3^1/2$oz) walnuts, roughly chopped

25g (1oz) brown sugar

1 tsp ground cinnamon

100g ($3^1/2$oz) ready-to-eat dried cherries and berries

CEREALS

Ever since Dr John Kellogg and his brother Will formed the Battle Creek Toasted Corn Flake Company in 1906, we've been besieged by cereals of all shapes, sizes, colours and tastes and the case for them is pretty compelling. They're frequently fortified with micronutrients such as the vitamins A, B, B_2, B_6, B_{12}, C and D, niacin and folic acid and minerals such as iron, and most will supply around 25% of the recommended daily vitamin intake – something that 'deskfasters' (the US cereal industry's name for people making do with a coffee at the office) miss out on. In the UK, cereals are eaten in over 90% of households and sales amount to over 414,000 tonnes in a market worth £1.1bn. In the world cereal-eating ranking, this brings us in second after Ireland, but ahead of both Australia and America. The two largest sectors of these RTE (ready to eat) sales are staples (simple corn flakes, for example) and children's cereals.

SWEET TOOTH

Scientists believe that we're all pre-programmed to go for the sweet things in life. Adult taste buds are located primarily on the tongue but infants have taste buds on the sides and roof of the mouth and are said to be conditioned to recognise sweet flavours because carbohydrates and sugars provide a readily available, generally safe source of energy. An acceptance and liking for the sour and salty is acquired in later life as our tastes mature – something that explains our childhood abhorrence of sprouts, cauliflower and the like! The industry certainly

seems to believe these claims: cereals aimed at the adult market are said to contain anything from 15–25g less sugar per serving then a typical 'kid-formulated' cereal.

In many of the recipes in this book we suggest using caster sugar because, being finer grained, it dissolves more easily than normal granulated sugar. If you don't have caster sugar however, don't worry. Use granulated instead. Indeed, caster sugar is basically granulated sugar ground up a bit more, while icing sugar just takes the grinding to the next stage. If you have a coffee grinder, try it!

One of Dr Kellogg's health goals was to introduce more fibre into his patients' diets. Almost 100 years later we still have a situation where it's estimated that as many as 44% of young children may suffer from constipation because of insufficient insoluble fibre. A daily bowl of cereal would go a long way towards curing that.

The most suitable grains for cereals are maize (corn on the cob), wheat, oats and rice, all of which can be puffed, shredded, flaked and extruded into all sorts of weird, wonderful (and to some of us, revolting) end products. Much of today's cereal packaging is aimed at the young market, but whilst you may see them trumpeting 'fat free' and 'vitamins added', you won't see them advertising 'up to 50% sugar'. That's what you could be buying . . . so if you're keen to learn what you're feeding your children, take some time and have a good look at the nutrition box on the package. The items to look for are 'sugar' and 'fibre'. The lower the first and the higher the second, the better the cereal.

So if you can't persuade the family to eat porridge every day and 'live to be a hundred' then try and steer them towards cereals that contain oats, nuts, raisins and other dried or freeze-dried fruits. Consumption of breakfast cereals also encourages the consumption of milk – a vitally important protein and calcium source for children of all ages.

For those of us with more gums than teeth, chomping on dried fruits such as the currants and raisins in muesli can be a painful and time-consuming business. Give up and soak them for a while (overnight is best) in boiling water or, better still, hot tea. No one seems to know why the latter is so effective, but in it, currants and raisins plump up beautifully and taste delicious.

CEREAL BARS

If you wonder what cereal bars have got to do with breakfasts, you've never been involved in ejecting young lay-a-beds out to the waiting school bus. As they dash – 'breakfastless' – for the door, a cereal bar is well suited to being passed to them like a relay-race baton. They're also a good and healthy filler for a lunch-box.

Preheat the oven to 180°C/355°F (gas mark 4) • Melt the butter in a small saucepan with the golden syrup • Stir in the muesli until evenly coated • Pour into a greased 14cm square tin and bake for 20 minutes until golden • Cool then chill in the fridge for 30 minutes before serving.

Makes 6
75g (2oz) butter
3 tbsp golden syrup
175g (6oz) muesli

YOGHURT

'Healthy' is frequently equated with 'yukky' in kids' eyes – indeed, a recent survey in Scotland showed that healthy eating was widely regarded as unpleasant and depressing – so we are indeed lucky that one of the healthiest foods of our age, yoghurt, is extremely popular. Just look at the kaleidoscopic range spread over our supermarket shelves!

Making this ancient food is extremely simple and certainly cheaper than buying it. Your home-made version will be additive free and you can monitor the amount of sugar that you use. You can also just make the flavours that your family enjoys so that you don't end up throwing out time-expired pots from the selection pack.

Your yoghurt can be made from any kind of cows' milk, as well as goats' and sheep's milk. Goats' milk yoghurt is common in Mediterranean countries and sheep's milk is frequently used to make Greek yoghurt – a great favourite in this country.

When you're adding fruit to your yoghurts, keep some of the yoghurt plain. It's a very healthy alternative wherever you might use cream: on your porridge, cereals, muesli, and of course, in a wide range of ways in general cooking (quickly reducing the heat of an over-exuberant curry, for instance).

Being fresher, the flavour of home-made yoghurt is not as sharp as the bought varieties, although both its taste and texture will depend upon the type of milk used, the yoghurt employed as the starter and the time the yoghurt takes to thicken. This is sometimes a bit hit-and-miss, so you will undoubtedly have to experiment. Take our advice and buy a simple yoghurt kit!

YOGHURT
- A useful source of calcium and phosphorous, important for strong bones and teeth.
- Contains vitamins B_2 (riboflavin) needed for healthy skin, eyes and nerve function, and B_{12}, important in the prevention of anaemia and needed for healthy cell growth and metabolism.
- May help to prevent bad breath, constipation and diarrhoea, as well as aid digestion.
- Is a healthy alternative to cream.

HOME-MADE YOGHURT

Bring the milk to the boil • Allow to cool to 38–46°C (100–15°F). Ideally you need a dairy thermometer for this – usually available at health food or cookware shops – but you can make do without it: the milk is ready for the next stage when you can comfortably hold your finger in it whilst counting up to ten. (If you think it's going to be too hot, use someone else's finger!) • Mix in the yoghurt • Pour into

Makes about 500ml (16fl. oz)
500ml (16fl. oz) pasteurised milk
2 tbsp plain active yoghurt

PROBIOTIC YOGHURTS

The healthy gut (large bowel) is home to 100,000,000,000 bacteria known as gut flora that, unbelievably, weigh nearly a kilo! It's claimed that the balance in the gut is upset by the increasingly sanitised food that we eat and our over-reliance on antibiotics that kill off the goodies and render us easy prey to the baddies.

Probiotic products are usually fermented milk drinks or yoghurts that contain live bacteria that are designed to colonise the gut, improving the microbial balance and so promoting health. Manufacturers' literature and anecdotal evidence suggest that this is true but the medical world is cautious as always and requires more proof. In the meantime, it can certainly do no harm to try them. Elderly people can fall prey more easily to stomach upsets and food poisoning so it might also be a good idea to introduce older family members to these yoghurts.

There are two major brands on the market, both packaged in small pots and so ideal for inclusion in youngster's lunchboxes. One has a very pleasant fruit taste; the other is not suited to all palates. If you choose the wrong one initially, persevere: it'll be worth it.

A yoghurt maker

two 250ml (8fl. oz) jars/containers and cover. (You can use a warmed vacuum flask in place of these) • Keep the mixture warm by wrapping in a towel or leaving in a warm place such as an airing cupboard • When the yoghurt is set (6–8 hours), stir in the required flavouring or fruit (see below) and refrigerate for 12 hours before use. If it hasn't set in that time, just leave it for another few hours.

YOGHURT FLAVOURINGS

Once you've made your yoghurt (or bought plain yoghurt from the supermarket), there are dozens of options as to what you can put in it:

- *muesli:* yoghurt muesli (or should it be muesli yoghurt?) is so healthy you can almost see it flexing its muscles! Adjust the proportions until you achieve the desired effect
- *crispy cereals:* there's such a choice of cereals these days that there's bound to be a few that the kids will love – usually the chocolate ones!
- *jam or honey:* add such sweeteners as runny honey or any good jam (preferably home-made)
- *fruits:* add any fresh or tinned fruit to hand – sliced banana, chopped or grated apples, chopped pears, fresh orange segments, tinned mandarin slices, halved grapes etc. Tinned grapefruit is particularly good with plain yoghurt.

FRESH FRUIT

One of the simplest, healthiest and most enjoyable ways of eating your way to good health – and setting the kids a good example for life – is eating fresh fruit. A long-running domestic and World Health Organisation campaign promotes the consumption of 'five a day' – five servings or portions of fruit and vegetables because they contain many essential vitamins and minerals, some of which can help combat heart disease and certain cancers. What is a serving?

Vegetables:
- one tablespoon for each year of life for children aged 1–3
- a quarter of a cup of vegetables or half a cup of salad for children aged 4–8
- half a cup of vegetables or a whole cup of salad for everyone else.

Fruit:
- a glass of fruit juice, a banana, an apple or a similar quantity of any other fruit, scaled down for younger children.

The following are just a few of the more popular fruits and vegetables commonly available in our supermarkets. Some of them may be beyond the family budget at times but there are still plenty of affordable ones that are brimful of goodness and easy to incorporate into the first meal of the day.

Bananas These are such a marvellous protein-rich, functional food that they deserve a chapter all on their own. They're a great source of fibre, are high in potassium, antioxidants, vitamin B_6, are naturally antibiotic and in general have a host of beneficial effects on the body. Best of all, they're instantly accessible – unzip a banana – which makes them ideal for youngsters (and adults) who're late out of bed and can't fit in a proper sit-down breakfast. They're also a simple lunch-box component for school kids which, together with a carton of real fruit juice, goes a long way towards the five-a-day regime. Nutritionally, bananas are best before they get to the riper, mottled stage when most of the beneficial starch has turned to sugar. For a quick burst of energy, however, go for the riper ones!

Berries Strawberries, raspberries, blueberries, cranberries, blackberries, redcurrants and blackcurrants and their relatives are an excellent example of just how clever Mother Nature really is. As recently discovered 'miracle' foods, their benefits are many and varied. With antioxidant vitamins C and E, they're especially important for immune health and neutralise what are called 'free radicals' in the body – responsible for a whole tranche of human ills, not least of them being cancer.

Fruit and vegetables are:
- a good source of soluble fibre
- low in fat
- just as good for you whether fresh, frozen or canned (as long as you watch the syrup!)
- much more sustaining than processed foods like cakes and biscuits.

MASCARPONE
Try this delicate and rich, soft cheese from Italy's Lombardy region with all sorts of fruit. It's wicked but it's wonderful!

Berries are at their best simply served on their own or with yoghurt, crème fraîche or cream; strawberries, raspberries and loganberries are a real luxury start to the day. Even tastier and healthier is the Summer Harvest recipe given later in this chapter (*see* p. 36).

Figs Fresh figs are a bit of a luxury but are a favourite accompaniment for raspberries and cream, or try them sprinkled with lemon juice and sugar. Once they're ripe they only last a couple of days so make sure you eat them at their best. Stewed dried figs have possibly never got over their 'keeps you regular' image but they're rich in potassium, calcium, magnesium and iron and may also discourage some cancers.

Kiwi fruit Almost as convenient as a banana, weight for weight the kiwi contains twice as much vitamin C as an orange and so is a vital weapon in the health armoury. Kids love them in an eggcup and they're great for their pack lunches – chop the top off, put it back in place and wrap up in cling film. The latest innovation is the golden kiwi which is slightly more pear-shaped and not quite so tart as the green variety.

Mango An opulent taste all of its own and with health benefits to match, being a good source of vitamins C and E, iron and carotenes. The easiest method of serving mango is to peel off the skin with a sharp knife or good potato peeler and then slice the flesh off the large flat stone. No accompaniment is needed but it is great with fresh strawberries.

Papaya High in calcium and vitamins A, B and C, this golden-yellow fleshed fruit is often regarded as a medicine! Also known as the 'pawpaw', it's a phenomenally fast grower in its native tropics and can reach 5m in something like 18 months.

Pears Unlike most fruit, pears improve in taste and texture if picked when they're still hard. They contain small amounts of phosphorous and vitamin A. Canned pear halves can also be used for breakfast, with yoghurt or crème frâiche decorating the hollowed-out centre.

Melons There's nothing simpler than a slice of fresh melon sprinkled with a little ground ginger or brown sugar and decorated with whatever garnish comes to hand. Melon is a healthy and attractive choice for breakfast. Although it can be stored for quite a while in the fridge, to get the best of its delicate taste take it out the night before serving and let it warm up to room temperature. The exception to this is watermelon, whose crunchy texture is best at low temperatures. Double-

---

DRIED AND TINNED FRUIT
There's a wide choice of tinned and dried fruits on the supermarket shelves that can be poached and eaten on their own or used in a fruit salad – figs, peaches, prunes, pears, apricots and apples, to name but a few. If preparing fresh grapefruit is too much for you (*see* p. 32), cool, tinned grapefruit is a great early-morning eye-opener, and there are many others that can be added to children's hot and cold cereals or used for brightening up pack lunches.

If left exposed to air, certain freshly cut fruits like pears, peaches and apples go brown due to the action of a particular enzyme. This is inhibited by acid, and dipping the cut fruit in acidulated water – water to which a small amount of acid in the form of lemon or lime juice has been added – will prevent this process. Jif produce bottles of lemon and lime juice which are always handy for such uses and for pepping up breakfast orange juice (see pp. 10–11).

Cut a thin slice off the bottom of melon portions so that they sit firmly on the plate.

wrap any melon going into the fridge with cling film to stop it absorbing any other flavours.

Getting hold of a really good watermelon in this country is a bit of a gamble, though. The test for ripeness is to bring the melon up to your ear and rap it sharply with your knuckles to hear if it sounds hollow. This doesn't guarantee that the inside is bright red and tasty but most greengrocers and supermarkets will have half melons on display so you can see what you're buying.

Unless you're going to sit on the back porch with a huge slice wrapped round your face, skilfully spitting the pips out at the scratching chickens, there's quite a bit of work in preparing a watermelon. Cut it into manageable wedges and then separate the flesh from the skin and carefully cut it into bite-sized chunks, de-seeding it as you go along. When finished, douse it liberally in sugar if you wish and store it in the fridge until it's icy cold. On the other hand, you could just give the family a big wedge each and leave them to sort the pips out for themselves!

Try making a mixed melon salad for a luxurious and healthy start to breakfast. Either cut your selected melons into bite-sized chunks or use a melon baller – or mix and match both. Add some orange or apple juice and a sprinkling of sugar and leave to blend overnight. If you want flavour rather than refreshing coolness, don't put it in the fridge. If you're including watermelon, however, cool it in the fridge overnight to improve its crispness and add just before serving. The sugar is not necessarily to sweeten the salad but to bring out the juices.

Pineapple Fresh pineapple just needs a sprinkling of sugar to turn it into 'exquisite fruit' – the translation of its original name in the Caribbean. With pineapples available all the year round, you might like to try frying or grilling slices of it with brown sugar for an unusual breakfast treat. As long as it's not consumed with over-sweetened juice, tinned pineapple is just as good for us as fresh, so tinned rings can be used for this simple dish as well.

Citrus fruits Anyone who has eaten citrus fruits in their country of origin will rarely if ever be satisfied with what's available in the UK. Whilst so many oranges are enticingly shiny and succulent-looking under the supermarket lights, when peeled they are – more often than not – chewy, dry and tasteless inside. The exception to this are the soft-skinned oranges (mandarins, satsumas etc.) that come in around Christmas, and the occasional batch in some of the better food retailers. *See* pp. 35–6 for a recipe for caramelised oranges. Skinned segments of orange also make an attractive addition to a bowl of tinned grapefruit. And to increase the eye appeal and pep up a citrus salad, use a potato peeler or zester to cut thin julienne strips of peel from oranges, lemons or limes and add to the mixture.

PEELING SOFT-SKINNED FRUIT

Carefully drop the whole fruit into boiling water for 10–30 seconds. The riper the fruit, the less time it needs. Remove, immerse in iced water and then peel the skin off with a knife.

Ice-cold grapefruit

Pitted fruit Peaches, nectarines, cherries, plums and fresh dates can all have a place on the breakfast table. Chopped or sliced, they can be added to muesli, porridge and a variety of breakfast cereals, or alternatively simply sliced and laid out attractively on a plate with some crème frâiche.

Try the recipes that follow, and go to pp. 10–13 for more information and ideas on fruit juices.

PAPAYA AND LIME SALAD

The British got the name of 'Limeys' because of the enforced consumption of lime juice in the Navy to combat scurvy. Scurvy has long gone but combine lime juice with papaya and you have a delightful dish brimming over with healthy bits and bobs! This salad can be served on its own or with a spoonful of yoghurt. It also makes a good topping for muesli.

Cut the papayas in half and scoop out the seeds with a spoon • Peel the halves and cut into manageable cubes • Finely grate the zest from the limes and sprinkle over the papaya • Squeeze the juice from the limes and place it in a small pan with the sugar • Heat gently until dissolved and allow to cool • Pour over the cubed papaya and toss well • Add the toasted almonds and serve.

3 ripe papayas

2 limes

2 tsps golden caster sugar

75g (3oz) flaked almonds, blanched and toasted

ICE-COLD GRAPEFRUIT

A marvellously refreshing beginning to a summer breakfast. Prepared properly, grapefruit is a delight to eat. Hastily done, it's a menace and you end up squirting juice all around and chewing on slivers of bitter skin. If you've got the time to spare, here's how to do it.

Cut the grapefruit in half across its equator • With a good sharp knife, cut round the central white pith and remove it. Take care not to penetrate the grapefruit skin or all the juice will seep out • Looking at the cut surface of the grapefruit you'll see that it's made up of many segments radiating from the centre. Each of these is bounded by a thin but bitter skin. Your task is to separate each segment of flesh from the skin on either side of it. This is done by gently sliding the tip of your sharp knife between the skin and the flesh, from the outer edge in towards the centre • When that's done, get out your special grapefruit knife (the one with the curved, serrated blade) and carefully cut the thick end of each wedge away from the white pith on the inside of the grapefruit skin. (If someone tells you that this takes a long time – don't believe them. It takes an eternity!) • Now sprinkle each half liberally with sugar, cover with cling film and store in the fridge overnight • If you eat a lot a grapefruit, it's worth buying some special grapefruit spoons that have a pointed end. With these you can daintily lift out each perfectly separated segment to the applause of the family.

GRILLED GRAPEFRUIT

A great tangy start to a cold winter's day. Cut and loosen the segments as before, sprinkle brown sugar or spread honey or marmalade (home-made, of course!) on top and then grill until bubbly brown. Another idea is to sprinkle a pinch of nutmeg or ginger over the surface before grilling. For a special breakfast, drain off some of the juice before grilling and replace with a teaspoonful of your favourite liqueur. Just as with the chilled grapefruit, the preparation can be done the night before and the grapefruit covered in cling film and left in the fridge.

APPLE COMPOTE

'Compote', 'poached' and 'stewed' all mean more or less the same thing, although 'compote' actually means a chilled dish of dried or fresh fruit that has been cooked very slowly in a sugar syrup so that it keeps its shape. If you make a mistake and boil it too vigorously, the fruit loses its shape and becomes a purée! Whatever you call your results, cold cooked apples for breakfast are very refreshing – either on their own with a sprinkling of sugar and perhaps a dab of yoghurt, or in porridge, muesli or conventional breakfast cereal.

Place the apples in a pan with sugar, a little water and the cloves and/or other flavourings • Cover with a lid and cook gently until tender – about 10 minutes. (If you prefer your apples to be a stew, add a little more water and simmer until the fruit breaks down) • Remove any solid flavourings, cool and refrigerate.

Serves 6

1kg (2.2lb) cooking apples, peeled, cored and cut into eighths
120g (4^1/$_2$oz) caster sugar
4–6 tbsp water
Optional extras
A few cloves tied in muslin
A good dash of lemon juice and a slice of lemon skin (just the zest – not the pith)
A 4cm (1^1/$_2$in.) piece of cinnamon stick

RHUBARB COMPOTE

Major cook books insist that rhubarb should never be eaten raw. Their writers must never have enjoyed the bitter-sweet treat of crunching through a stick of rhubarb and dipping the soggy end into a bowl of sugar between each bite. Always discard rhubarb leaves – they're extremely poisonous.

Wash and trim the rhubarb and cut into 4cm lengths • Place the rhubarb in a pan, and add all the other ingredients and a little water. (If the rhubarb has been grown in the open, it will be sourer than the 'under glass' variety and will no doubt need more sugar when serving) • Cover with a lid and cook gently until tender – about

Serves 6

1kg (2.2lb) young pink rhubarb
140g (5fl. oz) caster sugar
Two strips of orange and lemon zest (not the pith)
A pinch of cinnamon
4–6 tbsp water or orange juice

10 minutes • When cooked, remove the citrus peel and allow to cool • Serve chilled.

Sugar syrup can be flavoured with all manner of things – a vanilla pod or essence, cinnamon, cloves, lemon or lime juice and even wine or liqueur.

POACHED PEARS

Make some sugar syrup by gently dissolving the sugar in the water • Cover the pears with sugar syrup • Gently poach until the pears are soft.

VARIATIONS
Plums, nectarines, peaches and apricots can also be stewed in sugar syrup like this, either whole, cut in half or into slices. If halving the fruit, for extra taste stew the stones in the syrup (removing before eating, of course).

500g (1.1lb) caster sugar
1 litre (1³/₄ pt) water
Firm pears, peeled and either whole (with stalk) or halved

STEWED PRUNES

Soak the required number of prunes in cold water for 8 hours • Place in a pan and cover with natural apple juice • Add a few slices of lemon and the cinnamon stick • Stew gently until tender – about 10–15 minutes • Serve as it is or with yoghurt.

Prunes
Apple juice
Lemon slices
1 cinnamon stick

OTHER STEWED DRIED FRUIT

Dried fruit has fortunately cast off its wartime austerity image and there is now a wide range of temperate and tropical fruits on the market.

Wash the fruits thoroughly and soak in the water or tea for 12 hours • Place the fruit in its water in a pan • Add the sugar and lemon rind • Simmer gently until tender • Remove the fruit, reserving the juice • Boil the juice for a few minutes until it becomes syrupy • Strain the juice over the fruit and cool in the fridge overnight before serving.

Serves 4–6
450g (1lb) dried fruit (prunes, figs, apples, pears, peaches etc.)
600ml (1pt) water *or* tea (cold or hot)
225g (8oz) demerara sugar
Piece of lemon rind (just zest not pith)

AUSTRALIAN FRUIT COMPOTE

The combinations for a breakfast fruit salad are endless. Use any melons that are available – watermelon is particularly good if you can spare the time to de-seed it. Making more than you actually need is another good idea if you have hungry kids coming home from school – let them loose on this instead of the biscuit tin. Juices for fruit salads are also easy – use any fruit juice that comes to hand as long as it's not overpowering, although apple is particularly good.

Combine all the juice ingredients • Toss the fruit in the juice and leave in the fridge for an hour or more so that the mixture comes together • Serve on its own or with a blob of yoghurt, double cream or crème fraîche sprinkled with chopped nuts.

Serves 4–6
1 honeydew melon, cut into 2.5cm (1in.) cubes
1 cantaloup melon, cut into 2.5cm (1in.) cubes
2 apples, cored and cubed
2 ripe oranges, in sections
2 bananas, sliced
2 cups of grapes
1 cup of berries (whatever is available)
For the juice
115ml (4fl. oz) orange juice
1 tbsp clear honey
$^1/_2$ tsp orange blossom water
$^1/_2$ tsp rose water

BAKED APPLE

This can be served hot or cold (chilled in the fridge overnight), with or without cream or yoghurt.

Preheat the oven to 180°C/350°F (gas mark 4) • Remove the apple cores to about 2cm from the base • Run a sharp knife round the middle of each one, just cutting through the skin to allow for shrinkage • Fill with a mixture of dried fruit, nuts, a dribble of honey or brown sugar and a pinch of cinnamon • Place in a baking dish containing about 2cm of water or fruit juice • Cover and bake in the oven for about 40 minutes until tender but not mushy • If serving hot, dribble over the cooking juices. If serving cold, use yoghurt or crème fraîche.

1 large cooking apple per person
Dried fruit (raisins, prunes, figs, apples, pears, peaches etc.)
Mixed nuts, chopped
Clear honey or soft brown sugar
Ground cinnamon
Fruit juice (optional)

CARAMELISED ORANGES

Straight to the table from a night in the fridge, this zesty starter makes a delicious breakfast dish.

Heat 85ml (3fl. oz) of the water in a pan and dissolve the sugar • Bring to the boil and cook until the syrup changes into a rich brown caramel • Add the remaining

185ml (7fl. oz) water
175g (6oz) granulated sugar
8 seedless oranges

water and stir gently over a lowered heat until the caramel has melted • Leave to cool • Peel the rind and pith off all the oranges • Slice each orange into $^1/_2$cm slices across its diameter • Lay in a serving dish and cover with the caramel mixture • Leave for at least an hour but preferably overnight • Serve on its own or with double cream or yoghurt.

SUMMER HARVEST

This dish was the brainchild of Scottish fruit growers and processors, Rendalls of Blairgowrie, who sell it in frozen form. It's easy to make yourself, however, and there aren't many areas of Britain where you can't get hold of good quality berries and currants. It's brimful of colour, goodness and taste and is a very refreshing start to the day. It also makes an excellent light sweet to finish off other meals with a flourish.

Freeze all the fruit in a convenient rigid container or polythene bag • When required for use, boil the lemonade, dissolve the sugar in it and pour over the fruit salad, leaving to thaw for at least a few hours and preferably overnight. Don't be tempted to add more liquid – the soaking with sugar brings all the delicious juices out of the fruit • When thawed, taste and add more sugar if necessary before serving.

Serves 4–6

225g (8oz) raspberries
60g (2oz) strawberries
70g (2$^1/_2$oz) black currants
70g (2$^1/_2$oz) red currants
85g (3oz) blackberries
15g ($^1/_2$oz) seedless green
　grapes (for colour contrast)
210ml (7fl. oz) lemonade
1 tbsp caster sugar

FRESH BERRY COMPOTE

Like all fruit compotes, this can be a very useful breakfast accompaniment for adding to muesli, yoghurt, porridge, breakfast cereals and even French toast. Similar to the Summer Harvest recipe above but taken to the next stage, it can be made as follows.

Combine the sugar, lemon juice and water in a small pan • Heat until the sugar is dissolved, stir in the fruit and bring to the boil • Simmer for about 5 minutes or until the fruit is soft but still whole • Strain the fruit and return the juice to the pan • Add the honey and bring back to the boil, stirring well and cooking for about 7–10 minutes until the mixture will coat the back of a spoon • Allow to cool slightly and add to the fruit before serving.

Serves 4–6

100g (3$^1/_2$oz) caster sugar
Juice of 1 lemon
3 tbsp water
450g (1lb) fresh or frozen soft
　fruit
100g (3$^1/_2$oz) honey

SUMMER PUDDING

With its health-giving berries, this summer pudding is equally at home on the breakfast or lunch/dinner menu. Simple to make and great to look at, it can be served with a spoonful of yoghurt, fresh cream or whatever takes your fancy.

Place the berries and sugar in a small pan and simmer gently until soft (5–10 minutes) • Let the fruit cool and add more sugar if needed • Line a $1^1/_2$ litre ($2^1/_2$pt) pudding basin with bread slices, cutting so that they fit like a mosaic • Add the fruit and enough juice to moisten all the bread. Keep the rest of the juice • Cover the top with the rest of the bread • Lay a plate on top with at least a 500g (1lb) weight on it and leave in the fridge for at least a day or two if possible • Before serving, gently shake the pudding out on to a plate • Use the reserved juice to colour up any bits of bread that are still white • Slice and spoon out each portion.

Serves 6

750g (1lb 10oz) mixed berries
 – include redcurrants if
 possible
85g (3oz) caster sugar to taste
6–8 slices of stale sliced white
 bread, crusts removed

FRESH FRUIT KEBABS

A simple but luxurious dish that will put a smile on the face of the grumpiest breakfast companion. As an alternative to a herb in the marinade, try a tot of dark rum or a liqueur such as Cointreau.

Soak the skewers in water for an hour or two (overnight is fine) • Make the marinade by mixing the rosemary and honey with the water and bring to the boil over a low heat • Remove, cover with cling film and cool for at least a couple of hours or store in the fridge overnight • Thread a selection of fruit chunks on to the skewers and soak in the honey mixture for a minimum of 30 minutes • Preheat the grill to high, drain the fruit (reserving the liquid) and sprinkle with the sugar • Cook for about 5 minutes or until the fruit starts to brown. Brush with reserved marinade about halfway through • Serve hot, drizzled with the juice and some crème fraîche on the side.

125g ($4^1/_2$oz) clear honey
1 tsp fresh rosemary, finely
 chopped
2 tbsp water
450g (16oz) mixed fresh fruit,
 cut into equal-sized chunks
 (strawberries, kiwi, pineapple,
 mango etc.)
16 small wooden skewers or
 eight long ones cut in half
2 tsp caster sugar
crème fraîche to serve

breads, rolls and oatcakes

All bread is good for you whether white, brown or wholemeal and it's *not* fattening – it's what you put *on* it that can be! From baps to bagels, from muffins to huffkins and sourdough to soda bread, you could soon be enjoying your own home-made versions.

HOME-MADE BREADS AND ROLLS

There is an enormous selection of bread available these days, either from your local bakery (if it's survived) or from one of the in-store bakeries at the supermarket, some of which are very good. The ideal, though, is to make your own.

The words 'home-made bread' have magical properties. They summon up images of a floral-pinnied, floury-armed little old granny kneading dough on a huge farmhouse table with the old-fashioned black range glowing in the background – even if you don't have a granny like that yourself! The fact is that traditional bread-making is really very simple, extremely rewarding and the epitome of back-to-nature healthy eating. Although it won't be fortified with calcium, iron and the B vitamins like shop-bought bread, neither will your delicious home-made bread contain any preservatives so it will have a very much shorter life than the chemically-rich mass-produced variety. Kept at room temperature in an open polythene bag, it should stay fresh for at least 24 hours – even longer in a special bread bag – and after that it can be used for toast or breadcrumbs.

It has to be said, however, that home-made bread is not something you're going to knock up on a week day morning before you rush off to work. The proving times for conventional bread-making dictate that it's a weekend or holiday venture . . . unless you have a bread machine, of course!

Freezing bread Tightly wrapped, bread and rolls will easily keep for three months in the freezer. When needed they can be gently thawed at room temperature, placed on some absorbent kitchen paper to mop up any moisture released in the thawing process. If in a hurry, thaw rolls in a warm oven or in a microwave for about 15–20 seconds. Check your microwave manual for recommended standing times for bread and rolls after they've been thawed. They'll probably range from 2–3 minutes for rolls to 6–8 minutes for a large loaf. When you need some bread straight from the freezer, just slip a knife blade between the frozen slices to separate them and then pop them into a toaster or under the grill.

Raising agents Yeast is the raising agent used in hard (bread-making) flours produced in North America. Hard flours contain a high degree of gluten, which is elastic enough to contain the tiny bubbles of carbon dioxide in the dough, thus making it light. Flour produced from British cereals doesn't contain enough gluten to make good bread and, although we can still use yeast for some flour products, we can also resort to other methods of creating gaseous bubbles in the dough.

Baking soda, or bicarbonate of soda (to give it its proper name), is a chemical raising agent. If the dough contains sufficient acid then baking soda on its own will do the job. When that isn't the case, however, we must use baking 'powder'. In

- Don't store bread or rolls in the fridge. It goes stale up to six times faster than if stored at room temperature.
- When bread gets a little past it, refresh it by wrapping it in a clean, damp tea-towel and place it in a moderate oven (180°C/355°F, gas mark 4) for about five minutes. To freshen up dinner rolls, spray lightly with water and pop into a similar oven.

BREAD TINS

Although we've gone metric in the UK, imperial measures still hang on and you'll find bread tins sold as 1lb or 2lb, as well as small, medium, large and long etc.

addition to containing baking soda, this contains its own acid – usually cream of tartar – that acts with the soda to produce the carbon dioxide. Some baking powders have two acids incorporated, one that acts at room temperature (cream of tartar) and one that acts whilst the dough is in the oven.

You may come across recipes sometimes that assume you're going to use fresh yeast. Substitute dry yeast and cut the quantity by half. Yeast granules are a bit of a fiddle to measure and hardly worth bringing out the kitchen scales for. Most manufacturers supply their yeast in small boxes of individual sachets (usually 7g). If that isn't the case, either weigh it accurately or use measuring spoons: $^1/_2$ a heaped teaspoon weighs 2g; 1 heaped teaspoon weighs 4g.

HOME-MADE BREAD THE EASY WAY

This is a very simple recipe that doesn't require kneading. For white bread just substitute white bread flour for the whole wheat. These loaves freeze very well indeed.

Sift and mix together the flour, yeast and salt • Add the oil to about $^1/_2$ litre of the warm water and mix in quite quickly • Add enough extra warm water to make up a soft dough of dropping consistency • Make sure all the flour is thoroughly mixed • Cover the top of the dough liberally with more flour and gently press down the top into a nice round shape • Leave in a warm place until it doubles in size • Divide into four and, using a lot more flour so that you don't get covered in sloppy dough, form the pieces into oblongs – this is the nearest you get to kneading it and really all you're doing here is gently squeezing the dough into shape and covering it with more flour if the surface breaks • Put the dough into 4 x 1lb loaf tins (or squeeze into long sticks if you prefer) and leave to double in size • Bake in a moderately hot oven (200°C/400° F, gas mark 6) until cooked through. Loaves cooked in a tin obviously take longer than stick loaves, but as a guide, take a look at the sticks after 15 minutes and turn them around if they're cooking unevenly. Loaf tins are likely to need about 30–45 minutes but also may need turning around. Too hot an oven burns the top and leaves uncooked dough in the middle; too cool an oven makes the bread dry and hard.

Makes 4 loaves

750g (1lb 10oz) 100% wholewheat bread flour

1 double sachet (14g) dried yeast

3 dsp (33g) salt

100ml (3$^1/_2$fl. oz) vegetable oil (don't use olive oil for breakfast bread)

About 1$^1/_2$ litres warm water

Extra flour for rolling the dough (plain if preferred)

- If making your own bread, tap the bottom of the loaf with your knuckles. If it sounds hollow then it should be cooked.
- You can prove dough in your microwave – see the maker's instructions.

IRISH SODA BREAD (BROWN)

There are more recipes for Irish soda bread than you can shake a shillelagh at and this is just one version of the classic brown variety.

Preheat the oven to 230°C/445°F (gas mark 8) • Thoroughly mix together the dry ingredients and make a well in the centre • Add the milk and mix with your hands until you have a soft dough – don't over mix • Turn out on to a floured surface and shape into a round • Put on a floured baking tray and cut a cross on the surface to allow even cooking • Bake in the oven for 15–20 minutes • Reduce the heat to 200°C/400°F (gas mark 6) and further bake for approximately 20 minutes until the bread is cooked and sounds hollow when knocked on the base.

300g (10 oz) wholemeal flour

200g (7 oz) plain (white) flour

30g (1oz) coarse oatmeal

1 tsp salt

1 tsp bicarbonate of soda

2 tsp caster sugar

400ml (14fl. oz) buttermilk or soured milk

IRISH SODA BREAD (WHITE)

Preheat the oven to 220°C/425°F (gas mark 7) • Lightly grease a 23cm (9in.) round cake tin or a small loaf pan (23 x 13cm/9 x 5in.) • Thoroughly mix together the sifted dry ingredients and make a well in the centre • Add the milk and mix with your hands until you have a soft dough – don't over mix • Turn into the greased pan and bake in the oven for 10 minutes • Reduce the heat to 200°C/400°F (gas mark 6) and bake for about 45 minutes or until the bread is golden brown • Cool on a wire tray.

600g (1lb 6oz) plain flour

1 tsp baking soda

1 tsp cream of tartar

1 tsp salt

4 tbsp caster sugar

500ml (16fl. oz) buttermilk or sour milk

To sour milk, add 1 tbsp of either lemon juice or cider vinegar or 1 tsp baking powder to 300ml (10$\frac{1}{2}$fl. oz) fresh milk.

SOURDOUGH BREAD

Sourdough bread has – as its name suggests – a sour, tangy flavour and makes a tasty and healthy change from our run-of-the-mill batch breads. Thousands of years ago our ancestors discovered that a mixture of flour and water, left to its own devices, not only went sour but actually started to ferment and rise without the help of bakers' yeast. What was happening was that the mixture was being activated by wild yeasts present in the flour itself and by airborne wild yeasts. The resultant bread, although pretty solid (you could use it as a doorstop) has a characteristic nutty flavour and a consistency that lends itself perfectly to some breakfast dishes. Sourdough bread can be made with either rye or wheat flour. It's particularly good with rye flour since the lactic acid-forming bacteria in the sourdough really brings out the flavour of the rye.

TOAST

- Don't stack toast when it's just made, or serve it in a basket or on a plate in a napkin – it goes soft. Use a toast rack (or lean it against the cereal packet!).
- If using pre-sliced bread, ensure that it's thick.

METHOD 1

This is the traditional way of making sourdough and it works if you get the temperatures right. If you think your tap water has a high chlorine content, use bottled spring water instead. The method below will provide enough sourdough to make one large rye loaf, with a little left over to continue the sourdough process.

Day 1: Make a wet paste of 30g (1oz) rye flour with 60ml (1³/₄fl. oz) warm water at 30°C (the ideal temperature). Cover loosely with a lid, cling film or polythene bag and leave in a warm place.

Day 3: Take the Day 1 starter and add to it the same amount of rye flour and warm water (30g and 60ml respectively). Mix well and store as before.

Day 5: Take the Day 3 mixture and add the same amounts of rye flour and warm water once more. Mix and store as before.

Day 6: Do the same again.

Day 7: Take the Day 6 mixture and add 60g (2oz) rye flour this time, plus the usual amount of warm water. This will give you about 480g mixture in which the natural yeast spores have hopefully done their work.

You now have enough to make one sourdough loaf. If you were going to make a habit of baking sourdough bread, you ought to keep back a certain amount of the mixture as a starter for the next batch, but for this first time around, we suggest you use it all. The mixture will be quite wet so put it in a baking tin and place in a preheated oven (200°C/390°F/gas mark 6) for about 45 minutes. Remove from the tin and cool on a wire tray. If dubious about whether or not it's cooked, knock it on the base with your knuckles. If it sounds hollow, it's done. If it doesn't, pop it back in for another 10 minutes or so.

FRIED BREADS

Brighten up your fried bread by getting away from the conventional rectangular or triangular slice and use a round biscuit cutter instead. If serving youngsters, then try a novelty cutter – teddy bear or gingerbread man. Best to use bread that's one or two days old for fried bread and French toast – it holds its shape better and is easier to crisp. For a romantic breakfast, try using a heart-shaped cutter!

BASIC FRENCH TOAST

French toast . . . German toast . . . gypsy bread . . . eggy bread . . . Regardless of what name it goes under, this is a greatly under-utilised and attractive breakfast component whose versatility seems to be more appreciated in countries such as the United States and Australia. The French call it *pain perdu* ('lost bread') because it is a useful way of using up French bread which becomes dry very quickly.

Soak both sides of the bread in a shallow dish of the seasoned beaten eggs • Fry on both sides until golden brown • Cut into the desired shape and serve with a slice of cooked bacon topped by a slice of well-grilled tomato or perhaps a spoonful of your own fruit compote (*see* pp. 33–6).

Serves 2

4 thick slices of bread

2 eggs, beaten with 1 dsp milk

Salt and black pepper

Oil or butter for frying

FRENCH TOAST WITH MAPLE SYRUP

Here's a really exotic version of French toast.

Place the eggs, cream, cinnamon and sugar in a shallow bowl and whisk together • Soak the brioche in the mixture for 15 seconds on each side • Heat the butter in a frying pan until foaming • Place the brioche in the pan and cook for 3 minutes on each side or until golden • Serve with maple syrup and dust with extra cinnamon and icing sugar.

2 eggs

125g (4^1/$_2$oz) single cream

2 tsp ground cinnamon

1 tbsp caster sugar

8 slices brioche (ordinary bread will do at a pinch)

A knob of butter for frying

Maple syrup

Ground cinnamon and icing sugar

POOR KNIGHTS OF WINDSOR

French jam butties!

Beat together the eggs and milk • Make jam sandwiches with the bread using the butter and your favourite jam • Slice into fingers • Dip in the egg mixture • Heat the oil and butter in a frying pan • Fry the fingers until golden brown on both sides • Dust with caster sugar and serve.

1 egg, beaten

150ml (5^1/$_4$fl. oz) milk

8 slices white bread (crusts removed)

50g (2oz) butter

6 tbsp jam

1 tbsp vegetable oil

50g (2oz) butter

1 tbsp caster sugar

DORSET CREAM TOASTS

Mix the egg yolk with the sugar, cream and lemon zest • Place in shallow dish and soak the bread in this for about 5 minutes • Beat the remaining 2 eggs in a dish and dip the soaked bread into them • Heat the butter and oil in a frying pan until frothing • Add the bread slices and cook on both sides until golden brown • Dust with caster sugar and serve with lemon quarters.

1 egg yolk, beaten
2 tsp caster sugar
150ml (5¼fl. oz) single cream
Grated zest of ½ a lemon
6 slices French bread, 2½cm (1in.) thick
2 eggs
30g (1oz) butter
2 tbsp vegetable oil
Caster sugar and lemon quarters to serve

DEVONSHIRE HAM PANPERDY

This is a traditional English dish to which Devonshire or Somerset ham has been added to make a really substantial start to the day or midday snack.

Mix together the eggs, salt, pepper and parsley • Melt the butter in a large ovenproof frying pan • Cut the bread in half and dip into the egg mixture • Fry for 1–2 minutes on both sides until golden brown • Stir the ham into the egg mixture and pour into the pan, on and around the bread • Cook gently for 5 minutes and then place the pan under a preheated grill for 1–2 minutes until the panperdy is golden and set.

6 medium eggs, beaten
1 tbsp fresh parsley, chopped
50g (1½oz) butter
2 thick slices white bread (crusts removed)
100g (3½oz) ham, chopped
Salt and black pepper

IRISH TREAT

If you have the misfortune not to be in Ulster then just substitute your local versions of ham and cheese.

Preheat the grill • Spread the toast with the chutney • Top with the ham and then the cheese • Place under the grill until the cheese has melted • Top with sauce to your liking and serve.

Serves 2
2 slices Irish soda bread, lightly toasted
1 tsp chutney
2 slices of Ulster ham
4 slices of Irish Cheddar cheese
Brown sauce or tomato ketchup

Kentish huffkins

BAPS

Just as the French tiptoe through the morning dew to get their baguettes, so too do the Scots to get their baps – soft morning rolls dusted with flour.

Preheat the oven to 220°C/425°F (gas mark 7) • Sift the flour into a warm bowl with the salt • Lightly rub in the lard • In another bowl, cream the yeast and sugar with a little of the tepid milk • Strain the liquid into the flour mixture and make into a soft dough with the remaining milk • Cover with a towel and leave in a warm place to rise (about 1 hour) • Knead lightly, then form into 8cm (3in.) rounds • Brush with milk and dust with flour • Place on a greased and floured tin and leave in a warm place for 15 minutes • Press a finger into the middle of each to prevent blistering and bake in the oven for about 15 minutes • Dust with flour once cooked and cool on a wire tray.

Makes about 10

450g (16oz) strong white flour

1 tsp salt

50g (2oz) lard

15g (1/2oz) dried yeast

or 30g (1oz) fresh yeast

1 tsp sugar

300ml (10fl. oz) tepid milk or
  50/50 milk and water

A little milk for coating dough

KENTISH HUFFKINS

Mix together the sifted flour, salt, sugar and yeast • Rub the butter into the flour until it looks like breadcrumbs • Make a well in the centre of the flour and pour in the warm milk and water and mix to a dough with your hands – the dough should leave the sides of the bowl almost clean. If the dough is too wet and sticks, add a little flour. If it's too dry, add a little warm water • Place the dough on a floured board and knead for at least 10 minutes or until the dough is smooth and elastic. Alternatively, knead it in your food mixer using the dough hook • Divide the dough in half and in half again until you have 16 portions • Shape each into a flat oval and place on a greased baking tray, making a dent in the centre of each with your thumb • Brush each with beaten egg • Cover with cling film and leave in a warm place for about 30 minutes or until the huffkins have doubled in size • Meanwhile, preheat the oven to 230°C/450°F (gas mark 8) • Remove the cling film, place the tray in the oven and bake for 15–20 minutes until well risen and golden brown • Leave to cool covered with a clean tea towel to keep the crust soft.

Makes 16

750g (1lb 10oz) strong white flour

1 tsp salt

2 tsp sugar

1 x 7g sachet of fast-action yeast

75g (2$\frac{1}{2}$oz) butter, cut into small pieces

200ml (7fl. oz) warm milk, mixed with 225ml (8fl. oz) warm water

1 medium egg, beaten

ABERDEEN BUTTERIES OR ROWIES

This Scottish equivalent of the croissant has lard as well as butter and is a much richer version. Like the croissant, it's usually eaten warm for breakfast with butter and preserves. This recipe is suitable for part-baking and freezing – bake for just 10 minutes, cool and freeze. When thawed, bake at 200°C/400°F (gas mark 6) for 5 minutes.

Warm the sifted flour and salt in a large bowl by leaving it in a low oven for about 10 minutes • Dissolve the sugar in a little of the tepid water and add the yeast • Mix until creamy and add to the flour • Add as much tepid water as is needed to

Makes 16

450g (1lb) strong white flour

1 tsp salt

1–2 tsp caster sugar

285ml (10fl. oz) lukewarm water

15g ($\frac{1}{2}$oz) fresh yeast

150g (5$\frac{1}{2}$oz) butter

60g (2oz) lard

• It's said that Aberdeen rowies were developed as a long-life bread for the city's deep-sea fishermen who were often away for two or three weeks at a stretch. The higher the fat content of bread, the longer it will last.

• The Scottish 'plain' loaf (also called a 'batch' or 'square' loaf) was developed during the industrialisation of the late 19th and early 20th centuries and was baked as a batch bread to save oven space and keep costs down. They were (and still are) the perfect shape for sandwiches and were often filled with the square Lorne sausage. Loaves baked in a tin or a 'pan' were slightly more expensive – giving rise to 'posh' accents being referred to as 'pan loaf accents', meaning that the owners were rich enough to afford the more expensive 'pan' loaf.

make a softish dough and knead until it is smooth and elastic • Cover with a damp cloth or cling film and leave in a warm place until it has doubled in size (1–1$^1/_2$ hours) • Mix the butter and lard until they reach a spreading consistency • When the dough is ready, place on a floured surface and knead again • Roll out fairly thinly into a rectangle and mark out into thirds • Place half the fat mixture in the middle and fold each end over to make an envelope • Seal the edges, turn through 90° and roll out to original size • Place the remaining fat mixture in the middle and repeat the previous step • Roll out into a square about 1cm thick and cut into 16 small squares • Shape into rough ovals by turning the edges over – don't handle too much • Lay on a greased and floured tin or baking tray, allowing space between them, and put in a warm place for 30 minutes to prove • Preheat the oven to 200°C/400°F (gas mark 6) • When risen, bake in the oven for 15–20 minutes.

AUTOMATIC BREAD-MAKERS

Even simpler (in that it just requires the ability to read!) is the relatively modern bit of gadgetry, the automatic bread-maker. Seasoned bakers and pastry chefs will understandably turn their noses up at the thought of it, but for a hungry family it could be revolutionary. All the ingredients are just popped into the machine, a button is pressed and after the desired time a perfect home-baked loaf appears. The machine mixes, proves and bakes, and there's even a time delay that allows the machine to work its magic in the early hours and finish baking at breakfast time. In the process, of course, the irresistible aromas waft around the house.

A bread-maker

Many types of bread can be made in a bread-maker, from basic whites and browns to whole wheats and multigrains. As if that isn't enough, machines will also mix various doughs and give them their first rising so that you can take over and make – for oven baking – rolls, doughnuts, buns, muffins, pitta breads, pizzas, French sticks, naan bread, croissants and even Danish pastries.

BAGELS

Bagels are an Eastern European Jewish speciality which have become firmly associated with the classic New York breakfast of bagels, cream cheese and lox (unsmoked, salted salmon). Strictly speaking they are ring-shaped with a hole in the middle, but in this country you'll frequently see them just as round rolls with a slight indentation in the top. They have a shiny and chewy exterior with a dense and soft interior, and taste fantastic with cream cheese (Philadelphia or similar) and smoked salmon, cold ham, smoked streaky bacon . . . almost anything you fancy, including home-made strawberry jam!

In a bowl, sprinkle and dissolve the sugar and yeast into 100ml (3¹/₂fl. oz) of the water and leave for 5 minutes • Sift the flour and salt together in a large bowl • Make a well in the centre and mix in the yeast and sugar mixture • Add half the remaining water and mix in the flour, adding more of the water as necessary until you have a firm moist dough • Turn the dough out on to a well-floured surface and knead until smooth and elastic – about 10 minutes • As you knead, gradually work in as much additional flour as you can until the dough is very stiff and firm • Put the dough in a lightly oiled bowl, turning it to coat the surface with the oil • Cover with a tea towel and leave to rise in a warm place until it has doubled in size – about an hour • Knock back the dough and then leave to rest for 10 minutes • Cut the dough into 8 equal pieces and shape each piece into a ball (to keep life simpler, you can omit the next two steps) • Form each one into a ring by pushing a floured finger through the centre and widening the hole by working the finger in a circle • Twirl the ring around the index finger of one hand and the thumb of the other until the hole is about one-third of the bagel's diameter • Place the bagels

Makes 8

1¹/₂ tsp granulated sugar

2 tsp dried yeast

300ml (10¹/₂fl. oz) water

500g (1lb) strong white flour

1¹/₂ tsp salt

1 egg white, beaten

Poppy, sesame, caraway or
  melon seeds

The versatile English muffin

on a lightly oiled baking sheet, cover with a damp towel and leave to rest for 10 minutes • Bring a large pan of water to the boil and reduce to a simmer • Now, with a perforated spoon or egg slice, carefully lower the bagels into the water in batches of 2 or 3 at a time • Boil each batch until they rise to the surface – about 1 minute – turning them once • Remove with a spoon and leave to drain • At this stage you can brush the tops with beaten egg white and sprinkle with the seeds of your choice. Another option is to lay some thin strips of cheese on the top • Transfer the drained bagels to a lightly oiled baking sheet and bake in a preheated oven 220°C/425°F (gas mark 7) for 20 minutes or until golden • Leave to cool on a wire rack • Serve slightly warm • Cut them horizontally and spread with whatever goodies you fancy.

ENGLISH MUFFINS

Once sold through all the streets of the land by muffin men, these circular flat breads fell out of favour and – if you ignore the American-style sweet muffins available in our supermarkets – there are only a couple of traditional 'English muffin'-makers left in the country . . . until now, that is! In addition to using them in various breakfast dishes, muffins are handy for making mini pizza bases for the children. Just half them horizontally, lightly toast the cut side and then pile on the pizza topping.

Sieve the flour and salt together into a heatproof basin and either put in a warming drawer or barely warm oven until the flour is warm to the touch • Meanwhile, dissolve the sugar in 215ml (7^1/$_2$fl. oz) of the water and use 2 tbsp of this liquid to mix the yeast to a smooth paste • Stir in the rest of the sugar mixture • Tip the warm flour on to a working surface or into a large mixing bowl and make a well in the centre • Pour in the yeast mixture and the olive oil and mix vigorously to blend in the flour • Add more of the water if necessary to make a dough that is very soft but can just hold its shape • Knead to a smooth elastic dough then shape into a ball and put in a warm, greased bowl • Cover with greased cling film and put in a warm place for 1 hour to prove • Turn out the risen dough on to a floured work surface and divide into 10 equal pieces • Mould them into balls and set them on a thickly floured board • Dust the tops well with flour, cover them with cling film and leave to rise again in a warm place for 35–40 minutes • To cook, heat a lightly oiled griddle or thick-based frying pan and lay on 3 or 4 dough pieces • Cook over medium heat for 5–6 minutes, then turn over to cook for 6–7 minutes on the other side • The muffins will keep a better shape if they are held in by oiled 9cm (3^1/$_2$in.) rings on the cooking surface • Cool on a wire tray.

Makes 10

275g (10oz) strong white flour
  (bread flour)

1 rounded tsp salt

^{1}/$_2$ tsp caster sugar

215–300ml (7^1/$_2$–10^1/$_2$fl. oz)
  warm water*

1^1/$_2$ tsp (7.5g) dried yeast or
  15g (^{1}/$_2$oz) fresh yeast

1 tbsp olive oil

*The temperature you use to mix the dough is important. It should be 40°C (104°F) so that the yeast will start fermenting immediately.

OATCAKES

Oatcakes are one of man's earliest and simplest foods, basically comprised of ground oatmeal, salt, fat and water. Although Scottish oatcakes are probably the most famous, there are other UK versions which all offer a healthy option for the breakfast table. They can be served with the grill or fry-up, or eaten separately with butter, soft or hard cheese, smoked fish, Marmite, marmalade, jam or whatever appeals to you. In Lancashire they were traditionally served with eggs and black pudding. In Derbyshire and Staffordshire they're more like pancakes and are often served in place of fried bread – a much healthier option.

OATCAKES 1

Traditionally, oatcakes are made on a girdle or griddle but they can be just as effectively baked in the oven like the following coarse oatmeal version.

Preheat the oven to 190°C/375°F (gas mark 5) • Mix the oatmeal, baking powder and salt together in a bowl • Add the melted fat and most of the water • Stir well and knead until the mixture forms a ball. If it's too crumbly, add more of the water • Sprinkle a board or worktop with oatmeal or flour and roll out the ball as thinly as possible into a round. If the edges break, just pinch them back together • Cut the round in 4 and carefully lift each quarter on to a large baking tray • Bake in the oven for about 20 minutes until the oatcakes are light brown in colour • Cool on a wire tray.

Makes 4
225g (8oz) pinhead oatmeal
$^1/_2$ tsp baking powder
$^1/_2$ tsp salt
2 tbsp melted lard, bacon fat
   or vegetable oil
150ml (5$^1/_2$fl. oz) boiling water

OATCAKES 2

Preheat the oven to 110°C/210°F (gas mark $^1/_4$) • Add the salt and baking soda to the mixed oatmeal in a bowl • Add enough boiling water to mix to a fairly soft consistency • Turn on to a board sprinkled with oatmeal and knead well • Gradually work the mixture into a round shape, pressing it out with the knuckles • Sprinkle with fine oatmeal and roll out to just under 1cm thick • Melt the fat on a moderately hot girdle • Cut the oatmeal mixture into quarters and cook one side on the girdle until firm (about 3–4 minutes) • Finish by cooling in the oven until crisp.

Makes 4
A pinch of salt
A pinch of baking soda
60g (2oz) fine oatmeal
60g (2oz) medium oatmeal
Boiling water
Extra oatmeal for sprinkling
1 tsp dripping or bacon fat

OATCAKES 3

Mix together the dry ingredients in a bowl and make a well in the centre • Pour the melted fat into the centre • Add enough water to make a fairly stiff dough • Sprinkle the baking tray with oatmeal and turn out the mixture on to it • Roll out half the mixture at a time, as thinly as possible, into a circle • Cut each circle into 4 wedges and sprinkle with more oatmeal • Cook on a girdle, hot plate or cast-iron frying pan at medium heat for about 3 minutes or until the edges curl. Alternatively bake them in a preheated oven for 20 minutes at 160°C/320°F (Gas Mark 7^1/$_2$) • The oatcakes can be further crisped under a hot grill for a few minutes.

Makes 8
240g (8^1/$_2$oz) medium oatmeal
1 tsp baking powder
A good pinch of salt
1 tbsp dripping or bacon fat, melted
About 90ml (6 tbsp) very hot water
Extra oatmeal to sprinkle

DERBYSHIRE OATCAKES 1

These are also known as 'North Staffordshire' oatcakes. In Wales, a very similar recipe calls them 'crempog geirch' – oatmeal pancakes. Whatever the name, they'll keep for a few days and are excellent warmed up in the frying pan or toasted and served with butter and maple or golden syrup.

ANIMAL FATS

You'll see dripping and bacon fat recommended for frying many breakfast ingredients and that's because it tastes so good! Fat consumption in Britain is about the highest in the world and almost a quarter of our intake comes from meat and dairy products. Delicious and nutritious as it can be, it's known as 'saturated' fat and is the villain that increases blood cholesterol levels which in turn increases the risk of coronary heart disease.

But as with all such things, moderation is the key word and its sparing use will do no harm – especially if counteracted by the 'cholesterol-busting' foods mentioned in other chapters.

• *Dripping:* if you've never tried 'bread and home-made dripping' then you've missed a great treat! Dripping is the rendered fat from beef and adds an excellent savoury flavour –

the reason it is frequently recommended in breakfast recipes. You can buy blocks of dripping which will have at least a six-month 'best before' date. Alternatively, you can save the fat from a beef roast and that will keep in the fridge for up to two weeks or in a freezer for six months.

• *Lard:* rendered fat from pork, this is used mainly in pastry and charcuterie specialities such as pâté.

• *Bacon fat:* if the bacon is quite fatty it can be dry-fried without any oil and you can save what comes out of the bacon. Like dripping, it will keep for a couple of weeks in the fridge.

• *Goose and duck fat:* both are very rich and ideal for roasting or frying potatoes. Goose fat can be bought in tins.

Sift the oatmeal, flour and salt into a warm bowl • Dissolve the dried yeast and sugar in 1 tbsp of the warm water and add to the bowl • Add enough of the remaining water to make a thin batter • Set aside in a warm place until well risen (about 30 minutes) • Grease a large, heavy frying pan or girdle and heat • Pour cupfuls of the batter on to the hot pan and cook like thick pancakes (*see* p. 120) for 4–5 minutes on each side.

Makes 4–6
225g (8oz) fine oatmeal
225g (8oz) bread-making flour
  (white or wholemeal)
$^1/_2$ tsp salt
7g ($^1/_4$oz) dried yeast
1 tsp sugar
600–700ml (21–24$^1/_4$fl. oz)
  warm water

DERBYSHIRE OATCAKES 2

Use this recipe if you want smaller quantities. Mix all the ingredients together to a pouring consistency and cook as above.

Makes 1 or 2
2 tbsp plain white flour
2 tbsp fine oatmeal
1 tsp baking powder
A pinch of salt
A pinch of sugar
Warm water to mix.

SCONES

Scones are the great secret weapon of any good cook. Sweet or savoury, they can be rustled up in five minutes and cooked in ten. Soda scones are particularly appropriate for breakfast and very simple to make.

Sift together the dry ingredients • Rub in the fat • Add most of the milk and mix to a softish but not sticky dough, adding the remainder of the milk if necessary • Turn the dough on to a floured board and divide in 2 • Knead each piece gently and roll out into 2 large rounds about 5cm (2in.) thick • Cut each round into 6 triangles and cook on a hot girdle for about 5 minutes until each triangle has risen well and is brown on the underside • Turn over and cook for a further 5 minutes • If you can resist eating them immediately, cool them on a wire tray • Serve fresh or slice in half, fry in dripping or bacon fat and add to the breakfast grill.

Makes 12
225g (8oz) plain white flour
1 tsp bicarbonate of soda
2 tsp cream of tartar
1 tsp salt
A large knob of lard or butter
150ml (5$^1/_4$fl. oz) full fat milk

IRISH SODA FARLS

Slightly different from the previous soda scones, Irish soda farls use buttermilk and include sugar in the ingredients.

Sift the dry ingredients into a bowl • Make a well in the centre and gradually mix in the buttermilk • Turn out on to a floured surface and knead lightly, turning the corners into the centre and turning the dough as you do so • Lightly roll out to around 1cm thick and cut into quarters (or 'farls') • Warm a greased girdle over a low heat. It should be just hot enough to prevent the farls sticking • Place the farls on and cook for 5–6 minutes until they have risen and there is a white skin on top • Increase the heat and continue cooking until the farls are brown on the bottom • Turn over and cook on the other side until that too is brown • Cool on a wire tray and eat with cream or fry like soda scones.

Makes around 24

450g (1lb) plain white flour
1 tsp bicarbonate of soda
1 tsp cream of tartar
$^1/_2$ tsp salt
2 tsp sugar
300ml (10fl. oz) buttermilk

IRISH BREAKFAST

An Irish breakfast is very similar to other regional breakfasts in the UK, comprising eggs, local bacon, grilled tomatoes and mushrooms, and local versions of sausages and black and white puddings. It's said that an Ulster fry is an Irish breakfast with the addition of potato farls and/or soda farls.

BOXTY PANCAKES

Popular in the north-west of Ireland, boxty pancakes use grated potato instead of mashed and result in a quite different texture.

Grate the potatoes, put them in a colander to drain then sandwich them between kitchen paper to absorb as much moisture as possible • Sift the flour into a bowl and, stirring all the time, gradually add milk until you have a batter of single cream consistency • Add the grated potato and seasoning • Heat a girdle or heavy frying pan and add the fat • After it has foamed, drop in a tablespoon of mixture and cook for 3–4 minutes on both sides until golden brown • Remove and keep warm whilst you cook the remainder • You can ring the changes by adding chopped onions or a herb such as sage to the batter at the mixing stage.

Makes 4–6

450g (1lb) potatoes, peeled
125g (4$^1/_2$oz) self-raising flour
125ml (4fl. oz) milk
50g (1$^3/_4$oz) dripping, butter or bacon fat
Salt and freshly ground black pepper

POTATO PANCAKES

Not to be confused with the potato scones below, potato pancakes are very similar to Italian gnocchi but are fried instead of boiled. Great with bacon!

Mash or purée the potatoes and mix in the eggs, milk, flour and seasoning • Warm a frying pan to a moderate heat and add a little dripping • Using a tablespoon of the mixture for each pancake, fry for about a minute on each side.

Makes around 30
225g (8oz) boiled potatoes
2 eggs, lightly beaten
600ml (21fl. oz) milk
180g (6oz) plain white flour
Salt and black pepper
Dripping

POTATO SCONES 1

These are the traditional potato scones which are a great breakfast treat and so much easier to make than potato pancakes. In Ulster they are called potato farls, 'farl' meaning quarter (*see* Irish Soda Farls, opposite), and they can either be served fresh or made beforehand and refried until crisp. If you like oatmeal, replace 30–60g of the flour with an equivalent amount of pinhead or medium oatmeal.

Mash the potatoes with the butter, sifted flour and salt (if using cold potatoes then melt the butter before adding) • Turn on to a floured board and knead gently • Roll out into a circle about ¹/₂cm thick, flouring on both sides, and either cut into quarters or use biscuit cutters to produce small rounds, hearts, children's novelty shapes etc. • Grease a griddle with dripping or butter and either cook for a few minutes on each side or fry in bacon fat in a heavy frying pan until browned • They can be stored in the bread bin for a couple of days, fried in dripping or bacon fat and served with bacon and eggs.

Makes 4
480g (17oz) old potatoes*, boiled
60g (2oz) butter
120g (4oz) plain white flour
2 tsp salt
Dripping, butter or bacon fat

*Floury potatoes are by far the best – King Edward, Pentland Dell, Sante, Kerrs Pink, Golden Wonder, Fianna or Record.

POTATO SCONES 2

This recipe uses the same ingredients as above, but with self-raising flour instead of plain to produce a thicker and lighter scone. Roll out to a thickness of about 1cm, cut into triangles or rounds and cook on the griddle for about 4–5 minutes on each side.

preserves

Serving anything other than marmalade at breakfast used to be looked upon as dangerously progressive but, with our ever-increasing experience of continental diets, we've absorbed some of their breakfast traditions and preserves of all kinds are now commonplace on the breakfast table.

The days of jam-making being a bit of a chore are long gone with the introduction of special jam sugars (Tate & Lyle, Silver Spoon, Whitworths) that contain the correct balance of sugar and pectin. As a result, jams, jellies and marmalades require the very short boiling time of only 4 minutes, which means that the natural colour and taste of the fruit is retained and the result is far superior to the great majority of shop-bought preserves.

These sugars should be available from any good grocer or supermarket and both Tate & Lyle and Silver Spoon produce comprehensive leaflets. Take care when buying, however, since those companies also produce another sugar called 'preserving' sugar that doesn't have pectin in it but is large-grained so that it dissolves quickly for those who like to make their preserves in the traditional fashion.

So, with the help of sugar with pectin and a few baskets of PYO fruit, you can now become a kitchen deity amongst family and friends. Your own home-made raspberry and strawberry jams, bittersweet marmalade and lemon curd will just be the start!

JAM-MAKING KNOW-HOW

Jelly pan A proper jelly pan is highly recommended and you can often pick them up very cheaply in second-hand shops, charity shops or car boot sales. When jam achieves a rolling boil it rises up the pan like lava out of Vesuvius so, if you've been tempted to use a smaller conventional kitchen pan, you could be in trouble!

Setting point If you're not sure that your jam is cooked enough, take it off the heat and try the saucer test. Having placed a saucer in the fridge before you started making the jam, bring it out and put a teaspoonful of jam or marmalade on to it. Allow it to cool slightly and then gently push the jam across the saucer with your finger. If the jam is ready, it should wrinkle.

- To sterilise jam jars and prevent them cracking, wash and rinse them thoroughly then heat them in a paper towel-lined tray in a preheated oven (170°C/325°F/gas mark 3) for 10 minutes so that they are hot when you add the hot preserve. Alternatively, run them through the dishwasher cycle, after which they will be ready for use.
- When filled with hot preserve, seal immediately.
- Don't lay the hot filled jars on a cold surface or they may crack. Use a board or clean tea-towel.
- Try to avoid using self-adhesive labels – they're very difficult to take off when you want to reuse the jars.

Jam jars Whilst you can buy jam jars, why pay for them when you can collect your own for nothing! Save them (*and* the lids) throughout the year and, when it's jam time, give them another good wash and rinse with clear water before sterilising them. The beauty of collecting your own is that you can accumulate a range of shapes and sizes so if you have to give some to the school fête, you needn't give away the large ones!

Potting your jams Seasoned jam-makers will have their own way of potting their produce. Beginners should take care since jam temperatures are particularly high and spills can be dangerous. The safest way is to hold a heatproof jug over the pan and ladle the jam into it. When it's full, pour it into your jam jars to about $^1/_2$cm from the top.

Jar covers Traditionally, jam-makers buy packets of jam covers that include waxed discs for placing on top of the jam, cellophane or decorative paper covers, rubber bands and fancy labels. If you don't want to go to those lengths, just fill the jars as suggested and have fun matching each jar with its lid. If they're put on when the jam is hot, as it cools it creates a vacuum and your jam stays pristine for at least a year. Store in a dark cupboard and, just to be sure, have a look at them all now and again to make sure that there isn't a loose lid that has allowed a mould to form. If it does form, don't worry, it's harmless. Just remove it with a spoon and eat the jam as normal.

RASPBERRY JAM

Heat the raspberries gently in a preserving pan until the juices begin to run and the fruit softens • Add the jam sugar • Heat gently, stirring continuously until the jam sugar dissolves. Do not allow to boil • Add the knob of butter • Still stirring, increase the heat and bring to a full rolling boil – one that bubbles vigorously, rises in the pan and cannot be stirred down • As soon as this stage is reached, start timing. Boil for 4 minutes only • Remove from the heat • Pot and cover in the usual way.

Makes about 1.5kg (3lb 5oz)
800g (1³/₄lb) raspberries
1kg (2lbs 3oz) jam sugar
A knob of butter

STRAWBERRY JAM

Place the strawberries in a preserving pan with the sugar • Heat gently until the sugar is dissolved, stirring frequently • Bring to the boil and boil steadily for 4 minutes or until the setting point is reached • Skim with a slotted spoon and leave to stand for 15–20 minutes • Stir gently and pour into hot, sterilised jars.

Almost any other soft fruit can be substituted here, including ones with a high pectin content such as blackcurrants, whose intense taste is excellently preserved by the very short cooking time. About 850ml water per kilo of fruit needs to be added to the currants, and the stalks need to be removed but not the feathery tops!

Makes about 1.75kg (4lb)
900g (2lb) strawberries
1 kg (2lb 3oz) jam sugar
A knob of butter

To prevent the berries floating to the top, leave strawberry and raspberry jam to cool for the 15–20 minutes before potting.

MARMALADE

Marmalade is usually twinned with porridge when talking of a traditional breakfast and that's thanks to James and Janet Keiller of Dundee, who started making it in 1700. It wasn't until almost a hundred years later that the first factory was built there and marmalade's popularity spread quickly. One of its first strongholds in England was at Oxford where, known as 'squish', it was a favourite of under-graduates. The dark Oxford marmalade, now so popular, is said to have started life as Perthshire marmalade, which was the conventional product with black treacle added.

DARK AND CHUNKY MARMALADE

Place the oranges in a large pan with the water • Bring to the boil and simmer gently for 1½–2 hours until the peel is tender • Allow the mixture to cool, remove the oranges and reserve the liquid • Cut the fruits in half and scoop out the pulp and pips • Separate the pips and tough skin membranes and tie in muslin • Return the pulp to the pan • Cut the skins into chunks and add to the pan in a muslin bag • Bring to the boil and boil for 15 minutes • Remove the muslin, squeezing well • Add the sugar and treacle and stir until dissolved • Bring back to the boil and boil rapidly for 4 minutes or until setting point • Remove from the heat and skim off any scum • Stand for 10–15 minutes to cool until a thin skin forms • Stir gently then pot and seal • For a whisky flavour, add 75ml (3fl. oz) whisky after the first 15-minute boiling and continue as above.

Makes about 3.9–4kg (8½–9lb)
5kg (11lb) Seville oranges
4 litres (6pt) water
2.75kg (6lb) jam sugar
45ml (3 tbsp) black treacle

• To reduce cooking time even more, preheat the sugar in the oven before adding to the fruit.
• To virtually eliminate scum, add a knob of butter or paint round the pan with glycerine.

LEMON CURD

With a recipe that includes eggs and butter, this is not a true jam. It therefore needs to be made in small quantities and used reasonably quickly. Unopened, curds will keep for up to a month in a cool cupboard, three months in a fridge and six months in a freezer. Once opened they will keep in the fridge for up to a month. If using bought lemon curd, take care – some of them can be rather sickly and not a patch on the real thing.

Scrub the lemons to remove any wax • Finely grate the rind into the pan • Add the sugar and butter and heat very gently, stirring until the sugar dissolves and the butter is melted • Beat the eggs in a bowl and strain into the mixture • Stir over a gentle heat until thick enough to coat the back of a wooden spoon • Pot and seal as usual.

VARIATIONS

Different fruits can be used instead of lemons – grapefruit, oranges and even blueberries or blackcurrants. Tate & Lyle advise using 2 pink grapefruit in place of the lemons and – at the end of the cooking – colouring the curd a delicate pink with a tiny drop of red food dye. For orange curd, use 4 small blood oranges in place of the lemons. For blueberry or blackcurrant curd, use 225g (8oz) fruit, gently cooking first with 15ml (1 tbsp) water in a tightly covered pan until very tender. Press through a fine sieve before using.

Makes about 1kg (2lb 3oz)
2 large lemons
50g (2oz) unsalted butter
225g (8oz) granulated sugar
   (not jam sugar with added
   pectin)
3 eggs, size 3

Although not a jam or preserve, Marmite is such a traditional component of the British breakfast table that it can't go without mention. Many generations of youngsters have learned to love this salty yeast extract – especially on toast. Its wildly popular Australian equivalent is the even saltier Vegemite.

HONEY

Honey is one of nature's great wonders, highly prized since the earliest of times. Nectar gathered from blossoms undergoes the most complex of natural sugar chemistry, with changes in colour and flavour before it metamorphoses into honey. To date, over 200 different chemical substances have been identified in it.

Despite all its claimed health benefits, however, medical advice suggests that honey should not be fed to infants under 12 months old because of the rare chance of them contracting infant botulism.

Left to their own devices, bees will gather nectar from whatever source is available and the resulting honey can be a disappointing mixture of flavours. Therefore, for all pure honeys, such as heather, raspberry flower, clover, sunflower etc., the apiarists must move the hives to whatever blossom is in season – a routine that can happen up to six times a year. To ensure the purity of the resultant

Honey has many interesting properties:
- high in vitamins such as B and C
- sweeter than sugar so a great quick-fix energy source
- credited with numerous medicinal properties: antiseptic, antibacterial, calming coughs and hay fever, soothing peptic ulcers and stimulating the production of the mood-enhancing blood compound and neurotransmitter, serotonin.

honey, it must be harvested at the end of each flowering period.

In simple terms, harvesting consists of extracting the wax combs from the hives and draining and filtering the clear honey before bottling. The empty combs are then replaced in the hives. For white or set honey, a little of the previous year's crop with a smooth crystallisation is added. This imparts its crystalline characteristics to the new honey, which then goes rock hard. After warming slightly to soften it, that too is bottled.

Honey is conventionally used in ice creams and yoghurts, for glazing hams and for general sweetening. It is more hygroscopic (water attracting) than table sugar and will keep breads and cakes moister, losing water to the air more slowly and even absorbing it on humid days. One measure of honey is equivalent to about $1^1/_2$ of sugar. Clear honey makes an excellent porridge topping and is a good sweetener for a hot toddy.

PEANUT BUTTER

To many of us, eating peanut butter at breakfast (or at any time for that matter) ought to be made an offence. However, it has attracted generations of young fans since its debut as a health food at the 1904 St Louis World's Fair in America. American peanut farmers have calculated that Americans consume more than 700 million pounds of peanut butter every year – enough, they say, to coat the floor of the Grand Canyon. Probably the best place for the stuff.

Natural peanut butter comprises just peanuts and peanut oil: commercially produced versions may include any vegetable oil plus salt, sugar and additives to improve its creaminess. Apart from the fiddle of roasting the nuts to bring out their rich flavour, and removing the brown skins, it's simple to make your own. However, without any additives, the oil will separate from the ground peanuts and it must be stirred back in each time before use. Refrigerated, it should keep for around six months.

OVEN ROASTING PEANUTS
Preheat the oven to 175°C/350°F (gas mark 4) • Spread the nuts in a single layer on a shallow pan or baking tray with edges • Shaking the tray occasionally, bake for about 7–12 minutes. When the nuts are golden brown, they're done.

GRILLING PEANUTS
Spread them on a tray/pan/grill tray and grill them about 15cm (6in.) away from the heat for 3–5 minutes • Shake occasionally since they scorch very easily. When the nuts are golden brown, they're done.

- Peanut butter is a very convenient source of natural folic acid – a B vitamin that, for pregnant mums, can reduce the risk of birth defects and may be of help in preventing heart disease.
- Although high in fat, it is also a good source of protein, vitamin E, niacin, phosphorous and magnesium.
- As with any product involving nuts, thought must be given to allergies. Many products are now labelled with a warning that, to prevent nut allergy, women from families with a history of allergy or asthma should avoid eating nuts when pregnant or breast-feeding.

STOVE-TOP ROASTING PEANUTS

Spread the nuts in a good heavy-based frying pan • Roast over a medium heat, shaking frequently until the skins start to turn dark brown.

SKINNING THE NUTS

After the nuts have cooled, the outer skins have to be removed. Taking a small handful, rub them between your palms and gently blow the featherweight skins away – best done outside!

Purée the nuts in a blender until they're ground to a fine consistency • Pour in sufficient oil to bind the ground nuts together. If you want a crunchier version then keep some of the nuts back and chop finely with a knife or coffee grinder before adding to the ground mixture • Pack the mixture into a sterilised, lidded jar and store in the fridge.

Makes a jar

125g (4oz) peanuts, roasted
  and skinned

1–2 tbsp cooking oil (peanut if
  you have it)

eggs

'Farm', 'farm fresh', 'naturally fresh', 'country fresh', 'barn', 'perchery', 'free-range', 'freedom food', 'organic' . . . the different marketing tags applied to hens' eggs can be confusing and can conjure up all sorts of misleading images.

'Farm fresh' and 'naturally fresh' eggs sound great, but they can in fact be from battery hens. At the other end of the scale, 'free-range' may bring to mind contented hens pecking in the farmyard but don't be fooled. As The Soil Association says, '"Free-range" is a term often used simply to mean providing pop holes in huge chicken houses so that birds can access the outside when they want to. However, most birds in units termed as "free-range" have been reared inside and don't like to stray too far, so many may not even reach the pop holes. Those that do, tend to stay close to the house and their more familiar environment, so only a very few range properly.' Equally, 'barn' or 'perchery' sound like wholesome alternatives, but those eggs can be laid by hens with no access to the open air at all.

The modern trend to seek out more wholesome food, coupled with a growing interest in animal welfare, has resulted in a huge increase in public demand for free-range eggs and all supermarkets and catering suppliers now stock them. Consumption in the last few years has risen some 18% to 1.8 million free-range eggs a day. Because they're labelled 'free-range', a common public perception is that they taste better. Wrong. Blind tasting trials have shown that there is no actual difference between *commercially*-produced free-range eggs and battery eggs, given that both types are fed the same food.

The eggs that we regard as being *truly* free-range are those from hens scratching around in the farmyard or open fields, eating insects, seeds, worms, nettles and other goodies. These are the ones that will normally have a much deeper-coloured yolk – not produced by a dye food supplement – and a much richer, 'eggier' taste.

Galloping to the rescue of the 'eggophiles' among us without access to farmyard eggs is the latest development in the market — the organic egg. More expensive than commercial free-range eggs, these come from hens that have genuine access to outside pastures and are fed with a minimum of 80% of their feed grown to Soil Association standards. The routine, preventative use of antibiotics is prohibited and they can only be used to treat a specific illness, during which period the eggs cannot be sold as organic.

So, if you care about how your eggs taste and what they're doing to you, either buy them straight from the farm, small egg producer, local butcher or independent grocer, or plump for commercially produced organic ones. There is, of course, a risk of food poisoning from the consumption of any raw egg and dishes that use raw eggs such as mayonnaise and some ice creams. However, if the eggs are fresh, the dishes are not left at room temperature for more than an hour, and they're then eaten as soon as possible after they're made, that risk is minimal. It's a decision that only you can take.

Goose eggs These are four or five times bigger than a hen's egg. They have an oilier consistency and should be used when fresh.

Duck eggs Some of us like the slightly stronger, 'eggier' taste of duck eggs and eat them soft-boiled. Conventional wisdom and prudence, however, suggest that they are boiled for at least 15 minutes because of the risk of salmonella resulting from the eggs usually being laid in a dirty environment. Duck eggs can be used in any cooked dishes that normally ask for hens' eggs.

Quail eggs Tiny eggs that are usually hard- or medium-boiled, shelled and used in salads or fancy dishes.

Gull eggs Only the eggs of black-headed gulls can be collected under licence nowadays. Unlike other seabird eggs, gull eggs aren't fishy tasting and are excellent hard-boiled (5 minutes) and eaten cold with celery salt.

Ostrich eggs About 20 times bigger than a hen's egg and with a very thick shell, these are quite edible if they're fresh.

- The numbering system for eggs has been discontinued and they're now classified as small, medium, large and very large.
- The Lion returns. After the long-running debates and worries about salmonella in eggs, the industry resurrected the lion stamp as a sign of quality. Any eggs stamped with the red lion have come from birds that have been vaccinated against salmonella.
- There is no nutritional difference between brown and white eggs, but the moisture that evaporates through the porous shell does so more slowly through a brown shell than a white and the egg will therefore stay fresher marginally longer. Not worth worrying about however!
- Eggs hate heat and deteriorate quickly in such conditions so always keep them in a cool larder or in the fridge. To minimise moisture evaporation, keep them in their original carton in the cooler body of the fridge rather than in the door. Don't put them too close to the ice box or they'll start to freeze, and keep them away from strong smelling foods such as fish or they may become tainted.
- Store eggs pointed end down – there's an air sac at the round end of the egg and the yolk will rise and rest against this rather than touch – and possibly stick to – the shell.
- Egg whites will keep in the fridge for about a week; egg yolks (covered with water) for about two or three days; hard boiled eggs about a week. Cracked eggs should be broken into a small, airtight container and can be kept in the fridge for two days.
- Take eggs out of the fridge about half an hour before you need to use them.
- Don't shell eggs until just before use: their quality deteriorates rapidly if left to sit in the open.
- For beating, egg whites should be at room temperature. If there is the slightest trace of fat or egg yolk in them, however, they just won't whip. It's a good idea, therefore, to have three bowls when separating yolks and whites. One for the whites, one for the yolks and one to break the egg over just in case you puncture a yolk and contaminate a bowlful of whites.

BOILING AN EGG

It's often said of those who can't cook, 'They can't even boil an egg'. But for newcomers to the kitchen, boiling an egg isn't as simple as such criticism suggests, so here are a few tips for the uninitiated.

- Cold eggs + boiling water = cracked shells, so take the eggs out of the fridge well beforehand. If you've forgotten and are in a rush, pop them into a bowl of hot tap water for a few minutes.
- Bring a panful of water to the boil and use the smallest pan that will hold the eggs. If they crash around in too large a pan, the shells will probably crack and the white will seep out, overcook and create a nasty smell (hydrogen sulphide).
- Carefully lower each egg into the boiling water with a slotted spoon or tablespoon. The water will have gone off the boil now, so wait until it comes back and then lower the heat to a gentle simmer. This stops the eggs rattling around and produces a softer white.
- If you are in the habit of accidentally cracking your eggs, then put a table-spoonful or two of vinegar into the water – this solidifies the white and minimises the seepage.
- As soon as they're simmering, start your kitchen timer – an essential tool if you want consistently good boiled eggs. The old-fashioned hourglass timer filled with sand is not much good: the timing depends on the size of the eggs, how fresh they are and how you like them – soft, medium or hard.
- For soft-boiled, cook for 3–5 minutes: small ones would be 3 minutes and large ones would be 5, but if they're very fresh, they'll need up to 1 minute extra. For hard-boiled, cook for 10–12 minutes. Medium will obviously be somewhere between the two, depending upon your taste. When the cooking time is up, remove them with the spoon.
- Some cooks advocate pricking the broad end with a pin to allow the air to escape and prevent cracking but this shouldn't be necessary if they're simmered. Besides, pricking them sometimes actually causes the problem it is meant to prevent.
- If you're going to shell the eggs, dip them into cold water as soon as the cooking is finished. Even with that, very fresh eggs will still prove difficult to peel because the inner membrane sticks to the white.
- Remember that eggs continue to cook after being removed from the simmering water so if you've overdone them a bit, cut the tops off quickly before you serve them. If they're still a bit too hard, cheat and press a tiny knob of butter into the yolk and hope that this fools them all.
- If your family likes toasted soldiers, do the toast whilst the eggs are cooking

- To avoid the unsightly layer of greenish-grey on the surface of a hard-boiled egg, don't boil it for more than 10 minutes.
- You can tell a hard-boiled egg from a fresh one by spinning it round on its side. The hard-boiled one will spin easily; the fresh one (because of the liquid inside) will spin reluctantly and when stopped may start to spin again on its own.
- If hard-boiling eggs, plunge them into cold water after cooking. This causes a jacket of steam to form between the egg and shell which facilitates peeling.
- How your fried eggs turn out will depend a lot upon their age; the older they are, the more watery the whites will be and the more they'll spread over the pan.

and let it cool a bit so that the melted butter doesn't make it too soft. (Everyone knows that soldiers must stand to attention when being dipped!)
And you thought boiling an egg was simple!

SCRAMBLED EGGS

Beat the eggs together • Add salt and pepper • Add two-thirds of the cream, mixing well • Strain to remove any unseen shell fragments • Melt the butter in a thick-bottomed pan over a low heat • Add the egg mixture and stir until it becomes thick and creamy • Remove from the heat and stir in the last of the cream • Serve immediately.

8 eggs
Salt and white pepper
8 tbsp single cream
80g (2³/₄ oz) good quality
   butter

SMOKED SALMON AND SCRAMBLED EGGS

Line a coupe dish with cling film and then the smoked salmon • Heat up a heavy-bottomed or non-stick pan and add the butter • Stir the eggs into the pan with a wooden spoon • When the eggs are ready, stop the cooking process by adding the cream • Season and fill the coupe dish • Allow to rest for one minute, turn out on to a warm plate and serve • For an added extra, gently heat the crème fraîche in a pan • Add the herbs and pour around the salmon mixture • Arrange the tomatoes around the plate • Place a sprig of herb on top of the coupe.

Serves 1
40g (1¹/₂oz) smoked salmon,
   thinly sliced
10g (¹/₂oz) unsalted butter
2 medium eggs, whisked
2 tbsp double cream
Salt and milled black pepper
Optional garnish
2 tbsp crème fraîche
Fresh chives or dill, snipped
2 cherry tomatoes, halved

Smoked salmon and
scrambled eggs on toast

SCRAMBLED EGG TIPS

- On no account overcook scrambled eggs. The addition of cream at the end of cooking lowers the temperature and stops the process.
- If cooking without cream, take the pan off the heat whilst the mixture is still reasonably runny. It will continue to cook in the pan.
- If the mixture (for scrambled eggs or omelettes) is going to stand for any time before cooking, omit the salt until the last minute – it relaxes the egg whites and the mixture will become thin.
- After whisking the eggs, good chefs pour the mixture through a sieve to remove any tiny bits of shell or coagulated egg white. In the home it only adds to the washing up so don't bother – let the family take their chances!

VARIATIONS

As with so many dishes, the variations on scrambled eggs are limited only by your imagination and your ability to pair up interesting ingredients with the eggs:

- smoked salmon or trout: a classic addition either in slices beside the egg, or in morsels mixed in with the egg just before serving
- 50g (1³/₄oz) flaked smoked haddock or kipper
- 50g (1³/₄oz) chopped and lightly fried tomatoes
- 50g (1³/₄oz) fried diced bacon
- 50g (1³/₄oz) chopped ham
- 50–75g (1³/₄–2¹/₂oz) grated cheese
- 2.5ml (¹/₂ tsp) dried mixed herbs or 15ml (1 tbsp) chopped mixed herbs (usually a combination of marjoram or oregano, tarragon, sage, thyme and parsley).

FRIED EGGS

If you are having your fried eggs in an American diner you will be asked how you want them – 'sunny-side up', 'over-easy', 'over-medium' or 'over-hard'. 'Sunny-side up' is self explanatory; 'over-easy' is where the egg is turned over (flipped) and cooked for about 15 seconds so that the yolk is still runny; 'over-medium' eggs would be cooked for about 30 seconds; 'over-hard' for about a minute – all of this on a low to medium heat.

The perfect fried egg If you've cooked other elements of the breakfast in the pan first, the chances are that the fat may be burnt or discoloured, there may be bits of debris around and sticky goo on the bottom. The eggs will cook much more easily if you transfer the cooked ingredients to a warm oven or grill whilst you wash out the pan, or alternatively use a separate one.

Heat the pan on high for a few minutes and then add your oil or butter. The temperature is about right when the oil shimmers or the butter foams; if the fat starts spitting, it's too hot. Break the eggs into the pan carefully, tilting the pan to keep the white in one place if you suspect the eggs are a bit old. Leave them for about 30 seconds to solidify slightly and then turn the heat down to medium. Tilt

COOKING RINGS

Stainless steel cooking rings are excellent gizmos to add to your kitchen arsenal. Chefs use them for making towers of layered vegetables, mousses, rosti and many other cooking and presentation tasks. They're also ideal for frying eggs – especially if you have a lot to fry at one time.

There are quite a few *thin* rings on the market that can be easily bent: these are fine for most tasks but for egg-frying, go for the more substantial ones. Lakeland offer them in two sizes – 7cms (3in.) and 9cms (3¹/₂in.). The latter are the ones you're after.

Oil the inside of the rings, place them in your heated pan, break an egg into each and cook as normal. The heavy steel ring stops the egg white spreading and the heat conducted up its height helps to cook the egg. If you want a whitish film over the yolk, pop a lid on the pan or a flat plate over the rings.

Don't waste your time trying this with a thin and buckled frying pan – the ring won't sit squarely and egg white will leak out all over the place! You need a good solid-based pan or a griddle plate.

the pan and baste the yolk with oil or butter and you'll see a translucent white film forming over it which shows that it's cooked. Alternatively, you can pop a lid on the frying pan which reflects the heat down on to the eggs and cooks them that way.

If you like your egg easy-over then you can dispense with the basting and very carefully turn the egg over towards the end of cooking.

If possible, always drain eggs on absorbent paper before placing them on the serving plate. Less fat on the egg and the plate means less cholesterol in the arteries!

OEUFS AU BUERRE NOIR

'Eggs in black butter' don't sound as enticing as 'oeufs au buerre noir', and this dish *is* a traditional French speciality. The eggs are fried in butter and transferred to a warm serving dish. More butter is added to the pan and cooked quickly until it turns dark brown. A few drops of vinegar for each egg are added and then the mixture is stirred and poured over the eggs, with each being garnished with half a teaspoon of capers.

Following pages: Poached egg and ham buttie

CLASSIC POACHED EGGS

Bring a shallow saucepan of water to the boil • Add the salt and reduce to a simmer • Crack each egg on to a saucer • With a spoon, swirl the water so that, when you slip each egg in, the white wraps around the yolk • Slip the egg into the simmering water. (If, even after swirling the water, the white spreads too much when you slip the egg in, use a perforated spoon to gather it around the yolk again) • Allow to poach for 3 minutes • Remove with your perforated spoon and drain on a clean tea towel or piece of kitchen roll • Trim off any unattractive straggly egg white • Serve on the neat circles of buttered toast.

1 tsp salt

4 eggs

4 large circles of white bread, toasted

MICROWAVED POACHED EGGS

One of the simplest and quickest ways imaginable of poaching eggs. Just pour boiling water into a small cereal bowl or ramekin and break your egg into it. You may need to experiment with the timing, but start off with 20 seconds on 'high', have a look at the egg and, if it isn't cooked enough, give it another 10 seconds. Remember, though, that the egg will continue to cook even after you've taken it out of the microwave. When cooked, remove with a slotted spoon. Team this up with microwaved bacon (*see* p. 95) and you give new meaning to 'fast food'. (Your microwave instructions will probably suggest a slightly different method and will almost definitely tell you to pierce the yolk before cooking. We've yet to find that necessary. You'll also find the cooking times for more than one egg.)

• Cooked poached eggs can be kept for quite a time by transferring them to a bowl of cold water and then reheating them in hot water before serving.

EGGS BENEDICT

When regular diners Mr and Mrs LeGrand Benedict complained in Manhattan's famous Delmonica Restaurant that there was nothing new on the menu, Mrs Benedict and the maître d' conjured up this classic dish. Poached eggs and ham are the standard but it's also mouth-watering with scrambled eggs and smoked salmon.

Sauté the ham briefly in butter • Place each slice on a toasted half-muffin • Top with a poached egg • Cover with warm Hollandaise sauce.

4 slices of good cooked ham

A knob of butter

2 muffins, split in half and toasted

4 eggs, poached (*see* above)

285ml (10fl. oz) Hollandaise sauce, warmed (*see* below)

TRADITIONAL HOLLANDAISE SAUCE

This traditional French sauce (originally from Holland) needs a good heavy-based saucepan – not aluminium – or a double boiler. Be warned, however. Both the following recipes use uncooked egg yolks and could constitute a serious health risk. You must make your own informed decision as to whether or not to use it.

Melt the butter in a pan and skim off the surface froth with a spoon • Put to one side and cool until tepid • Whisk the egg yolks, water, wine and a little salt and pepper in the cold saucepan for about 30 seconds until combined • Put the pan on a low heat (if too high the eggs will become scrambled!) and whisk for about 3 minutes until smooth and creamy • Take the pan off the heat and gradually whisk in the butter a little at a time until the sauce thickens • Add the remainder – but not the milky residue • Stir in the lemon juice and season further if needed.

Makes 250ml (8³/₄fl. oz)
175g (6oz) unsalted butter, melted
3 egg yolks
2 tbsp water
1 tbsp dry white wine
Juice of ¹/₂ a lemon
Salt and black pepper

QUICK HOLLANDAISE SAUCE

Here's an easier way of making Hollandaise sauce that never fails.

Blend all the ingredients together except the butter on a low speed for 10 seconds • While the blender is still on, add the hot butter in a slow, steady stream until the mixture becomes creamy.

Makes 250ml (8³/₄fl. oz)
3 egg yolks
3 tbsp water
Juice of ¹/₂ a lemon
175g (6oz) unsalted butter, melted
Salt and black pepper

'POACHED EGGS' IN A POACHING PAN

In reality, eggs cooked in domestic egg poachers are not poached at all but are 'oeufs en cocotte' (*see* p. 78). The individual egg containers replace the traditional ramekins and the eggs are never exposed to water as in the genuine poaching process. But poachers are here to stay and will doubtless continue to be used in thousands of kitchens.

Half-fill the poaching pan with water and add a small knob of butter to each poaching cup • Bring the water to the boil • Break an egg into each cup • Sprinkle

Butter
4 eggs
Salt and black pepper
4 large circles of white bread, toasted

with seasoning • Cover with the lid and simmer until cooked • Break the seal around the top of the egg with the tip of a knife and slide the egg out on to a buttered round of toast.

OEUFS EN COCOTTE

Oeufs en cocotte are eggs cooked in individual heatproof dishes called ramekins and you'll see the resemblance to domestic 'poached' eggs discussed above. The beauty of eggs en cocotte is their versatility because all manner of savoury ingredients can be put into the ramekin before the egg – chopped ham or bacon mixed with parsley; chopped tomato and herbs; spinach; sweet peppers with ham and garlic; onion with fried croutons; shelled shrimps in a white sauce; flaked smoked fish (haddock, trout, salmon, kipper); black pudding or haggis . . . even tomato sauce. Slightly larger ramekins will accommodate two eggs. Another benefit of this recipe is that it's ideal for a large family where individual members want different bits and pieces with their egg.

Grease a ramekin with butter and season the salt and pepper • Break in the egg • Add the cream • Place in a bain-marie or conventional shallow pan • Fill the pan with water to halfway up the ramekin • Bring to the boil and cook until the egg white is just set and the yolks are still very soft • An alternative is to bake in the oven at 190°C/375°F (gas mark 5) for about 5 minutes. If left uncovered and without the cream, an attractive shiny skin forms on the egg. (This doesn't form if the egg is covered with kitchen foil.)

Butter
Salt and black pepper
1 or 2 eggs per person
1 tsp double cream

FOLDED OMELETTE

Almost every cook has a favourite way of making an omelette so we'll start with the simplest method imaginable.

Break the eggs into a good-sized mixing bowl, whisk until mixed but not frothy and season to taste • Heat a thick-bottomed frying pan (or omelette pan if you have one) and drop a knob of butter on to the base. A non-stick pan is a good idea and practice will show you how hot to have it depending upon whether you want your omelette brown-speckled or plain yellow • When the butter starts frothing, spread it over the base of the pan and pour in enough of the mixture to make one omelette • Stroke the base of the pan briskly with the back of a fork, breaking

2–3 eggs per person
Salt and black pepper
Butter
Filling of your choice
  (chopped, crisp-cooked
  streaky bacon; chopped,
  sautéed mushrooms;
  chopped ham and chopped –
  even tinned – tomatoes)

through the surface of the omelette. This brings uncooked egg into contact with the hot surface and introduces air into the egg, making the omelette lighter • If adding a filling, then do so when there is still some liquid egg left. Depending upon how you intend folding the omelette, spread the prepared filling either in the middle or in the centre of one half and fold over. Total cooking time should be about 1^1/$_2$ minutes • For the traditional half-moon-shaped omelette, fold the omelette in half when there is just a little liquid egg left, and slide it out of the pan on to a heated plate. An alternative and simpler method is to fold one-third of the omelette over the middle and then do the same with the remaining third, thus making an envelope.

OMELETTES

- For an omelette for one, use an 18cm (7in.) pan.
- Omelettes for two using 4–5 eggs should be cooked in a 23cm (9in.) pan.
- Don't over-beat the eggs – it spoils the texture of the omelette.
- Some omelette buffs prefer to separate the white from the yolks, beat it until stiff and then fold this into the beaten yolks just before cooking.

Omelettes with everything

FLAT OMELETTE

A flat or Spanish omelette is designed to hold a hearty portion of supplementary goodies such as chopped ham, potato, bacon, croutons, or tomatoes. The egg is really just to hold the filling together.

Mix the eggs as for the Folded Omelette above and pour into a buttered pan • Immediately add the desired filling and stir the eggs gently • Lift the edges of the omelette with a fork so that uncooked egg runs underneath • Cook until the omelette is almost firm on top and leave undisturbed so that the bottom can brown • Cover the pan with a plate and turn the pan over, transferring the omelette to the plate • Now slide the omelette back into the pan to brown the other side • Serve whole or in slices.

2–3 eggs per person
Salt and black pepper
Butter
Filling of your choice (*see* Folded Omelette p. 78)

FRITTATA

First cousin to the Spanish omelette is the famous Italian frittata, which finds great favour in America and Australia where they've taken it to new heights. It too is a flat or open-faced omelette into which go all sorts of tasty additions. The classic recipe contains potato, sweet peppers (bell or capsicums) and onion, although some recipes also include sautéed eggplant (aubergine) or courgette.

Boil (or microwave for 4 minutes) the potato until cooked and cut into 2cm slices • Preheat the oven to 180°C/355°F (gas mark 4) • Beat the eggs and double cream in a bowl and add the bread cubes, leaving them to soak for 10 minutes • In a large cast-iron frying pan or ovenproof/stove-top dish, pour in the olive oil and cook the onions over a medium heat until translucent • Add the sliced peppers and cook until al dente • Season well and, if you want to give someone a breakfast shock, add a generous sprinkling of the flaked chillies • Add the sliced potato and cook for a further few minutes • If you only have the one pan, remove the contents and keep them warm • Clean the pan, add the butter and heat on a medium setting until the butter foams • Add the egg mixture and then add the potatoes, peppers etc. • Cook until the bottom is just brown and then transfer to the oven and cook until the centre is firm – about 10 minutes • If you have a Desperate Dan in the family, serve it as a 'oner'. If not, cut into slices.

Serves 2–3
1 medium potato, peeled
5 eggs
55ml (2fl. oz) double cream
$^1/_2$ cup of day-old bread, cut into 2cm cubes
2 tbsp extra virgin olive oil
$^1/_2$ onion, thinly sliced
1 green, red or yellow pepper (or a mixture), cut into 2cm strips
Flaked chilli peppers (optional)
$^1/_2$ tbsp unsalted or lightly salted butter
Salt and black pepper

FRITTATA WITH TOMATO

Exactly as the basic frittata above but, instead of transferring it to the oven, sprinkle the grated cheese, thinly sliced tomato and dried rosemary on top and pop under the grill until the cheese bubbles and blisters.

Serves 2

1 medium tomato, sliced

2 tbsp Parmesan cheese (or good old dependable Cheddar), grated

A pinch of dried rosemary

SAUSAGE FRITTATA

This is real hearty 'come home to Momma's cooking' frittata with a bit of chilli pepper bite in it. A bit drastic for a British breakfast but probably great for brunch.

Preheat the oven to 180°C/355°F (gas mark 4) • In an ovenproof frying pan, sauté the peppers in the olive oil until al dente • Add the spring onions and cooked sausage slices • Add the ground pepper and chillies • Whisk together the eggs and cream and pour evenly into the pan • Cook on a low heat for a minute or two until the egg begins to set • Sprinkle the cheese over the top and put in the middle of the oven for 10–15 minutes until the top is puffed and golden • Cut into wedges and serve.

Serves 4–6

1 small to medium green, red or yellow pepper, chopped

1 tbsp olive oil

4 spring onions, chopped

8 breakfast sausages, cooked and sliced into 5cm (2in.) pieces

$1/2$ tsp freshly ground pepper

$1/2$ tsp red chillies, crushed

8 eggs

115ml (4fl. oz) double cream

115g (4oz) Cheddar cheese, grated

THE BRITISH FRITTATA

The beauty of the frittata is its flexibility – you can put into it whatever you and the family fancy. Most of the traditional British breakfast elements will be quite at home in the egg or – if you fancy living dangerously – the egg and cream mixture: sliced sausage as above, sliced tomatoes, left-over potato, chopped cooked bacon, black pudding, mushrooms, *anything* you like. You also have the choice of finishing it off in the oven or under a grill.

sausages

Sausages are one of those products that seem surrounded by mystique. But when you actually get down to it, they're surprisingly easy to make and you'll be amazed at how delicious they taste – no bulky extenders, no preservatives, no artificial colourings and no odd scraps.

Good Housekeeping's *Cookery Book* speaks of sausages as 'a most convenient way of utilising odd scraps of meat that are too bitty and diverse to make a proper cut or joint.' Therein lies the reason for the deep-rooted suspicion with which many commercial sausages have been (and still are) viewed – 'odd scraps of meat' and goodness knows what else! Most of today's generation of butchers take great pride in producing an ever-growing and innovative range of high-class sausages that have greatly raised their status. However, only experience will tell you which butcher in your area produces sausages to your liking. Look for one that enters competitions and wins awards and look for one that experiments with different ingredients. Remember too that very many butchers just work to a set recipe, the final ingredient being a bought-in, ready-made seasoning mix labelled Lincolnshire, Cumberland, West Country, Farmhouse or whatever their claimed local speciality sausage is.

MAKE IT YOURSELF

Once you've embarked on sausage-making, you'll hopefully be so impressed that you'll want to give your home-made bangers a permanent spot on the family menu. The simplest sausage comprises minced meat, breadcrumbs and some herbs. It's mixed up by hand, put into a piping bag and squeezed into sausage casing. If no casing is available then the sausages can be moulded by hand, dusted in flour and left for 12 hours to settle and – hey presto – you have skinless sausages. If even that's too much bother, then roll out the mixture, flour it and cut out sausage patties into whatever shape your biscuit or pastry cutters allow.

Freezing Whatever sausage mixture you don't use immediately can be frozen and has a storage life of three months – always freeze sausages or patties individually on a rack or on baking paper or foil before storing in a bulk bag or container. Defrosting eight large sausages in a microwave takes 5–6 minutes.

Experiment Regional sausages abound – especially in England – and there are many long-established favourites, some of which are included here for you to make yourself. Try them as they are and then incorporate your own changes – swap some of the herbs around, include leeks, cranberries or apple chips . . . dried apricots, chopped prunes . . . change the meats . . . the world is your oyster!

FRESH V. DRIED HERBS

Fresh herbs are obviously the best to use when cooking but of course that's not always possible. There is no hard and fast conversion rate between fresh and dried herbs as so much depends upon the age and quality of the dried versions. These have a shelf life of about a year, so have an annual clearout of the store cupboard. In general, however, the following can be used:

1 tbsp (3 tsp) chopped fresh herbs = $1\frac{1}{2}$ tsp dried/crumbled herbs = $\frac{1}{4}$ tsp ground herbs

If in doubt, initially always put in less of the dried or ground and then add to taste.

SAUSAGE-MAKING TIPS

Sausage casings There are two types of casing, natural and synthetic. Synthetic ones are difficult to obtain in small enough quantities for home use but natural ones can be obtained from a specialist mail order company listed in Appendix V under 'Sausage skins'. Natural casings vary from the 1½cm (1in.) diameter for pigs' intestines to the 10cm (3–4in.) diameter for the larger beef intestines. Casings are usually sold fresh, salted or frozen and the mail order ones mentioned are preserved in a salt solution and will last for a couple of years in the fridge. Varieties available are:

A mincer and sausage-filling attachment

- *hog casings:* for breakfast sausages and continental sausages like bratwurst and boerewors – 23m to make 9kg (20lb)
- *sheep casings:* for chipolatas, frankfurters and cocktail sausages – 45m to make 9kg (20lb)
- *beef runners:* for black pudding, white pudding and the highly-spiced Italian bologna –15m to make 13.5kg (30lb)
- *beef middles:* for Cornish hog's pudding, salami and cervelat – 9m to make 9kg (20lb)
- *beef bungs:* for haggis – 3m to make 4.5kg (10lb) of pudding.

Mincing Once through the mincer for coarse; twice for fine. Don't use a food processor – the blades break down the meat fibres into a mush.

WITHOUT CASINGS

Divide each 500g (1lb 2oz) sausage meat into 8 equal portions • Dust each with flour and roll by hand to form a sausage shape • Let them mature for 12–24 hours in the fridge to allow the sausages to settle and the flavours to permeate.

WITH CASINGS AND A PIPING BAG OR FUNNEL

(If using a sausage-maker, follow the manufacturer's instructions, which will be more or less the same as follows.) Put the sausage mixture into a piping bag using a 1cm (½in.) nozzle • To lubricate, moisten the nozzle and the inside of the bag with water before filling it with meat • Tie a knot in one end of the casing and push as much of the other end as possible on to the nozzle or funnel • Loosely holding the casing on to the nozzle or funnel, gently squeeze all the mixture into the casing, paying out the casing as required • Tie a knot in the open end • Pick the mid-point of the sausage length and press your finger down and twist the casing 3 times • Do this again with each half and then with each quarter until you have the required number of sausages (usually 8 to the ½kg or 1lb) • Let them settle for 12–24 hours.

Don't make your sausage too firm. You have to allow for twisting the length into individual sausages. To test, press down on the filled casing with your forefinger. If the top of the casing touches the bottom and stays there, the firmness is fine. If it springs back up under the pressure of the contents, then the casing is overfilled. To rectify this, lay the length on the work surface and gently stroke the contents towards the open end until you achieve the desired firmness.

An alternative method of forming the sausages themselves is to twist the casing after each sausage is filled. This is a little more time-consuming and the sausages may not be of a uniform size but it avoids early tribulations and casing splits.

SAUSAGE COOKING TIPS

- Source good-quality sausages – from your local butcher if possible.
- Always preheat the grill.
- If doing a fry-up, always cook the sausages before the bacon – they take longer.
- Ignore what your Granny said and don't bother pricking the sausages. This is a throw-back to the poor quality ones made after World War II that had a very high water content which resulted in them exploding when cooked – thus the name 'bangers'.
- Don't overload the grill pan. It increases cooking time and hampers turning the sausages.
- Tongs are very useful for turning sausages to ensure that they are evenly browned.

An interesting way of grilling sausages is to make one lengthways cut in the skin, press a small knob of butter into the cleft plus a sprinkling of breadcrumbs, oatmeal and/or herbs. The sausage opens up during grilling and has a nice crunchy feel to it when eaten.

ABERDEEN SAUSAGE

This is one of the few old Scottish sausage recipes about. They were apparently served cold, cut into slices and would make an interesting addition to the cold breakfast buffet. An alternative method of cooking is to put the mixture in a well-greased loaf tin and bake in a shallow container of water for about 1^1/$_2$ hours at 180°C/355°F (gas mark 4). Let it cool, turn it out, press the toasted oatmeal into all surfaces and then slice and serve as before.

Mix together the minced beef, bacon and fine oatmeal • Add the seasoning and spices • Grease a pudding cloth* and lay the mixture on it, shaping it into a sausage about 8 x 18cm (3 x 7in.) • Wrap the pudding cloth around it and secure it firmly • Boil the sausage in the stock until cooked through (2–3 hours) • Re-tie the cloth to take up any shrinkage and leave to cool • After cooling, remove the cloth and roll the sausage in the toasted oatmeal • Cut into slices and serve as part of a cold buffet breakfast.

*A pudding cloth is a piece of strong white cotton or linen. Before wrapping it around the mixture it should be well greased by rubbing butter or lard into it to prevent it sticking to the mixture.

Makes 14–18 slices
680g (1^1/$_2$lb) minced beef
340g (12oz) streaky bacon, minced
180g (6oz) fine oatmeal
^{1}/$_2$ tsp ground mace
^{1}/$_2$ tsp ground nutmeg
Salt and black pepper
1 litre (35fl. oz) brown meat stock
55g (2oz) pinhead oatmeal, toasted

CUMBERLAND SAUSAGES

A long unlinked sausage from the north-west of England.

Mix together the minced back fat, shoulder and bacon • Add the hot water to the breadcrumbs • Mix everything together by hand, adding the spices and seasoning • Test by frying a small spoonful and adjust the seasoning if required • Fill the casings • Allow to mature in the fridge overnight.

Makes 4 large sausages
360g (13oz) back fat, minced
960g (2lb) shoulder of pork, minced
1 slice of smoked bacon, minced
120g (4oz) stale white breadcrumbs
180ml (6fl. oz) hot water
Salt and black and white pepper to taste
2 generous pinches of nutmeg and mace
Sausage casings

GLAMORGAN SAUSAGE

Although called a 'sausage', this is a savoury rissole first mentioned in 1862 and then possibly adapted to a meatless version during World War II.

Separate one of the eggs, and mix its yolk with the other whole egg, reserving the remaining egg white • Mix together the bread-crumbs, cheese and chopped onion • Add the egg mixture to bind • Add the mustard and seasoning • If using casings, follow the instructions on p. 85 • If not using casings, divide the mixture into even-sized portions, roll into sausage shapes by hand and roll in the flour • Coat with the beaten egg white and cover with raspings.

Makes 4 sausages
2 medium eggs
150g (5½oz) fresh white breadcrumbs
90g (3oz) Cheddar-style cheese, grated
1 small onion or leek, finely chopped
A pinch of mustard
Plain flour and raspings* to coat, if not using casings
Salt and black pepper
Sausage casings

*Raspings are made by drying bread very slowly in the oven and then reducing it to crumbs.

GLOUCESTERSHIRE SAUSAGES

Tradition has it that these sausages have been made for as long as anyone can remember. Real 'Gloster' sausages are made from pork from Gloucestershire Old Spot pigs that frequently include windfall apples in their diet. Some recipes use fat pork instead of shredded suet.

Mix all the ingredients together by hand and squeeze into casings or, if doing without, form sausages by hand • Place in the fridge to mature for 12–24 hours.

Makes 20 full size or 40 chipolatas
900g (2lb) very lean pork, finely minced
350g (12oz) suet, shredded
225g (8oz) fresh white breadcrumbs
½ tsp dried sage
½ tsp dried thyme
½ tsp dried marjoram
1½ tsp salt
½ tsp freshly ground black pepper
Sausage casings

IRISH SAUSAGES

Mince the meat and the fat twice • Mix well with all the other ingredients, adjusting the quantities of the seasoning and spices to taste • Test them by frying a teaspoonful and adjusting the seasoning to taste • Fill the casings as usual and leave overnight in the fridge to mature.

Makes 10–12 sausages
720g (1lb 5oz) lean pork
240g (8^1/$_2$oz) pork fat (no gristle)
30g (1oz) breadcrumbs
^{1}/$_2$ tsp ground allspice
^{1}/$_2$ tsp dried sage
^{1}/$_2$ tsp ground ginger
^{1}/$_2$ tsp dried marjoram
^{1}/$_2$ tsp mace
^{1}/$_2$ tsp cayenne pepper
1 tsp salt
1 tsp freshly ground black pepper
Sausage casings

LINCOLNSHIRE SAUSAGES

One of the most famous of traditional English sausages, the Lincolnshire is made with a mixture of fat and lean pork, coarsely chopped or ground and combined with breadcrumbs and seasoned with sage, salt and pepper. Prize-winning sausage-makers will undoubtedly add their own additional secret herbs and seasonings, but this basic recipe should get you started.

Thoroughly mix together the meat, wet bread, sage and seasoning • Fill the casings and leave overnight to mature.

Makes 18–20 sausages
900g (2lbs) pork shoulder or belly (or a mixture), coarsely minced
160g (5^1/$_2$oz) large white loaf, soaked in water
4.5g (4 tbsp) dried sage
7.5g (1 tbsp) freshly ground black pepper
16g (1 tbsp) salt
Sausage casings

OXFORD SAUSAGES

Pork and veal Oxford sausages were famous as far back as 1799 but the modern recipe differs somewhat from the original.

Mince the meat very finely • Add the breadcrumbs, suet, herbs, seasoning and lemon rind and mix well • Add the beaten egg and bind the mixture together • Either fill the casings as usual or shape into sausage portions and roll in the flour • Leave to rest in the fridge for 12–24 hours.

Makes 24 sausages
450g (1lb) lean pork
450g (1lb) veal
240g (8^1/$_2$oz) white breadcrumbs
360g (13oz) suet
1 tsp nutmeg
1 tsp fresh mixed herbs, chopped (parsley, thyme, mint and marjoram)
1 tsp fresh sage, chopped
Grated rind of ^{1}/$_2$ a lemon
Salt and black pepper
1 egg, beaten
Sausage casings
A little plain flour for dusting

Lincoln sausages with red onion chutney

LORNE SAUSAGE

This is an uncased beef sausage mixture, formed in tins with a square section. Apparently the name 'Lorne' comes from a 'between the wars' Glasgow comedian, Tommy Lorne, who used to make rude jokes about the Glasgow square sausage by likening it to a doormat. If you've ever wondered what was in Lorne sausage, here it is – straight from the butcher's mouth courtesy of Douglas Scott of Scotts of Dunfermline. For visual appeal, butchers usually add some red food colouring, but that's been omitted from this home recipe. You can adjust the size and even the shape of Lorne sausage to suit, and can even form the mixture into conventional sausage shapes, rolling them in cling film and leaving them in the fridge overnight to firm up before cooking as required.

Mix the beef and dry ingredients thoroughly • Mix in the water • Mince all the mixture again and shape – with the help of a rectangular baking tray – into the traditional square shape or whatever shape you require • Place in the fridge overnight to firm up • Slice and fry or grill.

Makes about 20 slices
960g (2lb 2oz) beef (50% lean), coarsely minced
70g (2$^{1}/_{2}$oz) dry breadcrumbs
140g (5oz) rice flour
85ml (3fl. oz) water
34g (1oz) salt
Black pepper to taste

OATMEAL SAUSAGES

With a couple of changes to the Skirlie recipe (*see* p. 114), we have a mixture suitable for vegetarians and, with the substitution of margarine or vegetable oil for the dripping, also suitable for vegans.

Preheat the oven to 200°C/390°F (gas mark 6) • Sauté the onion in the dripping until soft • Stir in the oatmeal and cook until the fat is absorbed • Season well and add the water, cooking for 5–7 minutes until the mixture thickens • Pour into a bowl to cool • If not using casings, form into sausages and coat with egg and breadcrumbs • Bake in the oven for about 10 minutes until crisp and golden or alternatively, shallow or deep fry as preferred.

Makes 8

1 onion, chopped
60g (2oz) dripping
120g (4oz) medium oatmeal
300ml (10¹/₂fl. oz) water
1 egg, beaten
35–55g (1–2oz) dried
   breadcrumbs for coating
Salt and black pepper
Sausage casings

SUFFOLK SAUSAGES

Stories abound about local sausages and Suffolk boasted at least three types – Suffolk, Newmarket and Stowmarket. Indeed, sausages were such an important part of the Suffolk economy that they spawned a regional idiom – 'You can't judge a sausage by its skin', akin to 'Don't judge a book by its cover'. Stowmarket sausages – the recipe for which is lost – were famed during the era of steam trains. It's said that every train that passed through the town would pick up a supply, and the fireman (stoker) would lay them on a clean coal shovel and then cook them in the firebox.

Soak the breadcrumbs in cold water for 10 minutes and then squeeze dry • Mince the meat and the pork fat finely • Put the meat, fat, bread, seasoning and herbs into a bowl and mix by hand • Squeeze into casings or form into sausages by hand and dust with flour • Place in fridge to mature for 12–24 hours.

Makes about 20

200g (7oz) fresh white
   breadcrumbs
900g (2lb) lean pork (blade,
   collar or leg)
225g (8oz) pork back fat
1 tbsp fresh sage, chopped, or
   ³/₄ tsp dried
1 tsp fresh thyme, chopped, or
   ¹/₂ tsp dried
¹/₂ tsp ground mace
¹/₂ tsp nutmeg, grated
¹/₂ tsp freshly ground white
   pepper
2 tsp salt

VENISON SAUSAGES

Being a very lean and healthy meat, venison sausages need some unhealthy fat injected into them to give them more moisture, and this is usually provided by mixing minced venison with minced pork belly. As with other sausages, experimentation is the thing and some manufacturers offer venison sausages combined with a range of different flavours: wild boar; garlic and red wine; sweet peppers; fresh tomato; and whisky – even offering a spiced venison variety.

The following is a basic recipe from venison specialist Nichola Fletcher, to which can be added all sorts of optional ingredients. Pinhead oatmeal gives a good nutty flavour, but needs to be soaked overnight – about 170g (6oz) is fine for this recipe – and herbs and spices can be added to taste. Prior to turning into sausages, it's always safer to check your mixture for taste by frying a small quantity of it first.

Mix the venison and pork together • Add the various flavourings and mix well • Make as for conventional sausages and allow to rest for 12–24 hours • If you aren't piping the mixture into sausage casings, bind it with an egg and roll it out into the required shapes before dusting with flour • Place in the fridge to chill for 12–24 hours.

Makes 30–40 chipolatas
900g (2lb) lean venison, finely minced
450g (1lb) pork belly, finely minced
3 tsp salt
5 tsp cracked black pepper
Sausage casings

RED ONION CHUTNEY

This simple chutney is a very good accompaniment for sausages.

Melt the butter in a small pan • Add the onion and cook over a medium heat for 10 minutes or until softened • Stir in the remaining ingredients and cook for a further 10 minutes until reduced and thickened • Leave to cool and adjust the seasoning to taste.

25g (1oz) butter
2 large red onions, peeled and thinly sliced
75g (3oz) red currant jelly
15ml (1 tbsp) red wine vinegar
30ml (2 tbsp) orange juice
Salt and black pepper

SAUSAGE PATTIES IN A ROLL

Mix together the sausage meat, herbs, Worcestershire sauce and seasoning • Form the mixture into 4 patties • Heat a little oil in a frying pan • Add the patties and cook for 3–4 minutes on one side, turn them over and cook for a further 4–5 minutes until browned and cooked through • Split the baps in half, toast the cut sides and then spread with butter and mustard if required • Sandwich a patty between the two halves and serve.

Makes 4
450g (1lb) pork sausage meat
1 tsp mixed dried herbs
1 tbsp Worcestershire sauce
Salt and black pepper
Olive oil for frying
4 baps
Butter and English mustard to serve

bacon

The smell of cooking bacon joins those of freshly baked bread and brewing coffee as being one of the classic appetite stimulators.

It seems that the Romans started salting sides of bacon as far back as 200 BC and for many centuries it provided our ancestors with their only source of meat during the winter. Originally it was cured by soaking the sides in brine and then hanging them on hooks above the burning wood fires in huge farmhouse chimneys. As time passed, farmers' wives devised all sorts of interesting ways of improving the taste of their bacon – brown sugar, treacle, beer, cider and honey could all be added to the brine – and favourite cures were adopted by butchers to become local or regional specialities. As the decades passed, however, many of those fell by the wayside as supermarkets gained supremacy with their pricing policies that demanded mass production. Individual producers were taken over or went out of business and only a few specialist bacons survived.

But all is not lost. Modern tastes have turned full circle and we now have scores of butchers and small producers curing and smoking their own bacon, much to the delight of breakfast enthusiasts. The range of curing ingredients include salt, saltpetre, sodium nitrate and sodium nitrite which produces the attractive pink colour when the meat is cooked. They also dramatically reduce the risk of food poisoning by inhibiting the growth of the bacterium responsible for botulism. Other ingredients which may be added are sodium ascorbate, which accelerates the curing process, and sodium polyphosphate, which allows the bacon to soak up much more salty water during the curing and gives it a juicier texture. Then there can be sweeteners and flavourings added such as sugar, honey, molasses, juniper berries, spices and maple syrup. After curing, the bacon can then be smoked.

For real bacon lovers, the villain in the above list is the sodium polyphosphate. Although this produces a moister rasher, you end up paying a greatly inflated price for water, while the process also produces a milky white liquid that interferes with the cooking process and leaves behind a sticky brown residue in the pan or grill.

Despite the fact that Britons are the biggest consumers of bacon rashers in Europe – spending over £430 million (2001) on pre-packed rashers alone and consuming a staggering 560 million bacon butties every year – countries such as Denmark and Holland have developed their pig industries – and therefore their bacon production – to such a fine art that they've cornered the market. The most common cuts are:

- *streaky bacon:* made from the fatty chest meat of the pig, which becomes crisp if it's thin and well cooked
- *back bacon rashers:* lean since they're from the loin, and outselling streaky 9:1
- *middle or through-cut rashers:* combining the streaky bacon and the back to give us traditional cuts such as Ayrshire bacon
- *gammon rashers:* made, like gammon steaks, from the hind leg of the pig and delicious if thin-cut

but there's a much wider range of bacons available – smoked, unsmoked and

- Many chefs keep their cooking oil in a squeezy ketchup or mustard dispenser – the kind that you come across in fast-food outlets.
- To cut down on the oil you use when frying or grilling, use a refillable oil spray. It's also handy for summer barbecues and spraying precious pans to prevent rust.

traditional cures such as Wiltshire, Ayrshire, and Suffolk sweet-cure. Not so traditional are some interesting alternatives to conventional bacon. Pancetta is a wafer-thin, streaky Italian bacon which is proving so popular that some specialist UK producers are now supplying it. If you're a bacon fan, try and find a local butcher near you who cures his own – remember that you can ask them to cut it to whatever thickness you prefer. And if you can't source a local butcher, then try some of the mail order suppliers listed at the end of the book.

BACON SANDWICHES AND ROLLS

The bacon sarnie or butty really needs no explanation and is a great favourite with young and old at all times of the day. Grill or fry the bacon, it makes no difference and, to add even more taste, thinly sliced grilled or fried tomatoes can be added.

SPAM

Spam (spiced ham) was created in the US in 1926 and because it was not rationed during World War II it became an all-American and British staple food. To the many Marmite kids of that era we dedicate its inclusion here. Fried in a good hot fat so that it's crisp on the outside, it makes a tasty addition to a fried/grilled breakfast.

COOKING BACON

- Grilling is by far the healthier cooking method, although if the bacon is particularly lean, brush it with lard or vegetable oil beforehand to keep it moist. Always preheat the grill.
- Try grilling your bacon 'tile-style' to keep it even moister. Arrange the rashers on the grill rack with fat over lean, but only overlap as many rashers as you serve to one person – in grilling, the rashers tend to bond together.
- If frying, cook the bacon in its own fat with perhaps just a little oil to start it off. Try using a bacon weight (or an old fashioned flat iron) to increase the rashers' contact with the cooking surface.
- If cooking thick gammon rashers, snip all the way round the fat to prevent curling.
- Nowadays most bacon is rindless, but if it isn't, then cut the rind off with scissors and render the fat from it by cooking it slowly in the oven at 150°C/300°F (gas mark 2). It

will keep in the fridge for a couple of weeks. Then grill or fry the rinds until crisp, crush them up and freeze or store them in the fridge for seasoning soups and stews.
- For soft bacon, cook gently; for crisp, cook faster. Depending upon thickness, cook for 3–4 minutes until the bacon begins to curl and then turn. Cook for a lesser period on the other side – about 2 minutes.
- Use kitchen tongs for turning the bacon – they make life much easier.
- After cooking, ensure that you pat off the surplus oil with kitchen paper.
- You can't replicate the taste of grilled or fried bacon but, for a magically quick bacon butty or hurried fry-up, the microwave wins hands down. A couple of rashers will take 20–40 seconds to cook, depending upon the microwave power rating. Sandwich the rashers between two pieces of kitchen towel to absorb the fat/moisture and to prevent spitting.

Opposite:
Bacon and egg on a muffin

An open bap with bacon

BACON AND TOMATO BAP

Grill or fry the bacon and tomatoes until cooked • Spread the mayonnaise over the bap • Top with bacon and tomatoes and serve.

Serves 1

2–4 rashers of back bacon

1 tomato, sliced

1 tsp mayonnaise (reduced-fat version if that makes you feel better!)

1 bap, halved and toasted

FRIED BACON SANDWICHES

Grill the bacon lightly • Butter the bread and spread the non-buttered sides with the chutney • Put the cooked bacon on top and sprinkle with pepper • Put the remaining slices of bread on each sandwich and press down firmly • Cut into diagonal quarters • Dip each quarter into the beaten egg and coat evenly with the breadcrumbs • Shallow fry in hot oil on both sides until crisp and golden.

Serves 2

4 rashers of streaky or back bacon

4 slices of sandwich loaf

25g (1oz) butter

2 tbsp chutney

Freshly ground black pepper

1 egg, beaten

25g (1oz) dried breadcrumbs

Oil for frying

TOASTED BACON SANDWICH

We've suggested lard here for frying the egg because it's so tasty. However, if you've got an eye on your cholesterol levels then use vegetable oil.

Fry or grill the bacon as usual • Toast the bread on one side and then lightly toast it on the other • Butter the lightly-toasted sides • Fry the egg in the lard • Lay one slice of toast on a heated plate, toasted-side up • Place the fried egg on top and cover with the bacon • Top with the second slice of toast • Have kitchen roll handy to wipe egg yolk off your shirt front or dress.

Serves 1

2–3 rashers of back bacon
  or 4 rashers of streaky bacon
2 slices of thick toasting bread
Butter
1 egg
A knob of lard

PANS

As a fairly rigid rule, the thicker the pan bottom, the better the pan and the less likely it is that food will burn and stick to it. Some of the best pans ever to hit the UK market were the remarkably cheap imported sets of black cast-iron ones with removable wooden handles. Properly seasoned or proved (*see* below), they last a lifetime. Although new sets seem to have disappeared from the scene, they can still be found in various charity shops on sale for a matter of a few pounds.

• To 'prove' cast-iron pans, brush or spray with oil, being generous in the pan itself, and then bake for 1 hour in a cool oven (120°C/250°F). If the pans have wooden handles, remove them first!

• Over the months the treatment gradually wears off but all you have to do is prove them again.

• To stop cast-iron pans going rusty, rinse in clear water after washing and place on a hot ring for a minute until the surface is dry.

• To avoid damaging non-stick pans when storing and stacking, put a couple of sheets of kitchen paper between them.

If you're wary of the neighbours seeing you scouring the second-hand emporiums, then think stainless steel. Good ones (not the cheap offer ones which have thin bases) are expensive but hard wearing and will last a lifetime. The best ones will have a sandwich base of stainless steel and copper or aluminium to aid even heat distribution.

There are other excellent pans about, of course, and Aga owners will swear by that company's heavy cast-iron pans coated with vitreous enamel. The similar Le Creuset pans have long been a must-have kitchen fashion accessory for some.

Frying pans When it comes to frying, a stainless-steel surface is not the first choice. Food tends to stick to it very easily. A non-stick stainless steel frying pan, however, is another matter and it's well worth paying a king's ransom for a thick-based one with a really good non-stick lining on which metal utensils can be safely used. Ideally, you should have a couple of frying pans – one large and one small. Cast-iron ones are a very good and cheap alternative.

Omelette pan If you're serious about omelettes, you'll need one or more of these. They have shallow, sloping sides designed to facilitate easy turning and removal of the contents. Non-stick versions are ideal.

BACON AND POTATO CAKES

Cut the bacon rashers into small pieces • Pat the grated potatoes and onion with kitchen paper to absorb moisture and add them to the bacon • Work in the egg, flour and seasoning • Heat the lard in a frying pan and drop in tablespoons of the mixture • Fry until golden brown on both sides • Serve with fried or grilled tomatoes and/or mushrooms, or with fried eggs.

Serves 2

100g (4oz) bacon rashers

1 large potato, peeled and
  coarsely grated

1 medium onion, grated

1 egg, beaten

25g (1oz) self-raising flour

Salt and black pepper

A small knob of lard

BACON SCONES

Whether you pronounce them to rhyme with bones or dons, this recipe offers a really tasty savoury for breakfast.

Preheat the oven to 230°C/450°F(gas mark 8) • Heat the bacon in a frying pan until the fat runs (if it doesn't, add a drizzle of oil) • Add the onion and cook until the onion is soft and golden • Drain off the fat • Sift the flour, cream of tartar and bicarbonate of soda into a bowl and rub in the margarine or butter • Add the cheese • Mix with a little milk to make a soft but manageable dough • On a floured board, roll out the dough until 2.5cm (1in.) thick • Cut into rounds and put on a baking tray • Brush with a little milk and bake for 15 minutes until brown • Serve freshly baked, split and spread with butter.

Makes 10–12

3 back bacon rashers, rindless
  and finely chopped

1 medium onion, finely
  chopped

200g (8oz) plain flour

1 tsp cream of tartar

$1/2$ tsp bicarbonate of soda

50g (2oz) butter or margarine

50g (2oz) Cheddar cheese,
  grated

A little milk to mix

BACON ON CRUMPETS WITH MAPLE SYRUP

Fry the bacon for 2–3 minutes • Add the mushrooms and fry for 1 minute • To serve, place the bacon and mushrooms on top of the crumpet, drizzle over the maple syrup or honey and sprinkle with the parsley.

Serves 2

4 back bacon rashers, chopped

2 large button mushrooms,
  sliced

2 crumpets, toasted

Maple syrup or clear honey for
  drizzling

2 tsp fresh parsley, chopped

tomatoes and mushrooms

The Aztecs and Incas first cultivated tomatoes in around 700 AD – the word 'tomato' comes from the Aztec 'tomatl' – and today they are as familiar at breakfast time as they are at other meals during the day. Considering their health benefits, this is no bad thing. Comprised primarily of water (93–95%) and being low in fat, they are good sources of vitamins A, C and (when eaten raw) E, not to mention containing a range of other sugars, minerals and salts.

As you would expect, raw and grilled tomatoes contain the highest concentration of nutrients, although an interesting thing happens to them when cooked. Research suggests that people who eat more tomatoes, particularly processed ones, are better protected against the growth of cancerous tumours. Indeed, the benefit of 40g tomato paste is equal to that of 400g whole cooked tomatoes. This is because tomatoes contain the powerful antioxidant lycopene, which is more readily absorbed into the blood stream when the tomatoes are cooked, and especially with oils like olive oil and particularly corn oil. There is also a suggestion that this may be active in protecting the skin against UV damage from solar radiation.

Eating tomatoes clearly comes highly recommended, therefore, but the effects are said to be especially dramatic for men: eating tomatoes at least ten times a week can reduce the risk of developing prostrate cancer by 35% and half the risk of heart disease.

- As tomatoes are a subtropical fruit and dislike the cold, they should be stored at room temperature. Storing them in the fridge impairs their flavour.
- To ripen home-grown tomatoes, place them in a brown paper bag with a ripe tomato and keep at room temperature. Over-ripe tomatoes will go soft even quicker in the fridge.
- Tomato juice is an excellent hangover remedy.

CORING AND PEELING TOMATOES

If a recipe asks you to core and peel tomatoes, there are a couple of ways to do it – choose the one you find the most effective.

METHOD 1

Cut a small cross on the end of the tomato – opposite to the stalk end • Remove the core from the stalk end by cutting at an angle with a small sharp knife • Drop the tomatoes into a pan of boiling water and leave until the cross that you cut in the skin starts to curl (5–15 seconds) • Immediately remove the tomatoes with a slotted spoon and plunge them into cold water for a few seconds to halt the cooking process • Starting at the cross, cut in the base of the tomato and strip off the skin between finger and thumb.

METHOD 2

Place the tomatoes in a bowl • Pour over boiling water and leave for 20 seconds • Prick a tomato with the point of a sharp knife. If the skin splits and peels back, they're ready to be drained and peeled. If not, leave them for a few seconds more and check again.

SEEDING AND DRAINING TOMATOES

Depending upon the size and type of tomato and how it's going to be used, you can either cut them in half horizontally, cut the tops off (for round tomatoes) or cut them in half vertically (for plum tomatoes) and scoop out the seeds with a small teaspoon. As they will 'weep' slightly, turn them upside down on kitchen roll for about 10 minutes to drain off any excess liquid.

GRILLED TOMATOES

We could be forgiven for assuming that those sweet and tangy tomatoes of our childhood are merely an example of false memory syndrome. But they aren't and they'll be back one of these days. In the meantime, try this method of grilling tomatoes that will remind you of those bygone tastes. Serve them as an accompaniment to a host of other breakfast dishes or on toast or fried bread.

Slice each tomato horizontally through the middle • Sprinkle with just a touch of salt and more generously with brown sugar (white will do if brown isn't to hand) • Place under a very hot grill until cooked (about 10 minutes) and the top is caramelised to the point of being almost black. (They should be amongst the first items to go under the grill – at the same time as the sausages.) • When served, stand back and listen to the family's appreciative murmurs • If you have any lemon juice – the bottled kind will do – a drop or two on each half tomato before sprinkling with salt and sugar will further enhance the taste by heightening that bittersweet tanginess • For a tropical flavour, sprinkle a pinch of ground ginger, cinammon or nutmeg on each half before grilling.

Tomatoes
Salt
Brown sugar
Lemon juice, fresh or bottled
Ground ginger, cinnamon or
  nutmeg (optional)

TOMATO SCRUB
Tomato pulp is said to be very good for the skin. It refreshes, tones and aids circulation and will restore acidity to the face after cleansing. Blend together peeled tomatoes and lemon juice, remove from the liquidiser and splash on the face. Rinse off with tepid water.

STUFFED TOMATOES WITH EGG

Stuffed tomatoes are very versatile and, when it comes to filling them, you can let your imagination run riot. Instead of the bacon and mushroom below, you can use black pudding, white pudding, skirlie or even haggis (see pp. 114–18). For a simplified version you can obviously omit the eggs.

Preheat the oven to 180°C/350°F (gas mark 4) • Cut the tops off the tomatoes and scoop out the flesh and seeds • Season the inside of the tomatoes with salt and pepper • Dry-fry the bacon until crisp and lay aside • Fry the mushrooms quickly in the bacon fat until crisp and remove from the heat • Chop the bacon • Place the tomatoes in a greased ovenproof dish • Divide the bacon and mushrooms between the tomatoes • Bake for about 15 minutes until the tomatoes are soft • Take out of the oven, gently break an egg into each tomato and dot with butter • Bake for another few minutes until the egg is cooked • Garnish and serve on a slice of toast.

4 large beef tomatoes
2 rashers of streaky bacon
115g (4oz) mushrooms, finely
  chopped
4 small eggs
25g butter
4 slices of toast
Salt and black pepper

ROE-STUFFED BAKED TOMATOES

Preheat the oven to 180°C/350°F (gas mark 4) • Melt 25g (1oz) of the butter in a frying pan • Add the onion and fry until translucent • Add all but 4 tsp of the breadcrumbs and fry until golden • Break up the cod's roe with a fork and stir into the breadcrumb mixture • Add the lemon rind, cayenne and seasoning to taste • Fill the tomato halves with the stuffing and spoon over some orange or apple juice • Sprinkle with the reserved bread crumbs and add a knob of the remaining butter • Cook in the oven for 15–20 minutes until the tomatoes are just tender.

40g (1¹/₂oz) butter
1 small onion, finely chopped
50g (2oz) fresh white breadcrumbs
1 x 99g tin smoked cod's roe
Grated rind of ¹/₂ a lemon

4 large tomatoes, halved, seeded and drained
2–3 tbsp orange or apple juice
Cayenne pepper
Salt and black pepper

KIDNEYS IN TOMATOES

This mixture can also be used for stuffing mushrooms.

Preheat the oven to 190°C/375°F (gas mark 5) • Slice off and reserve the tops of the tomatoes • Scoop out the cores, seed and drain • Fry the kidneys quickly in the olive oil in a very hot pan, remove with a slotted spoon and save in a warm dish • Fry the mushrooms and add to the kidney dish • Add the cream and mustard to the pan and allow to bubble for 2 minutes • Return the kidneys and mushrooms to the pan, season and add the chopped parsley or chervil • Spoon 2 kidney halves and some sauce into each tomato • Put the tomatoes in a baking dish and place the reserved tops on them • Cook in the oven for 15 minutes or until soft • Serve with toast or muffins.

Serves 6
6 x 225g (8oz) beef tomatoes
12 lambs' kidneys, skinned, halved and cored
1¹/₂ tbsp olive oil
340g (12oz) mushrooms, wiped and chopped

1 x 142ml (5fl. oz) carton of double cream
1 tbsp Arran or other wholegrain mustard
Fresh parsley or chervil, chopped
Toast or muffins
Salt and black pepper

SKIRLIE TOMATOES

From Aberdeenshire and neighbouring Moray, these make an excellent accompaniment to a fried or grilled breakfast. Use beef tomatoes if making a feature of the dish, and ring the changes by using haggis or black pudding instead of skirlie.

To prevent fat spitting, sprinkle a little salt in the frying pan. If frying in butter, add a teaspoonful of oil to stop it burning.

Preheat the oven to 180°C/355°F (gas mark 4) • Slice off and reserve the tops of the tomatoes • Scoop out the flesh and mix with the prepared skirlie • Drain the tomatoes and fill them with the skirlie mixture • Replace the lids and bake in the oven for 15–20 minutes.

Large firm tomatoes
Skirlie (*see* p. 114)

ENGLISH MUFFINS WITH TINNED TOMATOES AND POACHED EGGS

The fruity acidity of tomatoes and the rich creaminess of egg yolk combine to perfection in this classic breakfast dish. Chefs normally avoid tinned tomatoes like the plague, but the health benefits have persuaded George to turn a blind eye on this occasion! For best results, the tomatoes must be cooked through so that the juices turn jammy and concentrate their flavour. The slightly chewy, dense texture of toasted muffins is the perfect raft because they don't go soggy like toast (for a muffin recipe, *see* p. 51).

Tip the tomatoes and their juice into a small saucepan with the sugar, Tabasco and a generous seasoning of salt and pepper • Cook over a medium heat for about 6 minutes or until the juices have reduced and thickened • Poach the eggs

Serves 2

1 x 400g tin Italian tomatoes, chopped

1 heaped tsp soft brown sugar

1 shake of Tabasco sauce

4 eggs

2 English muffins

Butter

Salt and black pepper

Tomato salsa on a bacon butty

(*see* p. 73) • Split and toast the muffins and spread with butter • Spoon the tomato mixture over the muffins • Remove the eggs with a slotted spoon, dry off on kitchen paper, then set on top of the tomatoes • Garnish and serve.

TOMATO PANCAKES

In these pancakes, diced tomato mixed with finely chopped onion is held in a soufflé-style batter. The mixture puffs up as it cooks and the pancakes give a delicious eggy background to the tomatoes. Serve them on their own, or with crisp streaky bacon and fried or poached eggs.

Separate the egg • Beat the yolk with the milk, flour and $1/2$ tsp of cooking oil to make a thick smooth batter • Season to taste and mix in the onions and tomatoes • Whisk the egg white until it's firm enough to stand in peaks • Fold into the batter • Heat the remaining cooking oil in a frying pan over a medium flame • Drop scoops of the tomato batter into the hot oil and fry for about 30 seconds on each side until set and nicely puffy.

Serves 2

1 large egg

100ml ($3^1/_2$fl. oz) milk

3 tbsp self-raising flour

2 tbsp cooking oil

4 spring onions, trimmed and finely sliced

4 large plum tomatoes, cored, peeled, seeded and sliced

Salt and black pepper

TOMATO SALSA

A tasty and fresh addition to a bacon butty. Put all the ingredients in a food processor and blend until at the desired consistency • Leave to mature for a few hours, but use within 2 days.

Makes 6 spoonfuls

2 normal or 4 small tomatoes

1 tsp capers

4 sun-dried tomatoes

1 tbsp fresh mixed herbs, chopped, or $1/2$ tbsp dried

2 tbsp olive oil

Jams with low sugar content, ketchups, tomato sauces and other tomato preserves risk contamination by moulds and bacteria if they are not heat-treated.

• Immerse your sterilised and filled jars/bottles in water in a large pan, heat the water to boiling point and simmer for 25 minutes (500g jars) to 45 minutes (1 litre jars).

• Leave the jars/bottles to cool in the water before storing.

• Always check that the seals have made a vacuum before storing by gently trying to lift the lids.

• To protect the jars/bottles so that they don't knock into each other and crack when in storage, wrap them in newspaper and place them on a metal rack or folded newspaper.

FRESH TOMATO KETCHUP

This is described as a 'grown-up' ketchup with a fruity, fresh, well-rounded flavour, a hint of chilli (Tabasco) and cinnamon. Both this and the Quick Tomato Ketchup (*see* p. 108) are designed to be used soon after they're made, but will keep in the fridge for a few days. Try pouring it into a bottle or jar and float a layer of olive oil on top each time you put it away.

In a pan, soften the onion and garlic in the olive oil with a pinch of salt • Add the red pepper and celery • Cover the pan and cook gently for 5 minutes • Add the tomato and apple • Cook uncovered for about 15 minutes until the tomato has cooked into juice with the core and skin floating around it • Pass through a sieve, discarding the residue • Add the vinegar and allspice • Simmer gently until reduced by half and very thick • Stir in the sugar, Tabasco and cinnamon • Cook for another 10 minutes and then remove the cinnamon • Taste and adjust with salt and a squeeze of lemon juice • Allow to cool and then chill before serving.

Makes about 425ml (15fl.oz)

1 small onion, chopped
1 clove of garlic, peeled and roughly chopped
2 tbsp olive oil
1 red pepper, cored, seeded and finely chopped
1 stick of celery, finely chopped
700g (1lb 9oz) very ripe tomatoes, coarsely chopped
1/2 a cooking apple, peeled and chopped
1 tbsp red wine vinegar
1/2 tsp ground allspice
3 tbsp white sugar
A few drops of Tabasco
5cm (2in.) stick of cinnamon
A squeeze of lemon juice
Salt to taste

TOMATO KETCHUP IN BULK

Ideal if you have access to a glut of tomatoes at the end of the season.

Combine the tomatoes, onion and peppers in a large pot over a medium heat and simmer, stirring occasionally until very soft • Push through a coarse mesh sieve, discarding the residue, and return to the pot with the sugar and mustard • Tie the cinnamon, allspice, cloves, mace, celery seeds, black peppercorns, bay leaves and garlic in a square of muslin and dangle into the mixture • Bring to a rolling boil, then reduce to a simmer • Continue to cook, stirring often and carefully – it tends to creep up over the edge – until the sauce is reduced by half • Remove and discard the spice bag • Stir in the cider vinegar, salt and paprika to taste • Reduce the heat and simmer for 10 minutes, stirring almost continually • Cool, pour through a funnel into sterilised bottles and preserve or store in the fridge. Use within a month.

Makes about 3 litres (90fl. oz)

6kg (13lb) ripe tomatoes, chopped
8 medium onions, peeled, halved and sliced
2 red peppers, seeds and white filament removed, chopped
175g (6oz) soft brown sugar
1/2 tsp dry mustard powder
7.5cm (3in.) cinnamon stick
1 tbsp allspice, whole
1 tbsp cloves, whole
1 tbsp mace, ground
1 tbsp celery seeds
1 tbsp black peppercorns
2 bay leaves
2 cloves of garlic, chopped
500ml (17 1/2fl. oz) cider vinegar
Salt and paprika

QUICK TOMATO KETCHUP

This is a quick-and-easy luxury version of a breakfast staple.

Quarter the tomatoes and place in a pan with all the other ingredients • Cover and boil hard for 5 minutes • Remove the lid and boil for a further 5 minutes until syrupy and reduced slightly • Pass through a sieve, discarding the residue • If it isn't the consistency of ketchup, simmer until it is • Cool and chill before serving

Makes about 350ml (12fl. oz)

350g (12oz) very ripe tomatoes

2 garlic cloves, peeled and roughly chopped

1 sprig of thyme

1 tbsp balsamic vinegar

1 tbsp olive oil

1 tbsp brown sugar

BAKED BEANS

Where would growing kids be without their baked beans on toast, and where would blow-out breakfasts be without their breakfast gravy? You're unlikely to rival Mr Heinz, but try this recipe which is one of many for baked beans.

Soak the beans overnight in cold water • Boil for 10 minutes and discard the water • Preheat the oven to 140°C/275°F (gas mark 1) • Place the beans in an ovenproof casserole dish • Tip the tomatoes and their juice into a liquidiser and blend • Add to the beans with the rest of the ingredients and stir together thoroughly • Bring to the boil, cover and cook in the oven for 8 hours. Check from time to time, adding more water if it starts to dry out • Remove the bay leaves and chilli before serving.

Serves 6

450g (16oz) dried haricot beans

900g (30oz) tinned plum tomatoes

350g (12oz) onions, finely chopped

2 garlic cloves, peeled and finely chopped

4 tbsp tomato ketchup

25g (1oz) demerara sugar

1 tsp dried oregano

2 bay leaves

1 tbsp English mustard powder

1 small red chilli

1 tsp black treacle or molasses

1 glass (150ml/5^1/$_4$fl. oz) dry white wine

1 tsp salt

2 tsp black pepper

MUSHROOMS

We have a 17th-century French botanist called Oliver de Serres to thank for discovering how to cultivate mushrooms, and they have remained a remarkably successful food product ever since. In recent years there has been a widespread awakening to the potential of wild mushrooms and there are now many professional mushroom hunters who supply discerning chefs up and down the country.

We're most familiar with common cultivated mushrooms, however, and we usually see them in three forms which are, in fact, just different stages in their growth cycle: button mushrooms are the youngest; cap or cup mushrooms are next; and the open, flat mushrooms are the last stage of growth. The pink gills evident on button mushrooms darken to brown as they grow to the flat stage.

None of these usually need peeling or de-stalking and there's no need to wash them – just wipe with a damp cloth if needed. Fresh mushrooms are best kept either in the fridge in their opened container covered with a damp cloth or piece of kitchen towel, or in a paper bag that has had holes punched in it.

Morels These are very flavoursome and are said to be the only serious rival to truffles. They're easily recognisable from their brown or beige caps covered in hollows in which the spores are produced, but they're very difficult to spot in the wild and the location of their woodland habitats are jealously guarded by collectors. Their season is early spring and summer but they can also be bought dried or canned. Because of their deeply pitted skin, cleaning morels requires that you soak them in a bowl of water for about five minutes. The French serve them with scrambled eggs, sautéing them gently in butter for about five minutes.

Ceps (boletus) In the eyes of gastronomes, ceps are high in the mushroom pecking order. Chubby little mushrooms (the Italians call them 'porcini' – 'little pigs'), they have a pungent and perfumed flavour that is said to encapsulate the smell and taste of the woods in which they grow during the summer and autumn. For breakfast they are best sautéed and served with scrambled eggs like morels.

Parasols These wild mushrooms like sandy soil and can be found from July through to November in pastures and woodlands and by the sea on cliff tops and edges. They're tall and conspicuous and the caps (covered with tiny scales) sometimes grow to about 20cm (8in.) in width. Only the heads are edible – the stalks are fibrous and tough – and they have a fragrant taste, delicious sautéed or grilled and especially good with ham and also Cheddar cheese.

Shaggy caps These are tall with blunt-ended elongated heads and a ragged, 'shaggy' surface. Best picked when small and white during the spring to winter season, they are good when grilled and served with bacon, eggs or ham.

Chanterelles The French love chanterelles sautéed in butter with scrambled eggs and bacon. These funnel-shaped, yellow mushrooms are found in beech woods from July to December but are also usually available in the dried or tinned form.

Shiitake This type of mushroom has great potential for breakfast since it's very good with bacon and ham. It's mostly grown on the logs of the Shii tree in China and Japan. Dried ones should be soaked in warm water for about 20 minutes before use.

Field and horse mushrooms   Both of these are found in pastures and meadows from late summer to autumn and their delicious, earthy taste knocks the cultivated varieties into a cocked hat. These wild ones will usually need peeling – especially the horse mushrooms which have a thick skin – and do check for small worms. Break off the stalk or cut one or two mushrooms open. If you come across any little lodgers, cut them out and don't tell the vegetarians in your family!

COOKING MUSHROOMS

As a breakfast accompaniment, fresh mushrooms can either be cooked whole or sliced and chopped. A small saucepan is usually the most convenient way of sautéing them since you can easily give them a periodic shake or stir to ensure even browning in the foaming butter, margarine or bacon fat.

Mushrooms contain a high degree of moisture and if you have too many cooking in the pan at the same time – or if you cook them with the lid on – you'll find that, instead of them frying, they're stewing. Either turn the heat up to evaporate the liquid or drain it off, rebutter the pan and start again. Also remember that mushrooms lose about half their volume when cooked, so don't underestimate the amount you need.

- All mushrooms are about 80% water, 8% carbohydrate and 1% fat. They are a good source of protein, riboflavin, thiamine, iron and copper, potassium and phosphates.
- Many edible mushrooms have poisonous lookalikes. On no account should you eat any wild mushrooms unless you are absolutely sure of their safety and they've been identified by an expert. Do not rely on your own identification from fungi books or charts.

MUSHROOM AND BACON TOASTS

If you don't fancy the cream cheese used in this recipe at breakfast time then omit it and just spoon the mushroom and bacon mixture on to a slice of buttered toast. You will probably need to serve this with grilled tomatoes to give some added moisture. Alternatively, you could spoon the mixture on to a bed of soft scrambled egg on toast.

Melt half the butter in a shallow pan • Add the chopped bacon and fry for 2–3 minutes • Add the mushrooms and half of the parsley, and season with salt and pepper • Cover the pan and cook gently for 6–8 minutes or until the mushrooms are tender • Meanwhile, toast the bread on both sides • Spread 4 of the slices on one side with the remaining butter and the cream cheese • Top each of these with the remaining slices of toast • Spoon the hot mushrooms and bacon over the top • Sprinkle with the remaining chopped parsley and serve.

75g (3oz) butter
6 bacon rashers, rindless and chopped
225g (8oz) button mushrooms, cleaned
2 tbsp parsley, chopped
8 thin slices of bread
100g (3$^{1}/_{2}$oz) full-fat soft cheese
Salt and black pepper

STUFFED MUSHROOMS

If you're using open mushrooms then you can stuff them with a variety of other breakfast elements, ranging from simply laying a slice of grilled tomato on top, to filling them with a spoonful or two of crumbled black pudding, with finely chopped apple and cream. Those could be further enhanced by wrapping each in a slice of streaky bacon and baking in a moderate oven for 15–20 minutes. Large, open mushrooms can also be used as a bed for scrambled eggs. Mushrooms can be fried before stuffing or stuffed raw and baked in the oven as in the following recipe.

Preheat the oven to 190°C/375°F (gas mark 5) • Remove and finely chop the mushroom stalks • Fry the chopped stalks and thinly sliced onion in butter until the onion is translucent • Add the bacon or ham, breadcrumbs and parsley • Add enough egg to bind the mixture and season to taste • Fill the open mushrooms, place in a greased tin, cover with kitchen foil and bake for 15–30 minutes until the mushrooms are soft and the filling is soft and crusty.

Serves 4–8

8 medium mushrooms
1 small onion or 2 shallots, thinly sliced
A knob of butter
3 tbsp cooked bacon or ham, chopped
5 tbsp breadcrumbs
1 tsp fresh parsley, chopped
1 egg, beaten
Salt and black pepper

CREAMED MUSHROOMS

Heat the butter in a small pan • Add the mushrooms and onion • Stir until the mushrooms are cooked and the onion is translucent • Add the cream, parsley and seasoning • Stir continuously until bubbling and the mixture thickens • Serve on toast.

Serves 2

A knob of butter
225g (8oz) button mushrooms, sliced
1 medium onion, finely chopped

1 x 140ml (5fl. oz) carton of single cream
Fresh parsley chopped
Salt and black pepper
Toast, crusts cut off

MUSHROOM OMELETTE

Make the omelette as on p. 78, but add the mushrooms while there is still some liquid egg left • Fold the omelette in half, and slide it out of the pan on to a heated plate • Alternatively, try folding the omelette in three, slitting it lengthways and spooning the cooked mushrooms into the slit.

50g (2oz) button mushrooms per person, sliced
Butter
2–3 eggs per person
Salt and black pepper

breakfast puddings and batters

White puddings, black puddings, haggis, pancakes . . . all make interesting additions to a conventional breakfast grill or fry-up. To dismiss them as bulky and inexpensive fillers (which they undoubtedly were in the poorer north of the country) is to ignore the new tastes and textures that they bring to breakfast, either as an accompaniment or as a stand-alone dish.

Whatever type of puddings you use, if you're not going to make them yourself, source them from a good local butcher whose product represents the best quality available. Try and avoid the mass-produced ones, most of which tend to be bland and devoid of that touch of originality that can elevate the pudding to an exciting breakfast component. And remember: always remove the inedible man-made skin before grilling breakfast puddings.

- For tips on filling sausage casings, turn to p. 85.
- Puddings absorb fat like blotting paper and will go soggy unless you cook them in a slightly smoking pan, or on a hot plate with a minimum of fat. It is far better to grill them.

WHITE PUDDING

White or 'mealie' pudding is very much a northern English and Celtic dish. It's basically a simple mixture of toasted oatmeal, onions, suet, pepper and salt, and is a good example of northern frugality in making a little oatmeal go a long way. Fried with bacon and egg for breakfast, it is difficult to beat.

Toast the oatmeal lightly in a heavy-bottomed pan and tip into a mixing bowl • Add the suet and chopped onions, allspice, salt, sugar and pepper • If using casings, half-fill 10cm (4in.) lengths, tie each end and prick them a few times with a knife point or skewer • Drop into boiling water and simmer for 1 hour • When cool, store in the fridge and, when required, slice and fry or form into patties and fry like skirlie (*see* below).

Makes 2
225g (8oz) pinhead oatmeal
125g (4$\frac{1}{2}$oz) shredded suet
1 small onion, peeled and
  finely chopped
$\frac{1}{2}$ tsp sugar (optional)
A small pinch of allspice
Salt and black pepper
Sausage casings

SKIRLIE
or WHITE PUDDING ON THE LOOSE!

These are the same ingredients as for white pudding but used loose. Serve a spoonful of skirlie as a breakfast accompaniment or use it to stuff mushrooms or tomatoes (*see* p. 104). It may need to be moister if used as a stuffing, so add a little water to the onions during cooking.

Melt the suet and dripping in a hot pan • Add the onion and cook until translucent • Add the oatmeal until it absorbs the fat • Season, cook for about 10–15 minutes and serve.

60g (2oz) shredded suet
60g (2oz) dripping
1–2 medium or 1 large onion,
  finely chopped
120–180g (4–6oz) medium
  oatmeal
Salt and black pepper

IRISH WHITE PUDDING

This differs quite markedly from the mainland UK versions in that pork predominates as an ingredient, breadcrumbs replace the oatmeal and they're not boiled but fried or grilled immediately prior to eating.

Mix all the ingredients thoroughly • Stuff into casings or shape into small, compact patties • Fry or grill until golden brown.

Makes about 6

400g (14oz) medium ground pork shoulder
400g (14oz) fine ground pork shoulder
2$\frac{1}{2}$ cups of breadcrumbs
2 eggs, lightly beaten
4 cloves of garlic, finely chopped or crushed
$\frac{1}{2}$ tsp salt
1$\frac{1}{2}$ tsp dried thyme
1$\frac{1}{2}$ tsp dried basil
1$\frac{1}{2}$ tsp dried marjoram
1$\frac{1}{2}$ tsp ground black pepper
1 cup of cold water
Sausages casings

BLACK PUDDING

Said to have been introduced by the Romans, this is – like white pudding – a very popular product in the Midlands, north of England, Scotland and Ireland. It found great favour with Scottish cattle drovers of old who herded their small black 'kine' (cattle) many hundreds of miles to the great cattle markets of the day. They would carry oatmeal with them, draw some blood from one of their cows and mix it with the oatmeal to produce a basic black pudding.

Scottish black puddings are usually finer in texture than other varieties since they use suet rather than the cubes of finely chopped back fat used in southern puddings. The Irish version is known as 'drisheen' and is made with pig or sheep blood.

George's first job as a 15-year-old in Falkirk was stirring a large heated vat containing the blood for the black puddings. Nowadays, however, the majority of butchers will use dried ox blood, together with pearl barley or groats, barley flour or fine oatmeal, onion, salt, pepper and various herb seasonings, depending upon their own recipe.

IRISH BLACK PUDDING

This differs in various respects from the Scottish and English versions, mainly in that it contains meat: pig's liver. It may not be feasible to make this these days because of the difficulty in obtaining pig's blood and beef casings, but if you want to persevere, speak to your butcher and he may help with the unrendered lard and dried blood.

Stew the liver in boiling salted water for about 10 minutes until tender • Remove and mince, reserving the cooking liquor • Thoroughly mix all the other ingredients together in a large bowl • Fill the casing with the mixture • Tie off in 30cm loops • Steam for 4 hours • Leave until cold • Cut into 1cm (1/2in.) slices as required and fry in hot fat on both sides until crisped.

If you can't get beef casings then pack the mixture into a conveniently sized heatproof dish or bread tin • Cover with kitchen foil that has been pleated down the middle to allow for any expansion, tying it securely around the edge of the container • Steam for 4–5 hours in a pan of boiling water • Cool, slice and cook as before.

Makes 8

450g (1lb) pig's liver

680g (11/2lb) unrendered lard, chopped

33/4 litres (6 pt) pig's blood

900g (2lb) breadcrumbs

115g (4oz) medium oatmeal

1 medium onion, chopped

1 tsp salt

1/2 tsp allspice

1 x beef casing

BLACK PUDDING ON TOAST

This is a Shropshire dish with added oatmeal. A tasty extra is to serve it with a small portion of sautéed or stewed cooking apples – a refreshing foil for the black pudding.

Toast the oatmeal in a hot dry pan, shaking it until it's evenly browned. Put on one side • Remove the skin from the black pudding and mash the contents up well with a fork • Melt the butter in a pan and gently cook the onion until translucent • Stir in the toasted oatmeal and cook for a further few minutes • Add the mashed black pudding and seasoning and mix well • Stir for another 3–4 minutes • Heap on to the rounds of toast, sprinkle with parsley and serve.

75g (3oz) medium or pinhead oatmeal

350g (12oz) black pudding

25g (1oz) butter

1 large onion, peeled and finely chopped

4 large rounds hot buttered toast

1/2 tsp salt

1/2 tsp black pepper

1 tbsp fresh parsley, finely chopped

HAGGIS

Haggis, of course, needs no introduction and whilst it has never been a tradition-al component of breakfast, it firmly deserves space on the plate. To many people it's still a bit of a music hall joke – the haggis shooting season; haggis has one leg shorter than the other so it can run round the hillside and escape the hunters . . . the old jokes are the best! (If anyone tells you that the plural of haggis is 'haggi', ignore them . . . it's 'haggises'.)

Apart from the basics, there's no hard and fast rule as to what goes into a haggis – craft butchers will doubtless have their own secret recipe. Some like a haggis to be hot and spicy, others like it with herbs, some like it dry, others like it wet. Some will use a pig or ox liver instead of the sheep's pluck.

Haggis is now becoming popular throughout the UK, so you should be able to

Opposite: Pancakes with Camarthen cheese and ham stuffing (*see* p. 122)

shop around and try different makes. A recent new product on the market that should find favour is bite-sized portions of haggis that are ideal for breakfast use. If you're an Internet buff, keying in haggis will produce a wide range of mail order suppliers. Whilst we don't expect you to rush off and make one of these fearsome beasties, here's a traditional basic recipe to show what's in the average haggis. After reading it you'll probably never eat one ever again!

Wash the pluck in cold water, scrape and clean well • Put it in a pan and cover with cold water, allowing the windpipe to lie over the side with a small dish or jar underneath to catch the drips • Bring to the boil and simmer gently until tender – from 1–2 hours • When cool, remove from the liquid and cut away the pipes and gristle, reserving the liquid • Toast the oatmeal in the oven until thoroughly dry • Chop up or mince the cooked heart and lungs and grate the liver • Add the oatmeal, herbs, onion, suet and seasoning and about 570ml (1pt) of the reserved liquid to produce a softish mixture • Mix well and use it to fill the sheep's paunch to just over half full (any fuller and the swelling oatmeal may burst it) • Press out the air, sew up the hole with strong thread and place in a large pan of boiling water • When the haggis begins to swell, prick it all over with a large needle • Boil gently without the lid for about 3 hours, topping up the water as necessary.

Serves 8

1 sheep's pluck*

250g (9oz) pinhead oatmeal

1 tsp dried mixed herbs or 2 tsp fresh mixed herbs

125g (4oz) shredded suet, finely chopped

4 medium onions, peeled and finely chopped

2–4 tbsp salt

1 tsp black pepper or ½ tsp cayenne pepper

1 sheep's paunch (stomach), thoroughly scrubbed and soaked overnight in cold salted water

*Those of a nervous disposition should not read this! The sheep's pluck is that bit of the sheep that has been plucked out of the stomach and includes the liver, heart and lungs which are all joined together with the windpipe at the end. There . . . now we've told you! For the squeamish, you can in fact order the liver, heart and lungs separately from your butcher.

PAN HAGGIS

This is a much simpler type of haggis without the blood and gore, and it's almost as good as the traditional version.

Simmer the liver and onions in the stock for 30–40 minutes • Meanwhile, toast the oatmeal in a heavy pan or grill until browned but not burnt, shaking the pan frequently to get even toasting • When the liver and onions are cooked, remove from the heat and retain the liquid • Mince the liver and onions into a bowl and add the oatmeal, suet, salt and pepper • Moisten with the reserved cooking stock to give a soft consistency • Put into a greased pudding basin and cover with pleated kitchen foil, tying it tightly round the rim of the bowl • Steam in a pan of boiling water for 3 hours • Reheat the required amount to spoon on to breakfast plates or turn into haggis bites (*see* opposite).

Makes about 20 spoonfuls

450g (1lb) pig or lamb liver

3 medium onions, peeled and finely chopped

250ml (½pt) stock (meat or vegetable)

100g (3½oz) pinhead oatmeal

150g (5½oz) shredded suet

1 tsp salt

½ tsp black pepper

HAGGIS BITES

Here's an even simpler way of incorporating haggis into your grilled or fried breakfast. If you can't get hold of a 'live' haggis, buy a tinned one and make these delicious haggis bites. Haggis is very rich and one or two of these on the breakfast plate will probably be enough for the uninitiated. These can be made the day before required, kept in the fridge and reheated in the oven, microwave, under the grill or in the frying pan.

Makes about 20 balls
1 tin of haggis
1 egg yolk
1 egg white, beaten
30–55g (1–1³/₄oz)
  breadcrumbs
Vegetable oil for frying

Open the tin and empty the haggis into a mixing bowl • Add the egg yolk and mix well • Take rounded teaspoonfuls of the mixture and roll into bite-sized balls • Dip each ball into the egg white and then roll in the breadcrumbs • Fry in the hot oil until evenly brown • Remove with tongs or a slotted spoon and dry off on kitchen paper.

CLOOTIE DUMPLING

Clootie or cloutie dumpling is a very traditional Scottish dish that has found its way on to quite a few breakfast menus – sliced and fried in butter as an accompaniment to the grill or fry-up.

A 'cloot' or 'clout' is a piece of cloth, in this case a square of cotton or linen in which the uncooked pudding is tied. When cooked, this gives us the shape of the traditional round Christmas pudding that we used to draw as youngsters. Traditionally – as with Christmas puddings – silver threepenny bits were wrapped in greaseproof paper and included in the mixture too.

Once cooked, a cloutie dumpling can be cooled, sliced and frozen ready for you to bring out a piece when required. Here's a recipe from the Clootie Dumpling Tearoom in the Scottish Highlands.

330g (11¹/₂oz) self-raising
  flour, sifted
150g (5¹/₂oz) wholemeal flour
180g (6oz) sugar
540g (19oz) raisins or mixed
  fruit
120g (4oz) shredded suet
3 rounded tsp mixed spice
1 tsp baking soda
1 large or 3 small carrots,
  grated
1 medium apple, grated
750ml (26fl. oz) milk
1 tbsp golden syrup
1¹/₂ tbsp black treacle

Half-fill a large pan with water and bring this to the boil • Mix all the dry ingredients together in a bowl and bind with the milk, syrup and treacle • Sterilise the cloot (a cotton or linen pudding cloth) by dropping it into the pan of water • Remove with tongs, then place the cloth into a large bowl and dredge with flour • Spoon in the doughy mixture and tie the cloot tightly, leaving enough room for the dumpling to swell • Remove from the bowl, put a plate in the bottom of the pan and place the dumpling on it • Simmer for a good 4 hours. Keep topping up with boiling water • Preheat the oven to 170°C/340°F (gas mark 3) • Turn out the dumpling very carefully on to a hot serving dish and dry off gently in the oven for 5–10 minutes • Wait until cool before cutting into slices for freezing.

PANCAKES

There's frequently some confusion about what's meant by a pancake. In England a pancake is really a crêpe – a light and paper-thin creation. In Scotland a pancake or 'drop scone' is much smaller and thicker, but not as thick as the North American 'hotcake'.

A great time-saver is to make up a large batch of the dry ingredients for pancakes and waffles, divide them up into quantities that suit you and bag and label them. Check the 'use by' date on the baking powder before you do this, though.

To check if baking powder is still alive and kicking, mix a teaspoonful into a small quantity of hot water. If it fizzes it's OK.

SCOTCH PANCAKES

Sift the flour, sugar and salt together • Add the beaten egg and a drop of milk, a little at a time, until you have a thick batter (use a balloon whisk or an electric hand mixer) • Heat a girdle or thick frying pan and add a smear of butter • Drop a few spoonfuls of the mixture on to the pan • Cook on one side until the exposed surface is covered in small bubbles • Turn over and cook until golden brown • Serve with whatever topping your heart desires.

- Throw dietary caution to the wind and decorate the hot pancake with a large knob of butter, immediately followed by a generous splash of maple syrup.
- A mixture of equal parts of yoghurt and maple syrup is known as 'maple cream' and is also delicious.
- Pancakes served with crisp, smoked streaky bacon and maple syrup are surprisingly scrumptious. Don't knock it unless you've tried it!

Any cooked pancakes left over can be eaten cold later in the day. Any leftover mixture can be kept in the fridge for use within the next day or so.

Makes about 12
100g (3¹/₂oz) self-raising flour
50g (2oz) caster sugar
A pinch of salt
1 egg, beaten
Milk
A knob of butter

MAPLE SYRUP

- Colonists learned from the North American Indians how to tap the maple tree for its sugary sap.
- Maple syrup is twice as sweet as sugar and takes 20–50 gallons of sap to make 1 gallon of syrup.
- Pure maple syrup is quite expensive, but well worth it. Don't make the mistake of buying maple-flavoured syrup – it's cheaper but not a patch on the real stuff.

CANADIAN HOTCAKES

If you've visited Canada or North America and sampled their pancakes for breakfast (also known as 'drop scones', 'griddlecakes', 'hotcakes' or 'flapjacks'), then you'll know how delicious they can be.

Here's a recipe that never fails to produce pancakes at least 2cm (¹/₂in.) thick (most diners will manage one or two). Ideally, the mixture should be made the night before and left in the fridge. If that can't be done, it doesn't matter – you'll still get excellent results from this instant mix.

Opposite: Bacon on crumpets with maple syrup

Sift the dry ingredients into a bowl • Add the beaten egg and some of the milk and blend with a whisk or hand mixer • Add the melted butter • Add more milk until the mixture is the consistency of thick custard • Oil a hot plate, girdle or cast-iron frying pan (in the absence of any of those, an ordinary frying pan will do, but take care of burning) • Transfer the mixture to a jug and pour the required amount on to the cooking surface (children tend to like smaller and thinner pancakes – 'silver dollars' they call them across the Atlantic) • When the surface is covered with bubbles, the pancake is ready for turning (or flipping, if you're brave!) • Pancakes should be served immediately but they will keep perfectly in a warm oven • Spread with fresh butter and pour over with maple syrup to serve.

Makes 4 large pancakes
150g (5^1/$_2$oz) plain flour
1 tbsp sugar
1 tbsp baking powder
^{1}/$_2$ tsp salt
1 egg, beaten
125–250ml (4–8^3/$_4$fl. oz) milk
1 tbsp melted butter

ENGLISH PANCAKES

These pancakes or crêpes can be stuffed with anything that takes your breakfast fancy: bacon and tomato, scrambled eggs, cheese and ham and even fruit and yoghurt. Try the stuffings that follow.

Makes 14–16
125g (4oz) plain flour
A pinch of salt
3 eggs, beaten
250ml (9fl. oz) milk
30g (1oz) melted butter

Sift the dry ingredients into a bowl and add the eggs • Mix with a whisk or electric hand mixer, adding the milk gradually until you have the consistency of thin cream • Leave it to 'prove' for about 30 minutes • Heat the frying pan and add some butter (ideally clarified). There are special crêpe pans available but, before you splurge on one of these, try a shallow-sided conventional frying pan • There's a bit of a knack to frying crêpes. Once the pan is hot (use a medium to high heat), drop in about a teaspoonful of batter; when it starts 'spitting', pour in a small ladleful of the mixture and tip and shake the pan to coat the bottom evenly. The idea is to get as thin a crêpe as you can • Cook quickly until the top is set and then loosen the crêpe with a spatula or similar tool • Using your fingers, lift it out and turn over to cook on the other side for about 20–30 seconds • The crêpes can be stacked between layers of greaseproof paper and kept warm before filling.

VARIATION

A healthier version uses 100g (3^1/$_2$oz) plain flour, 1 medium egg, 300ml 10^1/$_2$fl. oz) semi-skimmed milk and a pinch of salt. Cook as above.

STUFFINGS

- *Camarthenshire cheese and ham:* mix together 3 tbsp Welsh goat's cheese (or similar), ^{1}/$_2$ slice of diced Welsh ham and 3 ready-to-eat dried and chopped apricots in a bowl and fill one or more pancakes.
- *Fruit and yoghurt:* mix together 3 tbsp plain or vanilla yoghurt, 100g (3^1/$_2$oz)

red or white seedless grapes and 1 peeled and chopped kiwi fruit in a bowl and fill one pancake.

PANCAKES WITH BUTTERMILK

This recipe uses buttermilk and less sugar than the Canadian Hotcakes (*see* p. 120–2), and produces about a dozen thinner pancakes.

Sift the dry ingredients into a bowl • Add the beaten egg and some of the milk, and blend with a whisk or hand mixer • Add the melted butter • Add more milk until the mixture is the consistency of single cream • Oil a hot plate, girdle or cast-iron frying pan • Transfer the mixture to a jug and pour the required amount on to the cooking surface • When the pancake surface is covered with bubbles, it is ready for turning • Pancakes should be served immediately, but they will keep perfectly in a warm oven stacked between sheets of greaseproof paper.

VARIATIONS

* For whole-wheat pancakes, just substitute wholemeal flour for the plain.
* If you want to add any fruit such as fresh blueberries or raspberries, add them to the batter just before cooking.
* Butter and maple syrup is again the favourite topping, although you can also try honey.
* Don't forget to sample them with crispy bacon.

Makes 12

125g (4oz) plain flour
$^1/_2$ tsp caster sugar
$^1/_2$ tsp salt
1 tsp bicarbonate of soda
$^1/_2$ tsp baking powder
1 egg, beaten
2 tsp melted butter
225ml (8fl. oz) buttermilk
Butter for frying

CRUMPETS

Crumpets are not the simplest things in the world to make but if you have the time and patience, here's how it's done. You'll need some crumpet rings, but you can use the stainless steel rings recommended earlier instead (*see* p. 73).

Add the yeast and sugar to the bowl of lukewarm water and whisk until dissolved • Cover and leave in a warm place for about 10–15 minutes until the mixture froths • Sift the flour and salt into another bowl and make a well in the centre • Add the milk to the yeast mixture and whisk • Pour into the flour and beat vigorously until you achieve a smooth batter • Cover and leave in a warm place until the batter has doubled in size and just starts to shrink back • Dissolve the bicarbonate of soda in a drop of cold water and beat into the batter • Cover again and leave for about 5

Makes 6

1$^1/_2$ tsp dried yeast
$^1/_2$ tsp caster sugar
150ml (5$^1/_4$fl. oz) lukewarm
  water
225g (8oz) strong white
  (bread-making) flour
$^1/_2$ tsp salt
150ml (5$^1/_4$fl. oz) lukewarm
  milk (skimmed if prefer)
$^1/_2$ tsp bicarbonate of soda

minutes • Heat a girdle or thick-based frying pan and lightly grease it • Oil or grease the insides of the 9cm rings and place them in the pan • Half-fill each ring with batter • Cook for about 5 minutes on a medium heat until the top of each crumpet is covered with those characteristic holes and the surface is dry • Loosen the crumpets with a thin blade, turn over and cook for about 30 seconds until brown • Sit down, have a rest and enjoy them – you've earned a reward!

WAFFLES

Waffles are one of the world's great culinary inventions – a breakfast treat for young and old! Looking like a metallic block of chocolate, a waffle iron has two hinged, honeycombed sides. Batter, the consistency of thick cream, is poured into one of them, the lid is closed and, minutes later, out comes a crisp and delicious receptacle for all sorts of goodies, sweet or savoury. The most common form of waffle iron nowadays is an electric one where both top and bottom plates are heated, but stove-top versions are still available. The quantity of waffles depends upon the size of the waffle iron.

An electric waffle iron

WAFFLE-MAKERS

- Start off by sticking to the manufacturer's recommendation of how much mixture to use each time and then experiment until you get the waffle right out to the edge of the heating plate.
- You can have periodic looks at the waffle to see how it's cooking – no harm will be done.
- Ideally, waffles should be eaten as soon as they're cooked and they're nice and crisp. If you have to store them in the oven, don't stack them – like toast, they'll go soft. Lay them out on a wire tray if possible.
- If you end up with a soft waffle, a couple of minutes in a hot oven will crisp it up again.
- The top surface of waffle irons can get very hot so keep the kids away from it.

WAFFLE TOPPINGS

You can top waffles with savouries such as mushrooms, bacon, scrambled egg and even a fried egg. The youngsters will probably prefer the favourite waffle topping of butter and maple syrup, but try a good jam or fruit sauce plus cream or yoghurt . . . let your imagination run wild:

- *soft fruits:* 2 cups of berries, $1/2$ cup of honey and a few drops of vanilla. Crush the soft fruit, add the honey, simmer for 5 minutes and then add the vanilla
- *maple cream:* mix equal parts of yoghurt and maple syrup
- *banana and orange:* liquidise chunks of banana with some orange juice
- *Mars bar sauce:* don't let the local Health Board know about this one. Take 2 Mars bars, chop them into 4 pieces and place in a jug with 60ml (4 tbsp) milk. Microwave on 'high' for 2–3 minutes. If you haven't a microwave, use a double boiler or melt in a bowl over a pan of boiling water.

BASIC WAFFLES

Preheat the waffle-maker • Sift the flour, baking powder and salt into a large bowl and stir in the sugar • Put the egg yolks, melted butter and milk into another bowl and beat well. (Don't wash the whisks yet) • Add this mixture to the dry ingredients and beat to combine. (Wash the whisks now!) • Whisk the egg whites to a stiff consistency and fold into the other ingredients • Put 1–1$^1/_2$ large table-spoonfuls of the mixture into the middle of the waffle-maker • Close and cook until puffed and golden brown.

Makes 12

170g (6oz) plain flour

2 tsp baking powder

$^1/_2$ tsp salt

2 tsp caster sugar

2 eggs, separated

85g (3oz) melted butter

225ml (8fl. oz) milk

VARIATIONS

• *Chocolate waffles:* add 55g (2oz) melted chocolate and 3 drops of vanilla essence to the basic recipe. Melt the chocolate in a bowl over a saucepan of

The breakfast toad

boiling water and add it – together with the vanilla essence – when you whisk in the egg yolks, melted butter and milk. Cook as normal and serve with whipped cream, decorated with grated or powdered chocolate.

- *Cheese waffles:* add 55g (2oz) grated cheese to the basic recipe, combining it with the other ingredients prior to adding the egg whites. These can be served with cream cheese, sliced apples or crisp grilled bacon.

POTATO WAFFLES

Preheat the waffle-maker • Beat the potatoes, milk, flour and melted butter until smooth • Add the celery salt, pepper and eggs and mix thoroughly • Put 3 tbsp of the mixture into the centre of the waffle-maker • Close and cook until golden brown • For the topping, melt the butter in a frying pan • Add the spring onions and mushrooms and cook until softened • Add the cream and bring to the boil, stirring until thickened • Stir in the parsley and chives • Serve on top of the waffles.

Makes about 12
170g (6oz) potato, mashed
55ml (2fl. oz) milk, hot
6 tsp plain flour
30g (1oz) melted butter
2 eggs, beaten
Celery salt and black pepper

For the topping
45g (1¹/₂oz) butter
6 spring onions, chopped
340g (12oz) mixed mushrooms, chopped
256ml (10fl. oz) thick sour cream
1 tsp fresh parsley and chives, chopped

BREAKFAST TOAD

As Granny used to say, 'This'll put hairs on your chest.'

Preheat the oven to 220°C/425°F (gas mark 7) • Pour the oil into a roasting tin and heat in the oven for about 5 minutes • Add the sausages and return to the oven • Cook for 10 minutes until the sausages are brown • Meanwhile, sift the flour into a mixing bowl with the salt and pepper • Make a well in the centre and add the eggs • Add a little milk and whisk to a paste • Gradually whisk in the rest of the milk and the parsley until you have a smooth batter • Remove the roasting tin from the oven and arrange the sliced tomatoes and mushrooms evenly around the sausages • Pour the batter into the roasting tin around all the ingredients • Reduce the oven temperature to 200°C/400°F (gas mark 6) and cook for 30–35 minutes or until the batter is well risen, golden brown and crisp.

Serves a hearty 3
2 tbsp vegetable oil
6 sausages
125g (4¹/₂oz) plain flour
Salt and black pepper
2 medium eggs
300ml (10¹/₂ fl. oz) milk
3 tbsp parsley, finely chopped
4 button mushrooms, sliced
2 tomatoes, sliced

BLINI

Blini (the singular is 'blin') are small, yeast-raised pancakes from Russia that are traditionally served with smoked salmon or sour cream and caviar. They're usually made with buckwheat flour – a native Russian flour – but conventional western flours can be substituted. They are beautifully light, with an omelette-like taste and excellent served with any of our conventional breakfast elements – grilled tomatoes, smoky bacon, mushrooms . . . even baked beans.

Mix the dried yeast with 3 tbsp of the warm milk and the sugar • Leave until it froths (about 15 minutes). If it doesn't froth, the yeast is stale – give up! • Sift the flour into a bowl • Separate the eggs and add the yolks to a well in the centre of the flour, reserving the egg whites • Gradually pour the frothed yeast, remaining warm milk and the cream into the flour and mix well • Cover with a clean cloth or piece of kitchen roll and leave in a warm place for about an hour • Season, then whisk the egg whites into peaks and fold into the mixture • Having heated a heavy frying pan or girdle with the oil or fat, drop tablespoonfuls of the mixture in for small blini or about half a cupful for larger ones • Cook until bubbles appear on the surface (1–2 minutes), then turn over, cook until golden brown (about 1 minute) and serve.

Makes about 20 small blini
1 tbsp dried yeast
300ml (10¹/₂fl. oz) milk, warmed to 37.5°C (body temperature)
1 tsp sugar
340g (12oz) plain flour *or* 170g (6oz) each of plain and wholemeal flour
3 eggs
2 tbsp single cream
Salt and black pepper
Fat or oil for frying

POTATO BLINI

This recipe uses self-raising flour, which means you don't have to get up at the crack of dawn to let the yeast develop.

Mix the mashed potato, flour, egg yolks, soured cream, milk and seasoning in a bowl • Whisk the egg whites separately until peaked and fold into the mixture • Drop the required amount into a heated and oiled frying pan or girdle • Cook until bubbles appear on the surface (1–2 minutes) and then turn over and cook until golden brown (about 1 minute).

Makes 12–15
225g (8oz) floury potatoes, boiled and mashed with a little milk
5 tbsp self-raising flour, sifted
4 eggs, separated (reserve the whites)
3 tbsp soured cream (ordinary cream will do)
3 tbsp milk
Salt and black pepper
A pinch of cayenne pepper or chilli powder
Fat or oil or frying

comfort food

Bubble and squeak, fried potatoes, hash browns, cheesy tatties . . . we know we should spurn them but can't resist such temptations, so they're hidden in this chapter with some strange but comforting bedfellows.

RUMBLEDETHUMPS

A fancy Scottish name for bubble and squeak. Great for using up leftovers but tasty enough to justify making it from scratch. There are lots of recipes for this, colcannon being the Irish version which uses leeks instead of spring onions and can also contain ground mace. Many breakfast chefs will mould the mixture into small patties and fry until golden brown as shown on p.128.

Boil and mash the potatoes • If not using leftovers, boil or steam the cabbage or broccoli until tender • Mix together the potatoes, cabbage and spring onion, seasoning to taste • Divide into 110g (4oz) cakes and gently fry in the butter until brown.

Serves 2–4
450g (1lb) potatoes
450g (1lb) cabbage or
  broccoli, shredded
6 spring onions, finely sliced
Salt and black pepper
50g (2oz) butter

CHAMP

This is another Irish variation on bubble and squeak that uses chives or spring onions instead of cabbage. Just as with colcannon, small patties can be formed – if the mixture is not too wet – and fried individually.

Boil the potatoes until tender, then drain and mash • Combine the milk/cream and 60g (2$\frac{1}{2}$oz) of the butter in a saucepan • Heat until the butter is melted and add the chives or spring onions • Simmer for 3–4 minutes or until the greens are soft • Add the seasoning and blend in the mashed potatoes • Fill a small bowl, make a well in the top and add the remaining butter.

Serves 4–6
900g (2lb) potatoes, peeled
  and cut into 5cm (2in.)
  chunks
240ml (8$\frac{1}{2}$fl. oz) creamy milk
  or light cream
85g (3oz) butter
1 cup of chives or spring
  onions, chopped
Salt and black pepper

LAVERBREAD

A traditional Welsh dish, this edible seaweed is now usually bought ready-cooked in cans. Its preparation is quite lengthy – after it's been washed many times it's boiled for about 5 hours and then strained to form a gelatinous purée – after which it is often mixed with fine oatmeal, formed into small patties or cakes and fried in bacon fat. There are various other ways of serving it for breakfast:
- fry thick slices of bread in bacon fat, spread with hot laverbread and top with chopped bacon or ham
- mix laverbread with chopped, smoked bacon and use as an omelette filling.

SALT

The two major sources of salt are – not surprisingly – the sea and more commonly salt mines, which are just dried up salt lakes. Its name comes from 'salarium', the daily allowance paid to Roman soldiers to buy salt.

- Table salt is a fine grained salt with additives to make it free-flowing.
- Sea salt is the result of evaporated sea water and is more costly than mined salt. It comes in fine grains or larger crystals.
- Iodised salt is table salt with added iodine to aid thyroid functioning.
- Celtic salt is hand-harvested sea salt from

Brittany using a 2000-year-old Celtic process. Prized for its mellow sweet flavour.
- Rock salt is greyish, relatively unrefined salt used for more industrial purposes.
- Pickling salt is a fine-grained salt containing no additives that might cloud the pickling vinegar.
- Seasoned salt is normal salt combined with other flavourings, such as celery, garlic, onion etc.
- Kosher salt is an additive-free coarse-grained salt used for Jewish meat preparation. Also favoured by gourmet cooks.

COCKLES

Not a conventional breakfast dish for many of us but a great favourite in Wales where they're teamed with laverbread to accompany a more conformist fried or grilled breakfast. The cockles – which are usually bought already cooked and shelled – are gently fried in a little oil until brownish in colour. Being fairly moisture-laden they tend to spit quite a bit when fried so use a lid.

NETTLE AND POTATO CAKES

A real self-sufficiency recipe for breakfast.

Boil the potatoes in their skins with the peeled onion until they are soft • Drain, cool slightly and then remove the potatoes from their skins • Return them to the pan and mash together with the onion, butter, egg yolk and seasoning • Put the nettles into a saucepan with a little water and cook until soft • Drain well, squeezing out any excess water • Add the nettles to the potato mixture, blending well together • Shape into rounds on a well-floured board and fry in dripping or butter until golden brown.

450g (1lb) potatoes
1 onion, peeled
25g (1oz) butter
1 egg yolk
225g (8oz) nettle tops, washed and finely chopped
Salt and freshly ground black pepper
Butter or dripping for frying

CHEESY TATTIES

Boil, drain and mash the potatoes • Add the egg yolks and cheese, season to taste and mix well • Scoop out with an ice cream baller to get even-sized 'tatties', flattening them slightly by patting • Sprinkle both sides with a little flour • Pan-fry in a little oil or butter until golden brown.

Makes about 10
500g (1lb 2oz) floury potatoes
2 egg yolks
60g Cheddar cheese, grated
A little plain flour for dusting
Salt and black pepper
Vegetable oil or butter for
frying

OIL SMOKING POINTS

This is the temperature at which oil starts to smoke and smell acrid. If you've heated oil to this point, chuck it away because it will give whatever food you cook in it an unpleasant taste. The approximate smoke points of some oils are:

- *peanut* – 232°C/450°F

- *corn, olive, sesame* – 210°C/410°F
- *sunflower* – 199°C/390°F
- *lard* – 182°C/360°F
- *butter* – 177°C/350°F.

Chefs frequently sauté foods in butter, and to overcome its low smoking/burning point, they mix it with a little olive oil.

FRIED POTATOES

The best fried potatoes for breakfast use are usually leftovers. If you're going to prepare them from fresh, then we'd better be posh and call them sauté potatoes. Boil or microwave the required number of potatoes until they're just cooked, or else use leftover potatoes • Slice to 1cm ($^1/_2$in.) thick • Fry in butter, oil or good dripping until they're golden brown on both sides.

Potatoes
Butter, vegetable oil or
dripping

EGG PLANT

Egg plant, or aubergine as we know it, is a tasty and interesting breakfast ingredient. Named for its shape rather than for its taste, this vegetable (usually a deep purple in this country) can be sliced, fried (with the skin on) and served with bacon. It does tend to soak up the fat pretty readily so go easy on the amount in the pan and fry it at a high temperature. Alternatively, coat it with breadcrumbs or a batter mixture.

If you have the time, aubergines should ideally be degorged. This sounds bloodthirsty but is just a simple process of extracting excess liquid and any bitterness from vegetables. Cut the aubergines into 1–2cm slices, sprinkle generously with salt and set aside. After about 20 minutes rinse each slice and pat dry ready to fry. (It's nothing to do with breakfast, but degorging is the secret of traditional English cucumber sandwiches – try it.)

PEPPER

Said to be an appetite stimulant and an aid to digestion, peppercorns are the dried fruit of a tropical plant grown mostly in India and Indonesia.

- For black peppercorns, the tiny seeds are picked when green and left to ferment in the sun until black. For white pepper, the seeds are picked when red, soaked in water and then skinned and dried.
- The difference between the dusty pepper that you buy in those little cylindrical cardboard tubes and the real thing is, as they say, like chalk and cheese.
- As with all spices, pepper is best freshly ground. If you have a small electric coffee grinder (no kitchen should be without this inexpensive, jack-of-all-trades appliance), you can grind your own and fill your pepper shakers. If the holes in the pepper shaker are very small, just keep grinding until you reach a finer consistency. (Clean your coffee grinder by grinding a couple of lumps of bread afterwards!)
- Most recipes include pepper and in most we suggest you use black since black peppercorns are commonly available. If the use of black spoils the look of a dish then use white.
- A handheld grinder gives a ground pepper with a sharper, more lively flavour then the pre-ground variety.
- Give your taste buds a real treat and buy some more expensive peppercorns from a supermarket, a delicatessen or one of the many mail order suppliers.

Pepper corns

HASH BROWNS

A standard entry on North American breakfast menus, there are many variations of has browns, some using chopped-up cold potatoes (*see* 1 below), others using chopped-up or grated parboiled potatoes (*see* 2 below) and others using grated raw potatoes (*see* 3 below).

Try and make your own – they're so much better than the ubiquitous commercially manufactured ones that are available in the supermarkets and which seem to feature on so many menus from fast-food joints to top-class hotels!

HASH BROWNS 1

Chop the potatoes into small cubes • Season well and add any of the optional extras • Melt the mixture of butter and oil, dripping or bacon fat • Fry the mixture, turning it over continually until all sides are brown.

Another method is to press the potatoes cubes into patties whilst they're frying.

Serves 4–6

450g (16oz) cooked
  potatoes (leftovers,
  boiled the night before
  or microwaved)

Salt and pepper

Butter and oil, dripping
  or bacon fat

Optional extras:

1 small onion, finely
  chopped

30g (1oz) Cheddar
  cheese, grated

1–2 tbsp single cream

Any herbs

HASH BROWNS 2

Preheat the oven to 190°C/375°F (gas mark 5) • Parboil the potatoes for 10 minutes, drain and cool • Coarsely grate the onion and potatoes into a bowl and add the salt, pepper and vegetable oil • Mix well and form into 10–12 patties • Either bake in the oven for 20 minutes until golden brown or fry in oil or dripping for about 5 minutes on both sides.

Makes 10–12

450g (1lb) peeled potatoes

1 small onion, grated

Salt and black pepper

1 tbsp vegetable oil

HASH BROWNS 3

Grate the potatoes • Rinse them in cold water and squeeze as much liquid from them as possible (use your hand initially and then kitchen roll) • Season and mix with your choice of extras • Mould an appropriate amount of potato into a cake about 2cm (1in.) thick or press the potato into an oiled cake or egg ring. (A variation is to form the grated potato into one large cake that fills the pan and then cut it into portions after cooking) • Fry until golden brown on both sides • Sprinkle with paprika and parsley and serve • If wished, top each with half a rasher of grilled, streaky bacon.

Makes 10–12

450g (1lb) raw potatoes, peeled

Salt and pepper

Butter and oil, dripping or bacon fat.

Optional extras:

1 small onion, chopped

30g (1oz) Cheddar cheese, grated

Paprika and fresh parsley for garnishing

RÖSTI

Switzerland – probably where hash browns originated – gives us yet another variation on this dish. Put the grated potato into egg rings or ring moulds if you have them: if not, just follow the method below.

Parboil the potatoes in their skins for about 7 minutes (2–3 minutes in a microwave – check manufacturer's instructions) • Heat the butter in a frying pan until foaming • Remove the skin from the potatoes, roughly grate them into the pan and add the seasoning • With a palette or broad-bladed knife, gather the potato into a round • Fry gently for about 5–7 minutes on each side until golden brown, turning them carefully • Cut in half and serve.

350g (12oz) medium-sized potatoes, scrubbed

40g (1^1/$_2$oz) butter

Salt and black pepper

RÖSTI WITH BACON

Parboil the potatoes in their skins for about 7 minutes (2–3 minutes in a microwave – check manufacturer's instructions) • Leave to cool and then skin and grate them • Fry the bacon in some of the oil until crisp and cut into small pieces • Gently fry the onion in the oil until translucent, then remove from the heat • Mix together the potato, bacon and onion • Form in ring moulds or gently press them into patties • Fry on both sides in the butter for about 3 minutes until golden brown.

Serves 6

500g (1lb) large waxy
   potatoes, scrubbed
4 thin rashers of rindless
   bacon
2 tbsp oil
1 onion, thinly sliced
25g (1/2oz) butter

CORN GRIDDLE CAKES

Sift the dry ingredients into a bowl • Combine the sweetcorn, egg and milk, add to the flour mixture and mix well • Using 2 tbsp of the mixture for each cake, pat into flat rounds • Melt the butter in a pan and add the cakes • Cook until bubbles show on the surface and then turn over • Cook until golden brown • Serve with crisp rashers of bacon and maple syrup.

Makes about 10
225g (8oz) plain flour
1 1/2 tsp baking powder
1/2 tsp paprika
1/2 tsp salt
175g (6oz) sweet corn
   kernels (frozen or

tinned will do)
1 egg, beaten
125ml (4fl. oz) milk
2 tbsp unsalted butter
Bacon and maple syrup
   to serve

DEVILLED KIDNEYS

For kidney-lovers this is a real treat. The kidneys can be served on fried bread, muffins, toasted sourdough bread or on any savoury pancakes or blini. However, care must be taken not to overcook the kidneys – they should be very slightly pink inside.

Remove the transparent skin from the kidneys, cut them in half and remove the white core (easiest with good sharp scissors) • Cut each half into about 5 pieces • Melt the butter in frying pan and add the oil • When the pan is hot, add the kidneys, cooking quickly for a couple of minutes and turning until browned all over • Take them out and place in a warm oven or grill • Add the other ingredients to the pan, including the water, and bubble for a few minutes • Add the cooked kidneys, stir, serve on the triangles of fried bread and garnish with the herbs.

Serves 2
6 lambs' kidneys
Butter and sunflower oil
   for frying
1 tsp tomato purée
A pinch of cayenne
   pepper
A dash of Worcester-
   shire sauce
1/2 tsp English mustard

powder
Freshly ground black
   pepper
Salt (optional)
1 tbsp sherry
1 tbsp water
2 triangles of granary
   bread, crisply fried, to
   serve
Fresh parsley to garnish

how to cook a great British breakfast

Our grannies knew how to suck eggs and they knew how to fry them too. But in today's world we can't take it for granted that we've all inherited those essential kitchen skills. Cooking a big breakfast can be just as traumatic as cooking a full-blown Sunday lunch. In fact, many will claim that the Sunday lunch is easier.

Sixty seconds of overcooking can make a big difference to many of the breakfast constituents you use – especially the eggs – whereas a minute longer on your roast potatoes or Yorkshire pudding is neither here nor there. So, how do you do it and retain the image of the calm, unflustered 'wonder cook'?

Planning is more than half the battle. It's just a question of cooking all the elements in the right order. So here's your 25-step guide to cooking a fried breakfast to remember!

If you've forgotten to put the plates in the oven to warm and you're almost ready to serve, plunge them into a sink or basin of really hot tap water for a couple of minutes.

1 Get the table set, preferably by someone else! Press-gang the kids or your partner into helping, but keep an eye on them. They will invariably make a mess of it and forget the salt, pepper and – dare we say it – ketchup or brown sauce, not to mention some other essential element that you won't notice until you sit down.

2 Lay out the oil or butter and all the implements you intend to use: knives, egg slice, spoons, kitchen tongs, kitchen paper . . . the works.

3 Turn on the grill so that it has time to get up to operating temperature and run a basinful or sinkful of good hot soapy water.

4 Prepare all your breakfast bits and pieces: mushrooms chopped, tomatoes sliced, eggs whisked if appropriate, puddings cut into bite-sized pieces, toast sliced and popped into the toaster, sausage links separated etc.

5 Fill the kettle and get the tea or coffee out. If you're a real coffee fan, measure the required amount into the cafetière.

6 Turn the oven on low and pop the serving plates on to the lowest shelf. If you're going to serve breakfast on a large platter, then put that into the oven as well. You'll also need another plate or dish in there to hold the cooked ingredients; whilst in the oven, more fat will come out of them that you don't want on the serving platter.

7 If you're doing grilled tomatoes, put them under the grill now but keep an eye on them. Take them out when the top is nicely caramelised (a bit charred!).

8 Warm up your frying pan(s) and the small pan for the mushrooms.

9 Whether frying or grilling, cook sausages on a low heat (remember: don't prick them). Turn them frequently or use a pan with a lid and give it a gentle shake now and then to keep exposing a different surface to the heat.

10 Cook the mushrooms on a fairly high heat, shaking the pan or stirring the mushrooms frequently. Don't cook with the lid on the pan or the substantial moisture in the mushrooms won't evaporate and you'll end up with mushroom soup. If necessary, drain off that liquid and replace it with some more butter or oil and butter.

11 If there's space in the frying pan with the sausages, pop in any of the sliced puddings. If you have some, use kitchen tongs for turning them and for turning and removing the sausages.

12 As each ingredient is cooked, transfer it to the warm dish in the oven.

13 The tomatoes may well be ready by now and should be soft enough to need removing with a spoon and transferring to the oven.

14 Switch on the kettle and make the tea or coffee when it's boiled.

15 If making fried bread, fry it now. Make sure you put plenty of oil in the pan and heat it until you see a slight blue haze.

16 If you're using only one frying pan, it'll be pretty messy after the fried bread and the other previous ingredients. Get rid of the oil, give the pan a quick clean in the soapy water and rinse with fresh before

returning it to the stove to dry. Add some oil in readiness for frying the eggs.

17 Shout, 'Two minutes!' to the family and pop down the toaster.

18 Break the eggs into the pan and cook as required.

19 Whilst they're gently cooking, transfer the serving plates to the table and remove the platter and the dish of cooked ingredients from the oven.

20 Lay the ingredients out on the hot platter, dabbing any relevant items with some kitchen towel if they look too greasy.

21 Put the toast into the toast rack.

22 Shout, 'Get up to the table or it's going in the bin!'

23 Either put the cooked eggs on to the platter or leave them to serve directly on to the hot serving plates.

24 Carry the platter through and place on a mat or one of those candle dish-warmers.

25 Collapse in the chair exclaiming, 'After all that, I don't fancy anything!'

GHILLIES' GRILL

Even if you're not a ghillie*, this is a good excuse for a breakfast blow-out and really tests a cook's organisational skills! Lamb cutlets can take the place of the venison ones.

Put the grill on high and preheat the oven to 190°C/375°F (gas mark 5) • Put the tomatoes under the grill • Season the mushrooms and brush with butter • Place them in the oven for about 15 minutes • Brush the cutlets with oil and grill on high for about 1½ minutes on each side to seal the surface • Reduce the heat to moderate, add the sausages and cook for about 10 minutes, turning both cutlets and sausages so that they cook evenly • Add the bacon and kidneys about 5 minutes from the end, turning both once. The kidneys should be placed cut-side uppermost to start with to seal the surface and retain their moisture • Meanwhile, shape the cheesy tatties, pan fry them and keep them warm in the grill compartment until the cutlets, sausages, kidneys and tomatoes are cooked • You'll also have cooked the skirlie and filled the cooked mushrooms before serving • If there's room on the plate and you're still not demented, you could add fried or scrambled eggs to the feast.

If your grill pan isn't large enough to hold all the bits and pieces, you could chop the kidneys into quarters and pan fry them in a little butter and oil. It's better to undercook than overcook the cutlets and kidneys – both should be slightly pink in the middle.

*A ghillie is a Highland 'servant' who attends to your needs when you're salmon fishing or deer stalking.

To make life easier for the washing-up team (probably you), as soon as you've finished with a pan, plate or kitchen tool, rinse it and pop it into the basin of suds. If you have any spare time between tasks, wash them and let them drip dry.

4 tomatoes, sliced in half horizontally
4 large flat mushrooms, trimmed and cut to size
Butter, softened
4 venison cutlets
Vegetable oil
4 sausages
4 slices of bacon
4 lambs' kidneys, skinned, gristle removed and halved
200g (7oz) cheesy tatties (see p. 132)
60g (2oz) skirlie (see p. 114)
Eggs (optional)
Salt and black pepper

fish and seafood

When the words 'breakfast' and 'fish' are uttered in the same breath, most of us think of kippers – in other words, herrings that have been cold smoked. There are three main types of kipper – Scottish, Whitby and Manx – whose treatment, although traditional to a particular area, varies slightly according to the secret sub-recipes of individual smokers.

The Scottish kipper – especially the Loch Fyne variety – is reputed to be the Rolls Royce of the kipper world. The old-fashioned dark brown variety, coloured with a commercial coal tar dye introduced during World War II as an economy measure, should be avoided.

JUGGED KIPPERS

One of the easiest breakfasts imaginable. Just put the kippers tail up into a deep earthenware jug or similar container, fill it up with boiling water and leave for 5–10 minutes, depending upon size. Take them out, drain them and serve hot with bread and butter.

GRILLED KIPPERS

Almost as simple. Place your kippers skin-side up under a preheated grill until the skins start crisping and peeling away from the flesh – usually about 5 minutes. There should be no need to cook the other side – just take them out and serve hot with bread and butter.

FRIED KIPPERS

If you're using the grill for something else then you can fry your kippers instead. Put them into a hot, oiled frying pan skin-side down and cook them for 2–3 minutes on each side.

BAKED KIPPERS

Preheat the oven to 220°C/425°F (gas mark 7), then oil or butter some foil and wrap this loosely about the kipper before baking in the oven for about 5 minutes. If cooking a pair of kippers, butter the flesh sides and sandwich them together before wrapping them in foil. These should take about 10 minutes.

Oily fish such as salmon, whitebait, tuna, mackerel, herring and sardines provide so many health benefits that it almost justifies force-feeding them to the whole family! They contain omega-3 essential fatty acids, which can help strengthen the immune system, protect against heart disease and cancer, lower cholesterol and blood pressure, and improve inflammatory skin conditions, dry skin and rheumatoid arthritis . . . not to mention allegedly helping to reduce the appearance of cellulite.

MICROWAVED KIPPERS

The easiest and least 'smelly' method of cooking a kipper is to do it in the microwave. Put it on a plate with a knob of butter, cover loosely with clingfilm and zap it for about 2 minutes on high. Check the manufacturer's instructions since the time will vary.

KIPPER CAKES

These cakes are just as nice using mackerel or herring but, in each case, it's most important that you check the blended or flaked fish for bones. Pick them out with either a pair of tweezers or your fingers.

Place the kipper fillets into a food processor or blender and process until finely flaked • Stir in the egg, Worcestershire sauce and breadcrumbs • Divide the mixture into 8 and shape into 5cm (2in.) rounds • Chill in the fridge for 10–15 minutes • Cook under a low grill for 8–10 minutes, turning once • Serve with grilled tomatoes or scrambled egg.

450g (1lb) kipper fillets, skinned
1 egg, beaten
A dash of Worcestershire sauce
175g (6oz) fresh breadcrumbs

FINNAN HADDIE

Smoked haddock to most of us, this succulent fish is named after the coastal village of Findon, six miles south of Aberdeen where they first perfected the cold, peat-smoking of their catch. Although you may think the yellow colouring comes from the smoking process, it doesn't. Dye is used, so if you see the pale cream, undyed variety, buy that instead.

There are many recipes using finnan haddie and the following are just a few.

The custom of serving a slice of lemon with fish dates back to the Middle Ages. It was mistakenly believed that if a person accidentally swallowed a fish bone, the lemon juice would dissolve it.

GRILLED FINNAN HADDIE

Take 1 smoked haddock fillet, add a few knobs of butter, sprinkle with freshly ground black pepper and cook under a hot grill for 5–7 minutes.

POACHED FINNAN HADDIE

Another simple way to cook smoked haddock is to poach it lightly in milk to which a knob of butter has been added. Serve on a hot, flat plate that has sufficient depth to accommodate a good ladleful of the milk juice and accompany this with fresh white bread and a good butter to soak up all the goodness.

FINNAN HADDIE WITH SPINACH AND POACHED EGG

Preheat the oven to 180°C/350°F (gas mark 4) • Grease a shallow gratin dish with the butter • Place the fish skin-side down in the dish • Pour over the cream and grind some pepper on top • Bake in the oven for 20–30 minutes, giving it a shake in the middle of cooking to re-coat the fish with cream • Meanwhile, poach 4 eggs (*see* p. 76) • Remove the fish from the dish and place on a serving dish • Cover with the cream, which will have reduced slightly and thickened • Top with a poached egg and a spoonful of spinach to serve.

A knob of butter for greasing
750g (1lb 10oz) smoked
   haddock
250ml (9fl. oz) double cream
4 eggs
250g (9oz) spinach, picked
   and prepared
Freshly ground black pepper

HAM AND HADDIE

Here's a recipe from the Moray Firth in the north of Scotland.

Grease the bottom of the grill pan with some of the butter • Lay the fish fillets in and cover with small pieces of the remaining butter • Add the seasoning • Lay the rashers of bacon over the fish • Heat under a medium grill for 5 minutes • Meanwhile, poach the eggs (*see* p. 76) • Remove the fish from the grill, pour the cream over the bacon and fish and cook under a high grill until the cream starts bubbling • Serve on a hot plate and top with a poached egg.

Serves 2
25g (10oz) unsalted or slightly
   salted butter
2 fillets of smoked haddock,
   skinned
225g (8oz) unsmoked bacon
   rashers
2 eggs
2 tbsp double cream
Salt and black pepper

CHOPPING BOARDS

Contrary to expectations, modern agricultural and food-production techniques seem to have increased rather than decreased the chance of us catching something nasty from what we prepare and eat. It's a bit of a double whammy in that, not only have our body's natural defences been sanitised by over-zealous food hygiene, but the incidence of food poisoning has actually been increased by some modern, intensive farming methods. Since we can't beat them, we may have to join them and the best way of combating cross-contamination during food preparation is to buy a set of colour-coded, plastic chopping boards:

- red – raw meat
- blue – raw fish
- yellow – cooked meats
- green – salad and fruit
- brown – vegetables
- white – bakery and dairy.

If the budget won't rise to these, don't worry: the conventional wooden chopping board is quite adequate as long as it's properly cleaned in-between different produce categories. It's sensible also to wash knives at the same time.

SPINACH

Never, never boil spinach. Put the leaves in a very hot pan and stir briskly. It will wilt down and be ready for use in next to no time.

FISH FLORENTINE

This is a luxurious variation on egg florentine using smoked haddock and smoked salmon.

Soft-poach the eggs (*see* p. 76) and place them in a bowl of cold water • Boil the potatoes, cut them into a 15mm dice and keep them warm • Place the reserved haddock skin, bones, trimmings and a few shreds of onion in a pan with a little water • Simmer for 12 minutes and strain into a pan, discarding the residue • Put the haddock in food processor with a little salt and the egg white. Process until smooth and remove into a chilled mixing bowl • Gradually stir in the cream with a wooden spoon until you have a light mixture • Line 4 small ring moulds with cling film, leaving an overhang • Put the cooled mousse in a piping bag and pipe into the ring moulds • Level with a palette knife • Place in a steamer for 12–15 minutes until firm to the touch • Place the reserved haddock juices over a high heat and whisk in the diced butter, keeping this warm • Place a pan on the stove and, when hot, add a knob of butter • Add the spinach, season, and cook for 1 minute, keeping it warm • Place the poached eggs in simmering water to reheat • Make up the Hollandaise sauce and keep warm • When ready to serve, invert the mousse on to the middle of a deep serving plate • Put a spoonful of spinach in the cavity • Top with a drained poached egg • Strew the warm, diced potatoes around the dish • Add chopped parsley to the haddock juices and spoon over the potatoes • Top the egg with a spoonful of Hollandaise sauce • Crown with the narrow strips of smoked salmon.

4 eggs

60g (2oz) potatoes

250g (9oz) smoked haddock, boned, skinned and diced (bones, skins and trimmings reserved)

1 medium onion, finely chopped

1/2 egg white

1 x 140ml (5fl.oz) carton of double cream

60g (2oz) butter, diced and cooled

200g (7oz) baby spinach, picked and washed

10g (1/2oz) fresh parsley, chopped

4 tbsp Hollandaise sauce (*see* p. 77)

40g (11/2oz) smoked salmon, cut into neat strips

A pinch of salt

SMOKED HADDOCK SOUFFLÉ OMELETTE

This dish capitalises on the affinity between smoked haddock and eggs.

Melt half the butter in a saucepan • Add the haddock, cream and half the cheese and heat gently until the cheese is melted • Remove from the heat and season with salt and pepper • Stir in the egg yolks • Whisk the egg whites until stiff and fold into the haddock mixture • Melt the rest of the butter in a large frying pan • When sizzling, pour in the omelette mixture • Cook gently for 2–3 minutes until set, drawing the cooked edges towards the centre with a fork • Cut into quarters and turn out on to 4 warm serving plates • Sprinkle with the remaining cheese and garnish with herbs.

50g (2oz) unsalted or slightly salted butter

2 smoked haddock fillets, cooked, flaked and checked for bones

5 tbsp single cream

4 tbsp Parmesan cheese, grated

6 eggs, separated

Salt and black pepper

Fresh parsley, chervil or chives, finely chopped, to garnish

LUXURY KEDGEREE

This is a classic English dish brought back from India in the days of the Raj. Oatcakes make the perfect accompaniment.

Boil the eggs for about 6 minutes and leave on one side • Boil the rice in salted water according to instructions • Whilst it's cooking, add the herbs and spices to the boiling water • Put the haddock fillets and butter in a large frying pan and just cover with milk • Simmer for about 5 minutes until the fish can be gently pushed apart • Drain off and reserve the liquid • Add the salmon to the haddock and heat through • Drain and fluff the cooked rice • Gently mix together with the fish and the reserved liquid • Put on a serving dish with the lemon wedges, season and decorate with the halved quails' eggs or chopped hens' eggs.

Serves 6

6 quails' eggs *or* 3 hens' eggs

240g (8½oz) good quality rice

1 tbsp turmeric

1 tbsp ground cumin

1 tbsp ground coriander

1 tbsp fresh parsley, chopped

2 bay leaves

3 pale smoked haddock fillets

A knob of butter

Milk

360g (13oz) hot smoked salmon *or* lightly cooked fresh salmon, broken into small chunks

Lemon wedges

Salt and black pepper

ARBROATH SMOKIES

These are small haddock that have been cleaned but not split open, lightly salted, tied by their tails in pairs and then smoked until cooked. The outside is a beautiful copper colour and the inside is a much lighter cream. The important thing to remember is that Smokies are cooked and just need heating through. For breakfast they're best served simply – brush with melted butter, dust with ground pepper, wrap in buttered foil and heat in a low oven for about 15 minutes (or grill on a moderate heat, turning halfway through). When heated through, split them open along the backbone, remove the bone, pop in a knob of butter, close up and serve with a wedge of lemon.

To bone a herring, trout or mackerel, cut right along the belly, spread the fish open and lay it flesh-side down. Run a finger firmly up and down the backbone a couple of times. Turn the fish flesh-side up and the bones should come out easily.

TROUT

Trout is a very versatile breakfast dish and can be grilled, pan-fried, baked in the oven in foil or microwaved. There are three types – sea trout, brown trout and rainbow trout. Sea trout are very similar to salmon but tend to be smaller, not so fatty and have larger flaked but softer flesh. Brown trout are those beloved of serious anglers and you will rarely see them for sale anywhere – it's a case of catchers, keepers . . . and eaters! The trout we are all most familiar with are the rainbow trout – those of the fish farm variety. The best size for eating is 900g–1.8kg (1–2lb).

- *Grilling the whole fish:* slash the skin in 3 places, brush both sides well with fat or oil and a little lemon juice, season and grill for about 5 minutes on each side.
- *Grilling fillets:* brush the flesh liberally with fat or oil and season well. Lay skin-side down on the rack and cook under a moderately hot grill for about 3 minutes, brushing again with oil or fat halfway through.
- *Pan-frying the whole fish:* usually easier to remove the head first so the fish fits comfortably into the average frying pan. Dust lightly with seasoned flour or your preferred coating and fry in hot oil or a mixture of oil and butter for about 5 minutes on each side.
- *Pan-frying fillets:* toss lightly in seasoned flour or your preferred coating and fry in hot oil or a mixture of oil and butter for about 3 minutes on each side.
- *Oven baking the whole fish:* lay the fish in foil and brush with a little oil. Squeeze over a little lemon juice, season well and wrap up loosely. Bake in a moderate oven – 180°C/350°F (gas mark 4) – for about 25 minutes.

TROUT IN OATMEAL

This time the trout is boned. It should end up brown on the outside and soft and juicy on the inside.

Brush the trout fillets with a little melted butter • Season the oatmeal with salt and pepper and firmly press on to both sides of the fish • Heat the butter and oil in a frying pan • Place the trout in the pan, skin-side up • Fry for 3–4 minutes on each side • Garnish with lemon and chopped parsley and serve.

Serves 1–2
2 trout fillets
Melted butter for brushing
30g (1oz) medium oatmeal
Butter and oil for frying
2 lemon quarters
Fresh parsley, chopped
Salt and black pepper

TROUT STUFFED WITH HAGGIS

Preheat the oven to 180°C/350°F (gas mark 4) • Clean the trout thoroughly under cold running water • Fill the cavity with the cooked haggis • Brush the surface with melted butter • Grill for about 5 minutes on each side or wrap loosely in foil and bake in the oven for about 25 minutes • Garnish and serve.

Serves 1–2
1 fresh trout, gutted and
  prepared
Enough cooked haggis to fill
  the cavity
Melted butter for brushing

TROUT STUFFED WITH BACON

Preheat the oven to 180°C/350°F (gas mark 4) • Melt half the butter in a frying pan • Add the bacon and onion and cook gently for 3 minutes • Stir in the mushrooms and continue cooking • Remove from the heat and transfer the mixture to a bowl • Mix in the parsley, lemon zest and breadcrumbs • Season and bind with beaten egg • Stuff the mixture into the trout cavity • Melt the remaining butter and brush over the fish • Grill for about 5 minutes on each side or wrap loosely in foil and bake in the oven for about 25 minutes.

Serves 1– 2
15g (^{1}/$_2$oz) butter
30g (1oz) streaky
  bacon, chopped
^{1}/$_2$ small onion,
  chopped
30g (1oz) mushrooms,
  chopped
^{1}/$_2$ tbsp fresh parsley,
  chopped
^{1}/$_2$ tsp lemon zest,
  grated
30g (1oz) wholemeal
  breadcrumbs
1 egg, beaten
1 fresh trout, gutted
  and prepared
Salt and black pepper

Opposite: Herring in oatmeal

HERRINGS IN OATMEAL

It's said that the marriage of herrings and oatmeal was made in heaven.

Season the herring fillets and brush on both sides with melted butter • Spread the oatmeal on a plate or flat surface • Press both sides of the herring well into the oatmeal • Heat the fat or oil in a pan until sizzling and fry the herrings in it for about 3 minutes on both sides • Season and garnish each fillet with parsley and a lemon wedge, or accompanied by a small jug of malt vinegar.

4 herring fillets
Melted butter to brush
60–90g (2–3oz) coarse
  oatmeal
90g (3oz) unsmoked bacon fat
  or vegetable oil
1 tbsp fresh parsley, chopped
4 lemon wedges or malt
  vinegar
Salt and black pepper

RED HERRINGS

Red herrings are the result of one of the oldest methods of preserving fish, dating back to medieval times. Used extensively in East Anglia, the salting and lengthy smoking process (3–7 days) were designed to keep these strong, salty and by now red fish for as long a period as possible. They were so strong smelling that they were sometimes used to lay false trails and put hounds off the scent – hence our modern usage of the term 'a red herring'. At breakfast time serve them with scrambled eggs on toast.

To rid the fish of their strong briny taste, pour boiling water over them and leave for 30 minutes • Break a small piece of fish off and check for taste • Keep soaking until the taste is to your liking • When ready, drain, cut off the heads and tails and split them down the back • Smear with butter and grill until cooked.

FINNAN HADDIE TOAST

Many of the fish used lend themselves to being served on toast, finnan haddie being a case in point.

Poach the haddock in the milk and butter for about 5 minutes or until the fish will flake easily • Strain, flake and reserve the milk • Add the flaked haddock to the white sauce • Add the lemon juice and pepper • Spread on the buttered toast and pop under a hot grill for a couple of minutes • Garnish with whatever takes your fancy – a thin slice of twisted lemon, a herb or even a flower (see p. 188–9).

Serves 2
1 small/medium smoked
  haddock
225ml (8fl. oz) milk
A small knob of butter
White sauce (*see* opposite)
2 dashes of lemon juice
White pepper (black will do if
  white isn't available)
2 rounds of buttered toast

WHITE SAUCE

The classic white sauce made with milk is called 'béchamel'. If pepper is called for, it should always be white – black looks unsightly and might suggest that you had burnt the sauce! This recipe produces a sauce of medium thickness. For a thinner or thicker sauce, simply adjust the amount of butter and flour: 15g ($^{1}/_{2}$oz) of each for a thin sauce; 30g (1oz) of each for a thick sauce.

Although we've relied on the fish to flavour the sauce here, other flavours can be used – classic additions being a slice of onion, 1 tsp of peppercorns, a bay leaf, a blade of mace and parsley stalks. These would be added to the milk (or cream) when boiling and left to infuse for 10 minutes in the covered saucepan. The liquid would then be strained before adding to the butter and flour mixture.

Gently bring the fish stock to the boil and set aside • Melt the butter in a thick-bottomed saucepan • Whisk in the flour and cook until it foams – about 1 minute • Remove the pan from the heat and let it cool slightly • Add the hot stock to the flour mixture, whisking all the time until smooth • Return the mixture to the heat and, whisking constantly, bring it to the boil until it thickens • Add any seasoning and cook for another 2 minutes.

Makes 250ml (8fl. oz)
250ml (8fl. oz) milk (in this
 case, the strained, reserved
 stock from cooking the fish)
22g ($^{3}/_{4}$oz) butter
22g ($^{3}/_{4}$oz) plain white flour
Salt and white pepper

ABERDEEN TOAST

Kippers or Arbroath Smokies can be substituted for the smoked haddock in this recipe.

Cut the haddock into chunks and liquidise with the butter and enough of the cream to 'lubricate' the process • Transfer the mixture to a pan, add the dash of cayenne or chilli powder and cook for a few minutes • Heap on to the hot buttered toast, garnish and serve.

Serves 2
1 small/medium fillet of
 uncooked smoked haddock
A large knob of butter
142ml (5fl. oz) single cream
A pinch of cayenne pepper or
 chilli powder
2 slices of buttered toast

just for kids

Most children love to get into the kitchen and they gain in confidence remarkably quickly if they're included in the preparation or cooking process. It goes without saying that boys should know how to cook as well. How many of us know fathers and grandfathers who would have difficulty actually finding the kitchen, far less boiling an egg or making a pot of tea?

We therefore owe it to our boys, as well as our girls, to teach them the basics so that, by the time they leave home for independent living, they're not totally reliant on junk food and have enough knowledge and confidence to fend for themselves when necessary.

It's never too soon to get children involved and the pride that even toddlers display if you let them cut up lumps of cheese (with a blunt knife!) is heart-warming. Give them simple tasks and praise them to high heaven – as in all things in bringing up children, praise inspires confidence and confidence nurtures ability. And, at the risk of going too far down the Dr Spock route, ability greatly improves self-esteem, a lack of which seems to play a huge part in modern eating disorders amongst teenage girls.

Some of the following dishes are for you to cook for the children and some are suitable for them to have a go at. Although not translated into child-speak, the latter have been simplified somewhat for children who've become competent in reading. The kitchen is a dangerous environment and depending upon the children's ages, you can let them follow the recipes themselves or closely supervise them and step in to perform those parts which are risky.

Many of the dishes elsewhere in this book are perfectly suited for children and some of them are duplicated here in a slightly different and possibly more outlandish form.

It would be safer and quicker to complete some of the cooking steps in this chapter – heating beans or cooking bacon, for example – by using a microwave if you have one. You must make your own judgement about letting a child 'loose' with a microwave, however!

Children aged from 3–6 can:
- add ingredients to a bowl
- stir ingredients by hand
- wash fruit and vegetables
- tear up lettuce
- use a table knife or bluntish scissors to cut cheese or soft fruits.

Helping in the kitchen can teach them about:
- size and quantity
- colours and shapes
- hot and cold temperatures
- waiting for dishes to cook
- time and patience
- method – following recipe instructions with an adult.

BURNS AND SCALDS

In the unhappy event of a child getting burnt or scalded, the quicker the first aid, the less likelihood there is of scarring.

- Cool the scalded or burnt area with lots of cold water for at least 10 minutes. If the injury is on a hand or arm, then holding it under the cold running tap will do. If it's over a larger area, then there's nothing for it but to get the youngster into a cold bath as soon as possible. The poor child is not going to like this and neither are you, but it's essential to stop the injury penetrating deeper into the skin.
- If you can't get ice-cold water from your tap, put some ice or any packet of frozen food into the filled sink or basin. Don't apply ice

directly or indirectly to any wound, though.
- Gently try to remove any clothing that has been burnt or soaked. However, if it shows any sign of sticking to the injured area, leave well alone and seek medical advice.
- Cover the burnt area with a clean, non-fluffy cloth or dressing.
- Never touch any injured skin and never burst any blisters.
- Never, *never* apply any creams or ointments . . . and completely ignore any old wives' tales about putting butter on a burn.
- If you think the injury serious or you want reassurance, contact your doctor or local hospital.

KIDS' COOKING TIPS

Heating cooking oil When you first put cooking oil into a pan, it's pretty thick and doesn't move around the pan very easily. The hotter the pan gets, the thinner the oil gets and, when it's ready for cooking, there's usually a slight haze above it – a very thin smoke. That's when you put your food into it. If the recipe asks for oil and a little butter, it's ready when the butter starts foaming and sizzling.

Splashing and spitting When you put food into hot fat, the water in the food makes the fat spit and this can get on to your hands or clothes. It's best then to always wear an apron if you're going to use a frying pan.

Oven gloves These are insulated gloves that stop you getting burnt. If you're going to handle anything hot, make sure that an adult is present, and either have some oven gloves handy or a folded teatowel. Never use a damp teatowel, however, as the heat will turn the moisture into steam and it will come through the material to get you!

Washing frying pans Don't ever add water to a hot frying pan. It will react with the fat, bubble over and could easily burn you. Wait until the pan has cooled down before washing it.

Chopping and cutting Make sure an adult is present and always take great care if using knives or scissors.

- *A pinch of salt:* this is the amount you can pick up between your thumb and forefinger.
- *A knob of butter:* this is usually what you would put on the end of your knife if you were spreading a slice of bread.
- *A drizzle:* this is about a teaspoonful
- *Simmering:* cooking it on a very low heat so that it bubbles very gently.
- *Preheating the oven:* this means turning the oven on and setting the heat control to the required temerature. Check with an adult whether this is in °C, °F or a gas mark.

EGGCLOPS

A slice of fried bread surrounding a fried egg. This was the favourite dish of Cyclops, the Greek giant who only had one eye in the middle of his forehead.

Lay a slice of bread on the breadboard or work surface • Cut a hole in the centre of the bread with the pastry cutter and put this on one side. If you haven't got a pastry cutter, try and find a small cup or bowl of the right size and use that. If you can't find anything suitable, then cut a roundish hole with a knife – even a blunt one will do • Heat up the frying pan and put a little vegetable oil in it – about an egg cupful • When the oil is hot enough, place the bread in • While the first side of the bread is cooking, break an egg into a cup • Check the bread by lifting it up slightly with an egg slice and see how it's getting on • When it's brown, turn it over

Serves 1

1 slice of bread, white or
  brown
Vegetable oil
1 egg
Equipment needed:
frying pan, egg slice,
breadboard, cup or small bowl
to break egg into, 5cm (2in.)
round pastry cutter, teaspoon

Eggclops

and gently pour the egg into the hole • The egg will slowly cook as the bottom of the bread is browning (you might need to drizzle a teaspoonful of the hot oil over the top of the egg now and again to cook the yolk) • When it's done, use the egg slice to lift it on to your plate • Turn off the stove • If you want, you can also fry the circle you cut out and pop it on top of the yolk – Cyclops with his eye closed!

FRENCH TOAST

Break the egg into the bowl • Add the milk • Beat the egg and milk until it's frothy. If you don't have a whisk or old-fashioned eggbeater then you can use a fork but you might need some adult help with that • Add the pinch of salt and the pepper • Pour the mixture into a shallow bowl or dish and dip both sides of the sliced bread into the mixture for a few seconds so that it soaks it up • In the meantime, put a little butter or oil in your frying pan and heat it up on a medium setting • When the fat is hot enough, carry the bowl or dish to the frying pan and transfer the bread to the pan • Turn up the heat a little and keep having a peek at the side of the bread that's being cooked • When it's golden brown (not black!), turn it over to cook the other side • When cooked, transfer it on to your plate with a fish slice or the tongs • Turn off the stove.

Serves 1
1 egg
1 tbsp milk
1 slice of bread
Vegetable oil or butter
A pinch of salt
2 shakes or grinds of pepper
Equipment needed:
frying pan, egg slice or kitchen
tongs, bowl to mix egg in,
whisk, egg beater or fork, big
plate for soaking the bread on

VARIATIONS

Before dipping the bread into the egg mixture, you could cut it into interesting shapes with a round pastry cutter or a novelty cutter like a teddy bear, gingerbread man or heart. If you're cooking for a brother, giving him a soppy heart shape will really make him mad!

EGG IN A CUP

Your parents may have had this dish when they were toddlers, but it's still delicious even when you're older. Adults are too embarrassed to make this for themselves and they therefore pinch it from their kids. Stick up for your rights – don't let them have it!

Soft boil the free range eggs (fresh eggs usually need about 4–5 minutes boiling, but it does depend upon their size – ask an adult for advice) • When the eggs are cooked, pop each into an egg cup and chop the tops off • Scoop the egg out into a cup containing the knob of butter – you might need a bit of help with this because the eggs will be very hot. You can hold them with a bit of folded kitchen roll • Chop the eggs finely in the cup • Add sufficient breadcrumbs to make a moist paste • Sprinkle a little salt into the cup and eat it quickly before an adult sees it.

Serves 1

2 eggs – free range if possible
A knob of butter
Brown or white breadcrumbs
  (if you haven't got any of
  these, a slice of bread will do
  – just break it up into tiny
  pieces)
Salt
Equipment required:
small pan for boiling eggs, 1–2
egg cups, teacup, teaspoon,
knife, some kitchen roll

PIZZA OMELETTE

If you like pizzas then here's a kind of breakfast pizza that's very tasty.

HORRIBLE FOOD FACTS

- Most snakes can go without food for a whole year.
- Crocodiles carry a few kilos of stones in their stomachs. They don't chew their food, they just swallow it whole and it gets ground up by the stones.
- The Incas used to eat guinea pigs, while Romans used to eat flamingo tongues at their feasts as well as dormice, which they kept in small cages and fed on nuts. Mouse flesh was also thought a great delicacy in parts of India and China.
- Honey found by archaeologists in Egyptian 'mummy' tombs was still edible.
- Lettuce is the world's most popular green, whilst cabbage is 91% water – so drink your cabbage up!
- Bubble gum has got rubber in it.

Melt a knob of butter in a small pan • Peel and chop the onion into thin slices and put them into the pan • Fry gently for a few minutes until the onion becomes translucent (a bit transparent) • Whilst that's going on, break the eggs into a bowl and whisk them until they're mixed. You can whisk with a fork or a proper whisk or perhaps an adult will help you use an electric mixer of some sort • Go back to the onion pan, add the tomatoes and simmer the mixture until it gets thicker • Add a couple of shakes of pepper – or a couple of 'grinds' if you have a pepper mill • Take the pan off the heat and replace it with a frying pan • Add a knob of butter and, when it's melted and foaming, add the beaten egg • Cook until there's no runny egg left on the top • With a spoon, add the tomato mixture • Arrange the sliced mushrooms on top and sprinkle on the grated cheese • Place under a hot grill and cook until the cheese bubbles and it looks like the photograph on p. 152 • Cut into two portions and serve up using the egg slice.

Serves 2

1 small onion

A little vegetable oil or butter

3 large eggs

1 small tin of chopped tomatoes

60g (2oz) mushrooms, sliced

40g (1^1/$_2$oz) grated mozzarella cheese (Gouda or Edam will do, but failing that, just good old-fashioned 'mousetrap')

Black pepper

Equipment required:

small pan, chopping board, sharp knife, bowl for eggs, saucepan, egg whisk, frying pan, dessert spoon, hot grill, egg slice

---

BAKED BEANS

- Often referred to as 'breakfast gravy', a serving of baked beans on buttered toast with a glass of milk provides over one-third of the recommended daily amounts of iron and vitamins B$_1$ and B$_2$, as well as three-quarters of the amount of calcium.
- Did you know that in a large can there are about 420 beans?
- If you laid them end to end they would stretch to just under 6m.

- To make a circle of beans around the world you would need 7 million cans.
- To reach the moon you would need 56 million cans (a good few trolley loads).
- The biggest number of baked beans eaten with a cocktail stick in 5 minutes is 226 (*Guinness Book of Records*).
- Made in this country since 1928, the secret blend of herbs and spices which makes Heinz beans so popular is known to only 4 people in the world.

BEANS AND EGG

This dish looks like something nasty from another planet but it tastes great, is low in fat and full of protein and fibre which adults know are all very good for you!

Pop the beans into a small pan and heat gently (never heat beans quickly or the juice will stick to the bottom of the pan and burn). You may need an adult to open the beans – the pull-off lids can be pretty tough • Whilst the beans are heating, break the egg into a cup or a small bowl and beat it with a fork, mixing it so that the yolk is mixed in with the white • You shouldn't need any salt in this so just add a bit of pepper for extra taste • Once the beans are hot, pour in the egg and stir until it thickens and cooks • Serve it on toast or throw it straight into the bin if it looks too sick-making • If you like herbs, you could chop up some parsley and mix it in as well • If you're a spaghetti hoops fan, you could try this recipe using them instead of beans.

Serves 1

1 small can of baked beans

1 egg

Black pepper

1 slice of wholemeal toast

Equipment required:

small pan for beans, cup or small bowl, fork or small whisk

HAM FRITTERS

The bacon or ham needs to be chopped up into bits about the size of a 5p piece – if you're not allowed to use a knife then use kitchen scissors • Put the flour, salt and pepper, milk and vegetable oil into the mixing bowl and beat it with the whisk or fork until it's a smooth, thick and gooey batter • Heat the frying pan and add a drizzle of oil • When the oil is hot, add the chopped bacon or ham. If you're using bacon, you'll have to cook it for a few minutes, turning it over frequently with the egg slice. If you're using ham, it just needs warming and crisping so it won't need so long • When the bacon or ham is ready, take it out of the frying pan with the egg slice and pop it on to the kitchen roll to mop up any excess oil • Turn the heat down low under the pan • Tip the bacon or ham into the batter in the mixing bowl and give it a good stir • Turn the heat up under the pan and, after a minute, drip dessertspoonfuls of the mixture into it and press them down a bit with the egg slice. Since the mixture is pretty sticky, you might have to push each lump off the spoon with a teaspoon • Cook your fritters for about a minute on each side until they're nice and brown • Take them out with the fish slice and enjoy them!

Makes about 8 fritters
4 rashers of back bacon *or* equivalent in slices of cooked ham
55g (2oz) self-raising flour
5 tbsp milk
1 tbsp vegetable oil
Salt and pepper
Vegetable oil for frying
Equipment required:
chopping board, sharp knife or a pair of kitchen scissors, mixing bowl, whisk or fork, tablespoon, dessert spoon, teaspoon, frying pan, egg slice or kitchen tongs, kitchen roll

BACON 'N' BANANA

Preheat the oven to 150°C/300°F (gas mark 2) • Fry the bacon in a pan with a little oil until crisp and keep in a warm oven • Keep the pan hot • Peel the banana and slice it right down the middle and then cut each half crossways into 4 pieces • Carefully put each piece into the hot bacon fat in the pan – use kitchen tongs or a fork and spoon • Turn the banana pieces over now and again and cook until nice and brown • Remove from the pan using the kitchen tongs and serve with the bacon straight on to a warm plate or some hot buttered toast.

Serves 1–2
2 rashers of bacon
Vegetable oil
1 banana
1 slice of buttered toast
Equipment required:
frying pan, sharp knife, kitchen tongs or a fork and spoon

APPLE TREAT

Wash the apple, cut it into four, take the core out and then chop the quarters into small bits • Place in a cereal bowl with the nuts and raisins • Serve with or without milk or yoghurt.

Serves 1
1 eating apple
1 handful of nuts and raisins
Yoghurt or milk
Equipment required:
chopping board, sharp knife, cereal bowls

BACON, SAUSAGE AND APPLE

Preheat the oven to 150°C/300°F (gas mark 2) or turn on the grill to low • Put the sausages into a hot frying pan that has a little oil in it • Cook them gently for about 10 minutes making sure you turn them now and again using the kitchen tongs so that all sides get brown • Halfway through cooking the sausages, add the bacon, turning it once so that both sides are cooked • When cooked, remove the sausages and bacon using the tongs again, dry them on kitchen towel to get rid of the fat and keep them warm in a low oven or under a very low grill • Fry the apple slices on both sides in the bacon fat until soft • Add to the cooked sausages and bacon and serve on a plate.

Serves 1–2
2 sausages
Vegetable oil
2 slices of back bacon
1 large eating apple, peeled, cored and sliced
Equipment required:
frying pan, kitchen tongs or a fork, kitchen roll

BANANA DREAMBOAT

Preheat the oven to 220°C/430°F (gas mark 7) • Slit the skin of the banana lengthways • Put it into an ovenproof dish and bake in the oven for 10 minutes • Serve in its peel with yoghurt and a drop of jam or chocolate spread • Be careful since the banana will be very hot.

Serves 1
1 banana
Yoghurt
Jam or chocolate spread
Equipment required:
sharp knife, ovenproof dish or plate,

CINNAMON TOAST

Toast the bread on one side only under a grill • On the side that isn't toasted, spread the butter or peanut butter and then the honey • Sprinkle the cinnamon on top • Put back under the hot grill and leave until the butter and honey starts to bubble • It will be very hot, so remove it with an egg slice and let it cool before eating.

Serves 1
1 slice of toasting bread
1 tsp peanut butter or ordinary butter
1 tsp honey
$1/2$ tsp ground cinnamon
Equipment required:
hot grill, knife for spreading

BANANA TOAST

Toast the bread lightly on both sides • Spread it with butter or peanut butter • Lay sliced banana on top and spread with honey • Place the toast back under the grill until the top bubbles • Carefully remove with an egg slice and allow to cool before eating.

Serves 1
1 slice of bread, brown or
  white
Butter or peanut butter
1 banana, sliced
1 tsp clear, runny honey
Equipment required:
knife, grill, egg slice

ORANGE SHAKE

Mix all the ingredients in a blender/liquidiser until smooth and pour into a glass.

Serves 1
1/2 cup orange juice
1/2 cup plain yoghurt
  (preferably Greek)
1 tsp honey

1 ice cube
Equipment required:
1 blender/liquidiser,
glass or tumbler

STRAWBERRY SHAKE

You can use any fruits that are in season for this recipe or fruits from the freezer.

Mix all the ingredients in the blender/liquidiser until smooth and pour into a glass.

Serves 1
1 cup fresh or frozen strawberries
½ cup plain yoghurt (your own home-made yoghurt or bought Greek yoghurt)
1 tsp runny honey
1 ice cube (leave out if the strawberries were frozen)
Equipment required:
1 blender/liquidiser, glass or tumbler

HEALTHY EATING FOR CHILDREN

George and I both have youngsters who seem to grow overnight so we know the importance of making sure they have the right foods. Forgive us, therefore, if we preach a little by reproducing these tips courtesy of Tesco's Food Advice Service.

- Children need a large amount of calories and nutrients to meet their energy needs, for repair and maintenance and to fuel growth.
- Children have smaller stomachs than adults, so they need smaller more regular meals.
- They need a more concentrated form of calories and nutrients – not high fibre/low fat – to make up a well-balanced diet.
- They can still have low or reduced fat products and fibre-providing foods but neither to excess.
- It is recommended that children under 2 years old have full fat milk, but after that they can have semi-skimmed if the calories and nutrients are supplied by other sources in a healthy varied diet. Skimmed milk can be introduced from the age of 5.
- While children should not have a very low-fat diet, the balance of fats should be the same as for adults, cutting down on saturated fats in favour of unsaturated fats.

- Children's teeth are more at risk from tooth decay, so try and avoid too many sweets, especially the sticky chewy ones.
- Keep sweets and chocolates for after meal times only – banning them altogether doesn't usually work.
- Dilute fruit juices or give them fizzy water or milk to drink.
- Make sure they brush their teeth after eating sweets.
- Try not to encourage them to eat foods that are very salty – it will give them a taste for salty foods.
- A good variety of foods should ensure they get all the vitamins and minerals they need.
- Iron is important for young children. Meat and dark green vegetables are rich sources. It's also found in bread, eggs, nuts, beans and lentils.
- Calcium and vitamin D are important to growing children. Milk, cheese and yoghurt are good sources of calcium (even the low-fat varieties). It's also found in white bread, the soft bones of fish (e.g. canned sardines) and pulses such as baked beans.
- Vitamin D is found in foods like liver, oil-rich fish and eggs. It's also made in the body by the action of sunlight on the skin.

PACK LUNCHES

You could argue that pack lunches have precious little to do with breakfasts, but where youngsters' health is concerned, let's stretch a point. After all, most of us make them up just before or after breakfast.

In the health advice on p. 162, Tesco's make one especially good point which, when it's pointed out to you, is blindingly obvious: children's stomachs are not as big as ours and they therefore need to eat smaller portions more frequently. (The only exception to this is demonstrated by male teenagers who don't have stomachs at all – just bottomless pits!) This does explain one of life's great mysteries: an hour after a big meal, why do children say, 'Can I have something to eat?' It also explains why young school kids always want a snack for playtime or what we call a play 'piece' – a Scottish term thought to refer to youngsters being sent to work or school with a piece of cold porridge for mid-morning sustenance. Don't try that with your youngsters, but do give them something reasonably healthy and tasty from the suggestions that follow.

Although school lunches have improved tremendously we're told, they still seem to be a bit patchy and lots of children can't abide them. If that's a familiar story in your home or you're dissatisfied with the choice offered to the kids at lunchtime, give them a good healthy pack lunch instead. You can let your culinary imagination run riot and include all sorts of picnic-style goodies – pies, quiches, sandwiches, compotes, fresh fruit in season, fruit juices and your own home-made bread or rolls, jams, curds and chutneys. You don't make any of those? Don't worry . . . you can still produce superb pack lunches by the careful choice of components and sandwich fillings.

Sandwiches Whilst pack lunches are by no means composed of just sandwiches, with a bit of imagination the humble sandwich can be elevated to an art form. Don't restrict your choice of the sandwich 'holder' to the traditional pre-packed sliced loaf. These days there are lots of alternatives – the crusty French roll ('*petit pain*') or hunk of French bread (so beloved by supermarket in-store bakeries), and a wide choice of soft rolls, many of them wholemeal and dusted with seeds of one sort or another. Then there are all the excellent sandwich wraps and tortillas which really appeal to children. The beauty of these is that not only do most children seem to love them, but they're pre-wrapped and have a very long shelf life. There's also the humble pitta bread that's been with us for years: kids love the novelty of these and being able to pick out the filling with their fingers.

To keep children's interest, ring the changes now and again with the shape of sandwiches – triangles one day, rectangles the next, circles the next. It may be a bit wasteful but it does grab their attention and possibly make them the envy of their friends (always a good thing!). Wraps can also be cut into slices diagonally and, if you have some colourful fillings such as green, red or yellow peppers, the effect is very pleasing.

BREAD

- Ensure that whatever bread you use is fresh.
- If fresh, your own home-made bread or rolls would be ideal.
- If buying in bread, try and avoid using cheap sliced loaves – their plasticine-like consistency will do you no favours when chewed. Good soft morning rolls are an excellent substitute.
- If the youngsters aren't too keen on brown bread, give them wholemeal or soft grain. Alternatively, be sneaky and give them white for the top slice and brown for the bottom. If they turn their sandwiches over, of course, you'll be rumbled! But do persevere; they'll soon get used to it and they'll be a lot healthier for it.
- Generally speaking, use white bread for the more delicately flavoured fillings. Only use brown where its assertiveness is going to be matched by the filling.
- Use slightly salted or unsalted butter or low-fat spread.

Fillings The following are just a few suggestions to break away from the perennial ham, cheese and pickle choice that seems to greet snackers in so many establishments. You will no doubt have many ideas of your own and, of course, you can always pop into some of the major stores, peruse their sandwich selection and come home with a few ideas.

You can mix and match all sorts of ingredients depending on what you have in the fridge and cupboard and what you think you can get away with as far as feeding the children healthy food. Remember the versatility of rolls, wraps and pitta breads. Instead of cutting up slices of this and that, cut cubes and fill a pitta bread or a wrap instead; mix a meat or vegetable with cottage cheese; or cut hard cheese into cubes and pack it into a small container.

Drinks Here's another chance to contribute to the 'five a day' campaign by giving them a fruit or vegetable juice that they like. Avoid the expense and added sugar of the small cartons with a straw and fill up a container from the carton you would serve at breakfast.

Leak-proof and practical containers are sometimes a problem: one solution is to visit your nearest outdoor camping shop and choose from what should be a good range of small drink holders. Alternatively, some youngsters like the trendy water-filled sports bottles. They give them great 'street cred' in the playground and are marvellous for squirting their mates!

On cold winter days you might like to make up a vacuum flask (stainless steel will come home in one piece) of tea, hot chocolate or a favourite soup.

SAVOURY SANDWICHES

- any cold meat such as ham, tongue, beef, pork, chicken or lamb
- spam or other luncheon meat
- hard cheese such as Cheddar with pickle or even raw red onion
- cream cheese and Marmite
- cucumber and Marmite
- cucumber and lettuce
- ham and potato crisps (frowned upon by responsible grown-ups but actually delicious!)
- ham, cheese and pickles
- tuna or salmon with mayonnaise
- bacon, lettuce and tomato (BLT) – even when cold, these are still very tasty
- chicken and avocado
- coronation chicken
- egg mayonnaise
- hommous and sliced pepper or onion
- cottage cheese and grated carrot
- peanut butter

SWEET SANDWICHES

- home-made jam (see pp. 61–62) on its own or with peanut butter (see pp. 64–65)
- lemon curd (see p. 63), raspberries and cream
- lemon curd (see p. 63) and blueberries
- lemon curd (see p. 63) and tinned fruit salad
- peanut butter, chopped raisins, apple sauce and cinnamon
- sliced fresh or dried dates with honey
- mashed banana, lemon juice and honey

- mashed banana and raisins
- chocolate spread with or without chocolate chips
- cream cheese and sliced seedless grapes
- cottage cheese and chopped dried fruit such as apricot.

OTHER PACK LUNCH INGREDIENTS

- cheese biscuits and a sliver of cheese
- half an avocado wrapped up in cling film with a plastic spoon
- cherry tomatoes – they're usually very sweet and excellent eaten on their own
- crunchy raw carrot sticks and a pot of hommous or other mix
- mini pork pies
- cold, cooked sausages, with or without a ketchup dip
- a small container of dried fruit – sultanas, raisins, apricots, prunes, pears etc.
- their favourite yoghurt and a plastic spoon
- kiwi fruit – cut off the top and wrap in it cling film or foil. Include a plastic spoon
- bananas – captivate the young ones by lightly scratching a message on the banana skin. After a while it turns brown and is easily readable
- small tins of fruit – the easy-opening ones
- any fresh fruit that's in season, especially seedless grapes when they're cheap. Even melon can be chopped up and put in a container with a tooth-pick or plastic fork.

- If you're a family that still has a Sunday joint, then that makes the ideal source of cold meats for sandwiches.
- If you have any good gravy left over (not the stuff that comes out of a packet or jar), it will have gelatinised by Monday. Spread over the sandwich meat it will give lots of added taste.
- Try to avoid using the pre-packed slices of beef, chicken, turkey etc. They're often pretty bland and some of them may be made from 're-formed' MRM (mechanically recovered meat).
- Grating the cheese produces a less stodgy result.

If you can enthuse your youngsters by teaching them even the basics of cooking and follow that up with innovative and exciting pack lunches, you'll be giving them a great start to a lifetime of healthy eating.

the continental breakfast

As we sample other countries' lifestyles on our travels and become more aware of the impact of diet on our health, the continental breakfast or cold table becomes an increasingly popular alternative. A typical petit dejeuner in France comprises coffee, hot croissant and crusty baguette or brioche with butter and preserves . . . probably followed by a Gauloise! Elsewhere in Europe, diners push the boat out a little further with a selection of their national breads and rolls, plus fruit juices and a choice of cold meats, cheeses, yoghurts and – mainly in Scandinavia – fish.

If we take the best produce and ideas that other nations have to offer and team them with our own British fare, then we have the makings of a superlative cold table. The foods that we're looking at in this chapter are the cured or smoked meats and fish, mild and smoked cheeses, hard boiled eggs, smoked and unsmoked . . . anything, in fact, that can claim a legitimate place at a breakfast table.

CHEESE

For most people, breakfast is not the time for strong cheese so here's a small selection of mild ones that will go down very nicely with unspiced cold meats, fresh bread, rolls, oatcakes and bagels.

* *Brie:* made since the eighth century, this famous French soft cheese should be stored at room temperature and, as long as it's not 'high', is perfect for breakfast with fresh bread or oatcakes.
* *Caerphilly:* this famous Welsh cheese is made from cows' milk and is quite similar to Wensleydale with a mild and slightly sour taste.
* *Cheddars:* there are many mild Cheddars available; it's just a matter of experimenting until you find a consistently good one.
* *Cream cheese:* you can't have bagels without cream cheese, and probably the most commonly available is Philadelphia.
* *Dunlop:* a favourite with oatcakes, this Scottish cheese has a Cheddar-type texture with a bland and buttery taste.
* *Edam:* a mild and bland Dutch cheese made from cows' milk with a butter-like consistency and a red wax coating.
* *Emmental:* this famous Swiss cheese has a delightfully sweet and nutty taste and has large holes – eyes – spread throughout. An excellent breakfast cheese.
* *Gouda:* made in wheels like Edam, this mild Dutch cheese is tastier than Edam and has a yellowish natural rind.
* *Gruyère:* a hard Swiss cheese that's also made in France and Germany. It's similar to Emmental in looks and nutty taste but doesn't have so many holes.
* *Jarlsberg:* this is a relatively new cheese from Norway (1959) which is usually white or light yellow. Made from cows' milk, it has a dense and waxy consistency, a mild and nutty taste and is recognisable by the large holes spread throughout it.
* *Wensleydale:* if you like a slightly sour and salty cheese with a buttermilk flavour, then this well-known Yorkshire cheese is for you.

For storage, cheese should be wrapped in kitchen foil or greaseproof paper

The holes in Swiss-type cheeses such as Emmental and Gruyère are caused by a special bacterium that lives off the lactic acid produced by other bacterium. This gets converted into prodigious amounts of carbon dioxide, which collects in pockets and forms the holes.

Hard cheeses such as Emmental and Gruyère are best cut with a cheese 'shaver'.

and then in a plastic bag and stored in or near the salad compartment. Try and bring it out to 'warm up' for at least an hour before you require it. The range of smoked cheeses has grown over the years and many are available through mail order direct from the smokehouses. All will be vacuum-packed, which gives them a storage life (unopened) of 14 days in a good fridge and 2–3 months in a freezer.

COLD AND CURED MEATS AND SAUSAGES

A selection of cold meats on a platter makes a refreshing change and the choice is bewildering. Hams – raw, cooked, smoked, unsmoked – sausages, cured meats, cooked and raw: the following list is by no means exhaustive but gives you an idea of the choice that awaits you. You may well find vacuum-packed versions in the major supermarkets.

- *Ardennes ham:* this is a Belgian ham that is rated alongside Bayonne, Parma and York hams.
- *Bayonne ham:* this is from the Basque region and is soaked in a brine of red wine, olive oil and rosemary. It is then wrapped in straw and smoked.
- *Bradenham ham:* cured to a recipe dating back to 1881 and is a sweet, unsmoked ham that needs to be cooked before eating. Legs are cut from bacon pigs, cured in dry salt with saltpetre and sugar, placed in a marinade of molasses and spices and then hung to mature. The whole process from fresh meat to matured ham is 5–6 months.
- *Bresaola:* this is an air-dried salted beef from the Lombardy region of Italy. It's usually served as a starter but would be quite at home in a breakfast selection. Usually served with a really good olive oil, lemon juice, freshly ground pepper and possible some fresh shavings of Parmesan cheese.
- *Carmarthen ham:* as for Welsh hams (*see* below) but matured for a further 3–6 months.
- *Carpaccio:* Italian in origin, Carpaccio consists of thin shavings of raw beef fillet usually served with the same accompaniments as bresaola.
- *Cumberland ham:* unsmoked ham for cooking and not well known outside the Lake District. The hams are dry-salted for a month with salt and saltpetre and then dried and matured at an ambient temperature for three months.
- *Cumbria air-dried ham:* Unsmoked, cured ham for eating raw, they are usually from Large White and Landrace Cross pigs.
- *Devonshire ham:* smoked or unsmoked cured ham for cooking and on the go

for about 150 years. The hams are brined for 12 days in 60% salt solution, then cold-smoked in oak plus a little beech.

- *Irish hams:* there are two well-known varieties, Belfast and Limerick, both of which are dry cured and smoked over – yes, you've guessed it – peat!

- *Parma ham:* this superior – and expensive – uncooked ham comes from Italy's Parma region, also the home of Parmesan cheese. The pigs in Parma are fed on a diet of chestnuts and whey (from the cheese-making process) and the resultant hams are seasoned, cured in salt and then air-dried. Thinly sliced Parma ham can be eaten on its own or served with a slice of melon or fresh figs.

- *Pastrami:* any veteran TV watchers will remember New York cop Kojak and his 'pastrami on rye' sandwiches. Usually made from brisket, which is rubbed in salt and a seasoning paste that can include garlic, peppercorns, cinnamon, cloves, allspice, coriander seeds and nutmeg, it's then dry-cured, smoked, cooked and thinly sliced.

- *Prosciutto:* you may see pre-packed cold meats labelled thus, but it's just the Italian name for ham and describes a ham that has been seasoned, salt-cured and air-dried. Parma ham is a proscuitto from Parma.

- *Salami:* there's a bewildering array of salamis to choose from – French, German, Danish, Hungarian, Milano, Toscana, Genoa etc. They're all fairly heavily smoked and 'garlicked' and your choice (if any) depends upon how seriously you want to repel friends, loved ones or vampires. Delis and deli counters in supermarkets are usually quite happy to give you a taste before you buy, so try some out.

- *Salt beef:* a good old-fashioned treatment for beef and especially tasty when cold (*see* p. 172).

- *Smithfields:* this ham is named, not after London's meat market, but after the US town of Smithfields in Virginia. It, and the similar Virginia ham, are given a fairly conventional curing and then smoked over hickory, rubbed with pepper and aged over about 18 months.

- *Smoked meats:* many specialist smokehouses around the country produce – and offer a mail order service for – such delicacies as smoked venison, chicken, duck, lamb, pork, pheasant, grouse, pigeon, partridge, quail, guinea fowl and even more exotic products. Most of these will be available in a good deli or supermarket deli counter.

- *Suffolk ham:* this is a cured, smoked ham dating back to at least the early 1800s and in many old farmhouse chimneys in Suffolk the hooks for hanging the hams can still be seen. In the modern recipe they are brined in salt, saltpetre and water and then pickled for 3–4 weeks in a mixture of black treacle, sugar, salt and stout or cider. They're then smoked for 5 days over oak sawdust and matured for at least a month. The hams used to be considered at their best between 1–2 years old.

- *Tongue:* we're told that the tongue of all domestic animals tastes good but let's restrict ourselves to the most commonly available dish in the UK which is the very tasty beef (ox) tongue. For continental breakfast use this can be fresh or salted and then poached and pressed. It can also be smoked.

- *Welsh ham:* this cured, uncooked ham is made by placing the raw hams in a bed of dry salt containing a very small amount of saltpetre, a mixture which is rubbed in several times a week for six weeks. The hams are then dried and matured for three months.

- *Westphalia ham:* the best of the German hams, which ranks with Parma and Bayonne. This rich and dark raw ham undergoes a lengthy ageing process after it has been cured and smoked.

- *Wurst:* Schinken, Kalbfleischwurst, Zungenwurst, Mettwurst, Bierwurst, Jagdwurst, Knoblauchwurst, Weisswurst . . . 'wurst' is the German for 'sausage' and those mild versions that are suitable for the breakfast table are cooked, with some of them being lightly smoked. Once again, don't be afraid to experiment at the deli counter and ask for a taste.

- *York ham:* these have been renowned for centuries in many parts of the world. The raw hams are cured for a month, drained for 3 days and then matured for 4–24 months, depending upon the manufacturer. A word of warning, however. Much of what goes under the name of York ham is describing the process and not the origin of the ham or the cure.

Salting or pickling for recipes like Salted Tongue (*see* p. 172) can be wet or dry. Wet is the easiest and is best done in cool weather. You'll need a non-metallic container – a basin or pail that's large enough to hold the tongue. You'll also need a lid or cover of sorts to prevent dust settling in the liquid.

PRESSED OX TONGUE

Some of the preparation for this dish is not for the squeamish but the end result is well worth it.

Put the tongue in a large pan and cover with cold water • Add the other ingredients • Bring to the boil and simmer for 1 hour per 450g (1lb) • Remove the tongue and plunge it into cold water, straining and reserving the liquid • Cut out any bones or bits of gristle from the base of the tongue and then skin it • Curl the tongue round tightly and place in a tin or pan that provides a tight fit • Cover it with the reserved stock • Put a saucer on top of the tongue and a weight or heavy object on the saucer • Leave to set overnight in the fridge • Turn out on to a plate and garnish or slice as required.

1 small beef tongue (larger ones can weigh up to 2.3kg /5lb)
1 carrot, sliced
1 turnip, sliced
1 onion, peeled and cut in half
A few peppercorns
1 bouquet garni

SALTED TONGUE

Bring the water, salt, saltpetre and sugar to the boil, and simmer for 20 minutes, skimming continuously • Strain it into your chosen container and add the tongue • Put the lid on and leave for 4–5 days in a cool place, stirring about once a day • At the end of the salting period, remove the tongue and wash it thoroughly under cold running water • Soak it in cold water for about an hour before cooking • Cover it in fresh water and bring to the boil, simmering for 30 minutes per 450g (1lb) – about half the time required for an unsalted tongue. The main criterion, however, is that the meat should be tender – test it with a skewer.

4½ litres (1 gallon) cold water
700g (1½lb) salt
2 tbsp saltpetre
175g (6oz) brown sugar
1 small beef tongue

NORFOLK SALT BEEF

Mix the salt, sugar, saltpetre and water in a very clean, large plastic tub • Put the beef into the brine and keep it submerged by placing a large plate on top of it, surmounted by a weight • Cover the tub to keep dust out and leave in a cool place for 5–7 days, turning periodically • To cook, place the salt beef in a large saucepan, together with the carrots, onions, bay leaves, peppercorns and bouquet garni • Cover with water and bring to the boil • Skim and leave to simmer for 2–3 hours, or until tender.

450g (1lb) Maldon or other
    coarse sea salt
225g (8oz) brown sugar
50g (2oz) saltpetre
3.6 litres (6pt) water
1.3–1.8kg (3–4lb) silverside of
    beef
4 carrots, sliced
2 onions, chopped
2 bay leaves
12 black peppercorns
1 bouquet garni

BRINING

Brining is the term used to describe the pre-smoking process of salting the produce – either by storing in dry salt for a period (called, not surprisingly, 'dry salting') or soaking in a salt solution. The salt is used to draw moisture out of the food, so the brine must have a salinity of at least 20%. If an egg floats on the water, you've achieved the right strength. When the solution contains other ingredients such as herbs, spices, vinegars and even wines or spirits, plus a curing agent, it's called a 'cure' or 'pickle'. These not only impart their own flavours into the produce, but assist the cold-smoking process by facilitating the penetration of the preserving and flavouring agents in the smoke.

Saltpetre The addition of saltpetre (potassium nitrate) to a brine inhibits bacterial growth and helps to keep the meat's natural colour. In modern times its use as a constituent of gunpowder makes it a little difficult to source. Most chemists can get hold of it, however, although you may have to buy as much as 500g at a time and you might get a visit from Special Branch!

Water Tap water could contain chemicals that would interfere with the curing process so use bottled instead.

BOUQUET GARNI

You can buy teabag-style bouquet garnis but, if you have the herbs, it's much better to make them yourself. The classic contents are parsley, thyme and bay leaf, which are either tied together and hung over the side of the pan or placed in a piece of tied or knotted muslin.

FISH

Sweet-cured smoking is the traditional cure for the 'king of fish'. Sides of salmon are marinated in a mixture of rum, molasses and juniper and then slow smoked over smouldering oak shavings. Others worth trying at breakfast time are as follows.

- *Dill-cured salmon:* here the raw sides of salmon are not smoked but marinated in a dill brine with sugar, air-dried to reduce the moisture content and then matured for 2–3 days with dill weed. The Swedish product is known as 'gravadlax' or 'gravlax' (*see* p. 181).
- *Hot-smoked salmon:* this is a relatively new way of treating salmon which has proved very popular. After marinating in brine and cold smoking for some hours, it is hot-smoked to cook it. This results in a dark pink flesh and a flaky texture.
- *Lox:* this brine-cured, cold-smoked salmon can be saltier than other smoked salmon products and is a favourite in Jewish–American cuisine, especially with bagels and cream cheese.
- *Rollmop herring:* usually eaten with dark brown bread and butter, fillets of raw herring are rolled up around pieces of onion or pickled cucumber and marinated in a spiced vinegar. Most delis and supermarket fish counters now stock them.
- *Smoked trout:* invariably farmed rainbow trout, it's often said that smoked trout has a superior taste to salmon. It certainly has a finer texture and a more subtle taste – and it's about 30% lower in calories.
- *Sweet-cured smoked trout:* these are usually large rainbow trout cured in the same way as sweet-cured salmon (*see* above).
- *Hot-smoked trout:* a similar treatment to hot-smoked salmon (*see* above).
- *Hot-smoked mackerel:* again, a similar treatment to hot-smoked salmon, this can be plain or peppered.
- *Orkney herring:* there is an excellent proprietary brand of Orkney herring on the market with two different marinades.
- *Bismark herring:* these are Baltic herring filleted and marinated in vinegar with onion rings for 2–3 days.

Recipes for Gravadlax and Marinated Raw Fish can be found in World Breakfasts on pp. 181 and 183 respectively.

world breakfasts

If you like good food, a huge part of the enjoyment of overseas travel will be involved with experiencing new dishes and new tastes. It's regrettable, therefore, that so many holiday spots have felt obliged to ditch their own centuries-old cuisine and pander to what many of our compatriots insist on when they travel abroad – British fry-ups and fish and chips (plus, of course, copious quantities of lager).

Even business travel is affected by this globalisation and ethnic breakfasts in international hotels are slowly being squeezed out to make way for the 'safe', westernised versions that will be acceptable to the majority of guests.

USA

A nation's food tends to represent its ethnic make-up and its agricultural diversity, and the United States offers an excellent example of this. Although American breakfasts are very similar to British ones in many respects (bacon, eggs, toast, tea, coffee etc.), a pot-pourri of other influences have been overlaid from Europe, Scandinavia and America's near neighbours. In turn, many of those influences have been re-exported to us in the form of cereals, fruit juice, waffles and hotcakes, to mention just a few.

Pastries and specialist breads play a huge part in US breakfasts, with the national sweet tooth being pampered with continental-style offerings such as cinnamon rolls, Danish pastries, coffee cakes, German apple cake, cherry turnovers, Belgian waffles, apple pancakes and a host of muffins incorporating a bewildering range of fruits and spices. Specialist breads originate from throughout Europe, with the nation's favourite being those delicious Jewish bagels.

The medley of dishes and just a taste of the ethnic mix is exemplified by this fast-food menu from Schneithorst's Kaffee Haus somewhere in Missouri.

Southern Pride: 2 farm fresh eggs, golden hashed brown potatoes and authentic Southern-style biscuits and gravy

Steak and eggs: 7oz charbroiled strip steak, 2 farm fresh eggs, golden hashed browned potatoes and toast

Continental breakfast: choice of home-made pastry with orange juice and a cup of fresh brewed coffee

The triple play: ham, sausage, bacon, 2 country fresh eggs, golden hash browned potatoes and toast

Pancake sandwich: 4 buttermilk griddle cakes served with 2 strips of bacon and a fried egg

Waffle sandwich: Belgian waffle and 2 strips of bacon with 1 fried egg

Country ham and eggs: served with home-made hash browns and toast

2+2+2+2: 2 eggs, 2 bacon strips, 2 links sausage, 2 buttermilk pancakes and toast

Corned beef hash: with 2 eggs, hash browns and choice of toast

Traveller's delight: 2 eggs, bacon or sausage, hash browned potatoes, toast and jelly

Three-egg omelet: with a choice of bacon, ham, cheese or sautéed mushrooms, served with toast, jelly and hash browned potatoes

Two eggs: any style served with hash browns and choice of toast

Chicken, fried steak and eggs: served with hash browns and toast

PANCAKES AND FRENCH TOAST

Blueberry pancakes • Belgian waffles • Hot griddle cakes • Pecan Belgian waffle • French toast

TOAST AND ROLLS

Bagel with cream cheese • Cinnamon or Danish rolls • Apple coffee cake • English muffin or toast • Blueberry or bran muffin

FRUIT JUICES AND CEREALS

Half grapefruit • Hot oatmeal • Biscuits and gravy • Kellogg's best cereal • Chilled juice (orange, grapefruit, apple, V-8, cranberry)

HEALTH TIPS

The following items are available for the health conscious: egg beaters, skim milk, low calorie syrup, margarine.

CANADA

With its huge border with the US and a similar, but not so extensive, ethnic mix, it's not surprising that Canadian breakfasts are very much in line with American ones. Hotcakes – or griddle cakes – with maple syrup and Canadian back bacon must be the favourite dish of all. And appetites tend to be big, as can be seen from Mars Diner – offering three large griddle cakes served with three sausages and ham and bacon!

Two-scoop plate: salmon, tuna, chicken salad, chopped liver or chopped egg – choice of any two items with bread or roll and butter

Big time: 3 eggs, 3 slices of peameal bacon, 3 slices of toast, small juice and coffee

Grand slam: griddle cake, fried egg, bacon, sausages, home fries, butter and syrup, coffee

Corned beef hash: with fried egg, home fries, toast and coffee

Mr Mars special: 3 eggs with 6oz steak, toast, coffee and small juice

Belgian waffle: with coffee

Griddle cakes: 3 large griddle cakes served with syrup and butter

Griddle Cakes: 3 large griddle cakes served with 3 sausages, ham or bacon

French toast (made with 2 eggs): with syrup and butter

French Toast (made with 2 eggs): with 3 sausages, ham or bacon

NEW ZEALAND

Butter, lamb and kiwi fruit are the food products that immediately spring to mind when thinking of New Zealand and it has to be said that the country has never produced a distinctively national cuisine of its own. Rather it has refined and supplemented its British culinary heritage with its own unique produce. This menu comes from Remarkables Lodge in Queenstown, South Island.

TRADITIONAL ENGLISH BREAKFAST

A hearty selection of:
* breakfast buffet
* a generous platter of fresh and preserved fruits
* hot fruit compotes
* assorted cereals
* yoghurts
* fresh berry muffins
* fresh pastries and croissants
* a choice of toasted breads
* fresh fruit juice
* tea and freshly ground coffee

Followed by your choice of the following sample menu:
* our hot selection
* the Lodge's fresh free range eggs cooked to order with honey cured bacon
* smoked salmon scrambled eggs
* the Lodge's stuffed omelette
* ricotta hotcakes drizzled with local comb honey
* savoury and fresh fruit waffles

AUSTRALIA

Not surprisingly, Australia's culinary roots lie in Britain. But just as in America, the ethnic mix has altered in recent decades and out of that has come fusion cooking – the mixing of different national dishes to great and exciting effect.

The following menus of the Pelham Bay Diner and The Fenix Hotel, Richmond, Victoria, both display these characteristics admirably.

PELHAM BAY DINER

Eggs: 2 ranch eggs served with potatoes and tomatoes, English muffin or bagel

Australian breakfast: 12oz New York strip steak and eggs served with home fries and toasted bagel or English muffin

Irish breakfast: 2 eggs, Irish bacon, Irish sausage, black pudding and grilled tomatoes

Bronx breakfast: pancakes or French toast or waffles with bacon, ham, sausage and 2 eggs

Bagel 'all the way': Nova Scotia lox, cream cheese, sliced red onion, green leaf lettuce, tomato and Kalamata olives

Eggs benedict: 2 poached eggs with Canadian bacon, served over English muffin and topped with hollandaise sauce

Any cheese omelette

Western omelette: with ham, onion and peppers

International omelette: with pepper, onion, sweet sausage, melted mozzarella and Cheddar cheese, topped with Spanish sauce

Bacon, ham or sausage omelette

Mushroom omelette

Garden omelette: with fresh garden vegetables

Greek omelette: with feta cheese and tomato

Pelham Bay friccata omelette: plum tomatoes and sweet sausage topped with melted mozzarella

Tomato, basil and asparagus omelette: fresh tomatoes, basil, asparagus, melted cheese with a touch of garlic and red onions

FENIX HOTEL

Orange juice

Selection of poached and fresh fruit platters

Home-made muesli with sheep's milk yoghurt

Selection of croissant, Danish, pain au chocolate and muffins

Toast, preserves, honey and butter

Freshly brewed Grinders coffee and Boutique Lipton teas

Eggs Benedict: with cured ham. hollandaise sauce, grilled vine ripened tomato

Eggs any style: with chicken and parsley sausages, bacon, vine ripened tomato served with grilled sourdough

Toasted brioche: with warmed winter fruit, star anise and King Island cream

Buttermilk and hazelnut pancakes: with whipped marmalade butter and orange syrup

French toast: with cinnamon mascarpone and caramelised pineapple

Pan-fried mushrooms: with flat parsley, extra virgin olive oil and grilled sourdough

Home-made baked borlotti beans: with tomato and garlic bruschetta and lemon infused oil

Fritatta: with kipfler potatoes, bell peppers and spicy Italian sausage

Soft poached free-range eggs – with black pudding, apple wood smoked bacon and thyme potatoes

SCOTLAND

This sample menu from the world-famous Gleneagles Hotel in Perthshire shows that, of all countries, Scotland certainly knows how to 'Breakfast like a king'. The choice of dishes reads like a culinary roll of honour . . . summer berries, morning rolls, porridge, potato scones, Finnan haddock, Loch Fyne kippers, smoked

salmon, Ayrshire bacon, artisan cheeses, Scotch pancakes . . . mouth-watering in the extreme!

AUTUMN À LA CARTE BREAKFAST

Fresh fruit juice • Scottish summer berries • Peach sparkling water • Buck's fizz or kir royale • Walnut bread horseshoe and farmer's twist • Stone-baked Scottish rolls and breakfast pastries • Assorted breakfast cereals and muesli • Prunes, apricots, grapes and lychees • Natural and fresh fruit yoghurts • Artisan cheeses

MADE TO ORDER

A choice of cream or traditional porridge

Heart-warming Scottish breakfast: Ayrshire bacon, pork and herb sausages, fried eggs, potato scones, grilled tomatoes and fried mushrooms

Vegetarian breakfast: including crispy sausages, potato scones

Tomatoes and fried mushrooms

Scrambled eggs and smoked Tay salmon

Poached Finnan haddock and poached eggs

Loch Fyne kippers and potato scones

Omelettes of your choice

The Devil's dish: spicy beans, sliced sausage, crispy bacon and a generous dash of Tabasco

Trio of muffins: topped with scrambled eggs, Lyonnaise potatoes, bacon and maple syrup

English Breakfast tea • Earl Grey, herbal or fruit teas • Colombian, espresso, cappuccino and decaffeinated coffees • Hot chocolate • Café au lait or try our Frothee (a coffee with plenty of froth and a delicate taste of chocolate)

FROM THE BUFFET

Omelettes and fried eggs • Scotch pancakes with streaky bacon, grilled tomatoes and mushrooms • Banana waffles with maple syrup • A choice of cream or traditional Scots porridge • Scrambled eggs and smoked Scottish salmon • Pork and herb link sausages or vegetarian sausages • Home-cured bacon and potato scones • Grilled trout fillet with lemon and chives

COOKED TO ORDER

Poached Finnan haddock • Baked beans on toast • Black pudding, cloutie dumpling and venison sausages • Egg benedictine

---

EUROPE AND SCANDINAVIA

It was temperate Europe that gave us the 'continental' breakfast and most countries there have similar dishes – boiled eggs, cold meats, cheeses, spiced sausages, local bread, butter, jams, yoghurts, fruit and fruit juices, together with tea, coffee, hot chocolate and milk.

Germany has over 1500 types of wurst (sausage) and 300 types of bread, one of the favourites being the crusty rolls or *petit pain* often accompanied by excellent cherry jam and sweet continental marmalade. If something more substantial is required, then there is always the universal open omelette, here masquerading as *Bauernfrühstück* – 'farmer's breakfast'. With potatoes, bacon, ham, tomatoes and chives embedded in whisked eggs, this can see a diner through until evening.

Dutch breakfasts follow the European norm but have a local delicacy known as *groene haring* ('green herring'). These are small, lightly pickled herrings that are usually eaten by picking them up by the tail and dropping them into your mouth. A popular drink at breakfast time is *anijsmelk* – warm milk flavoured with aniseed.

Austrians have a very similar breakfast to the Germans but tend to eat very lightly early in the morning and then indulge in a more substantial feast at 'fork breakfast' or *Gabelfrühstück* in one of the country's renowned coffee houses.

Swiss breakfasts are very much like those of their German neighbours, plus, of course, a couple of dishes that the Swiss invented: muesli (*see* p. 22) and rösti (*see* p. 134).

Scandinavian countries have a record of healthy eating and we carnivores should take note that fish tends to replace red meat in most diets there. Norwegian breakfasts in particular offer an enormous variety of fish, meat, cheese and bread, served from a cold buffet with coffee and boiled or fried eggs. Instead of using milk on their cereals in Norway and Sweden, breakfast diners will often have *filmjölk*, a thick, slightly sour milk and quite a shock to the taste buds if you don't know about it.

GRAVADLAX

This delicious Swedish dish is very simple to prepare and is best served with bagels and cream cheese. It will keep for a couple of days in the fridge.

45g (1¹/₂ oz) salt
30g (1oz) granulated sugar
15 peppercorns, crushed
2 fresh salmon fillets
A large bunch of fresh dill

Sprinkle the salt, sugar and crushed or roughly ground peppercorns on the flesh side of one fillet • Cover with a generous layer of fresh dill • Place the second fillet face down and head to tail on top of the first • Place a heavy cutting board or a weighted plate on top • Cover loosely and refrigerate for two days, turning the fillets over about every 12 hours and basting with the juice that has been drawn out • At the end of this period, discard the seasonings and the dill • Using a very sharp knife, cut the fish in thin, diagonal slices.

Spain and Portugal tend to go to work on a milky coffee and a roll with butter and jam. Cooked breakfasts usually involve eggs, fried and in omelette form – the Spanish omelette being related to the many other open omelettes that we've discussed. In some areas (Catalan especially), bread is often served with olive oil rather than butter. An interesting variation of that is said to be an ancestor of the American pizza. Olive oil is brushed on to a thick, grilled slice of bread that is topped with garlic, tomato and a slice of ham. An indulgent chocolate masterpiece from the nation that introduced chocolate from Central America is *chocolate con churros*, also a favourite in Mexico. Thick hot chocolate is used as a dip for a deep-fried pastry filled with chocolate or jam and coated with cinnamon sugar . . . enough to keep Spanish stroke units on permanent standby!

Unlike their near neighbours the Turks, the Greeks aren't great breakfast fans and will often make do with fresh fruit, yoghurt and Greek coffee – Turkish coffee by another name. In common with other light breakfasters, many Greeks will have a midmorning snack that includes bread, meat, cheese and pastries.

Turkish breakfasts are extremely healthy, usually involving freshly baked bread, sheep's milk cheese, olives, tomatoes, cucumbers, butter, honey, jam and often a boiled egg. If they go down the cooked route then one of the favourites is *menemen* – Turkish scrambled eggs. This is really a misnomer since it is our old friend the open omelette with onion, tomatoes, hot green peppers and paprika.

Street cafés abound in larger Turkish towns and cities and all of them offer an enticing choice of bean and meat stews that will set you up for the day. As in many other Mediterranean countries, falafel is another staple offering – small, deep-fried balls of highly spiced chickpeas with yoghurt sauce that seem to be eaten at any time of the day.

The West has enviously looked at Bulgaria's large population of centenarians and put it down to yoghurt – which the majority of Bulgarians seem to eat at least once a day together with a diet similar to their Turkish neighbours: sesame bread, butter, cheese, honey, olives, tomatoes and boiled eggs.

Egypt's favourite breakfast dish seems to be *ful mesdames*. Served by street vendors and leading chefs alike, this dish comprises a hard-boiled egg covered with hot fava beans (broad beans, to you and I) and spiced with cumin and garlic.

Travelling north from Turkey, we see the Russian equivalent of the *menemen* and the *Bauernfrühstück*, the *Krestianskiy Zavtrak*, or the egalitarian 'peasant breakfast': cubes of pumpernickel bread, smoky bacon, onion and bratwurst, all sautéed with eggs added and then baked in the oven and garnished with fresh chopped dill. Other breakfast favourites are strong black tea and a variety of bitter black breads, blini (*see* p. 127), cucumber pickles, sausages and fried eggs. *Kasha* is popular for breakfast – a cereal that is served with a soft curd cheese or sour cream and sugar.

ASIA

Almost all of us are familiar with Chinese food, but not for breakfast. Bacon, eggs, toast and coffee don't form part of the Chinese diet or culture. At home, many Chinese will have rice porridge, soy bean milk soup or a slice of cold rice cake. City-dwellers favour breakfast vendors, who ply their trade in the streets from about 5 a.m. to 8 a.m. Some will just sell the ingredients for a home breakfast while others will offer the fast-food version from a makeshift stove on a tricycle or through the hatch of a tiny shop. What's a bit disappointing about the Chinese breakfast is that frequently the same dishes are eaten at lunch and dinner.

The huge geographical spread of China means that there are very many quite different styles of cuisine and a huge variety of sweet and savoury dishes – porridge (*zhou*), noodles (*mian*), doughnuts (*gao*), buns (*bao*), soups (*tang*), pancakes (*bing*) and many others.

Like China, the Indian subcontinent is host to numerous cuisines and different areas have their own specialities. Our own kedgeree (*see* p. 146) comes from the Hindi dish of *khichri*, which is a rice-based dish with lentils and spices to which, in the days of the British Raj, we added smoked haddock, eggs and cream. Another popular dish is scrambled eggs with spices, onions and potatoes. Fresh fruits and yoghurts are an inexpensive choice and other favourites include thin rice pancakes filled with spiced meats or potatoes and vegetables and rice noodles with meat curry or sweetened coconut milk.

In Japan, trendy westernisation has brought fruit juice, coffee, toast and eggs to the tables and restaurants in many towns and cities. In rural areas, however, they will still enjoy the traditional rice (possibly flavoured with seaweed and strengthened with raw egg), miso soup and various pickles.

MARINATED RAW FISH

Japanese dishes such as sushi and sashimi have made quite an impact in the West and, whilst we're not going to suggest you make either of those, here's an interesting way of preparing raw fish. The lemon juice 'cooks' the fish and the olive oil keeps it moist. Try this with salmon, trout, sea bass and even kipper – boned and thinly sliced.

1 fish fillet of your choice
Olive oil
Lemon juice
Salt and black pepper
Fresh herbs (chives, chervil or tarragon), chopped

Cut paper-thin slices from the raw fish fillet and lay them in a single layer on a serving platter or on each individual plate • Sprinkle 1–2 tbsp olive oil and a few drops of lemon juice over each serving plus the herbs, and season • Chill for 15–30 minutes and serve.

THE AMERICAS

Despite having a westernised menu, Las Mañanitas Hotel in Fundador, Mexico, still says 'Buenos dias!' to its breakfast guests with some red-hot ethnic dishes that include the following:

* *chitaquiles:* fried tortilla strips with chicken in green chilli sauce and a cream and cheese topping
* *melletes:* toasted rolls with beans and a melted cheese topping
* *puntas de filete a la Mexicana:* sirloin tips in chilli sauce and beans
* *puntas de pollo a la Mexicana:* chicken in chilli sauce
* *huevos rancheros:* baked ranch-style eggs.

The latter is a fascinating dish. The salsa base is made of onion, garlic, red peppers, red chillies, tomatoes, tomato paste, oregano, cumin and fresh coriander, and the eggs are broken into a well before the whole lot is baked in the oven and served with chopped avocado and salad.

Other Central American countries also favour egg dishes and various sausages including chorizo – a highly seasoned, coarsely ground, pork sausage flavoured with garlic, chilli and other spices. Tortillas – the area's pancake-like everyday bread – together with sweet bread (*pan dulce*), fresh fruit and fruit juices and fried plantains also figure largely in the diet. Plantains are cooking bananas and are very popular in this area and parts of Africa and Asia.

Out in the Caribbean, one of Costa Rica's favourite breakfast dishes is *gallo pinto* – spotted rooster – a lightly spiced mixture of black beans and fried rice that can be served with sour cream or fried/scrambled eggs.

It's not surprising that coffee plays a huge part in the South American culinary scene and breakfast is no exception, where it is frequently accompanied by bread, sweet bread or small croissants called *medialunas*. Like so many of their Mediterranean soul mates, South Americans often indulge in a mid-morning snack to keep them going until lunchtime and the siesta.

Such a tremendous variety of dishes demonstrates that real and exciting food does still exist outside the confines of the hotel dining-room. Hopefully you'll be enticed to experiment with some of the goodies that await the culinary explorer, whether they're to be found in a back street café in Istanbul or on the international shelves of your local supermarket.

appendices

CONVERSION TABLES

For ease of use, both imperial and metric measurements have been given in these recipes, so use whichever you like but don't skip between the two. Teaspoons are usually level unless the recipe specifies rounded. If you lose some of the small weights from your kitchen scales, use coins instead: 20p = 5g; £1 = 10g; 2p = $^1/_4$oz.

TEMPERATURE

Oven temperature The heat bands given (cool, warm etc.) are the UK definitions. Beware if you follow American or Australian recipes. Theirs are very different.

Fan ovens Check the manufacturer's instruction booklet, but in general terms either reduce the oven temperature by 10–20° (20–50°F) or reduce the cooking time by 5–10 minutes per hour.

Deep-fat frying The temperature of hot fat can be judged by the time it takes for a $2^1/_2$cm (1in.) cube of bread to turn golden brown:
- 20 secs: 196–202°C
- 40 secs: 190–196°C
- 60 secs: 177–185°C
- 65 secs: 174–9°C

Gas	°C	°F	Band
	70	160	
	80	175	
	90	195	
	100	210	
$^1/_4$	110	230	Cool
$^1/_2$	120	250	Cool
	130	265	
1	140	285	Warm
2	150	300	Warm
	160	320	
3	170	340	Moderate
4	180	355	Moderate
5	190	375	Fairly hot
6	200	390	Fairly hot
	210	410	
7	220	430	Hot
8	230	445	Hot
9	240	465	
	250	480	Very hot
	260	500	
	270	520	
	280	535	
	290	555	

Mrs Beaton had a novel, if not entirely safe, method of testing the temperature in cookers where there was no heat regulator – usually solid fuel cookers of the farm kitchen variety.

- *Hot oven:* a piece of white paper placed in the hottest part of the oven (usually the top) will turn a rich brown colour in 3 minutes, or – if you like a bit of danger in your life – the hand held in the same hottest part should begin to sting after about 8 or 9 seconds.
- *Fairly hot:* the paper becomes brown in about 3 minutes.
- *Moderate oven:* the paper becomes yellow.
- *Warm oven:* the paper doesn't discolour at all.

WEIGHTS

IMPERIAL TO METRIC

Conversion factors:

- ounces (oz) to grams (g) x 28.35
- pounds (lb) to kilos (kg) x 0.4454

oz/lb	g/kg
$1/2$	15
1	30
2	55
3	85
4 ($1/4$lb)	115
5	140
6	170
7	200
8 ($1/2$lb)	225
9	255
10	285
11	310
12 ($3/4$lb)	340
13	370
14	400
15	425
16 (1lb)	450
$1^1/2$lb	680
2lb	900
3lb	1.4kg
4lb	1.8kg
5lb	2.3kg
6lb	2.7kg

METRIC TO IMPERIAL

Conversion factors:

- grams (g) to ounces (oz) x 0.03353
- kilos (kg) to pounds (lb) x 2.2

g/kg	oz/lb
15	$1/2$
30	1
50	$1^3/4$
100	$3^1/2$
125	$4^1/2$
150	$5^1/2$
175	6
200	7
225	8
250	9
300	$10^1/2$
325	$11^1/2$
350	12
400	14
425	15
450	16
500	1lb 2oz
750	1lb 10oz
1kg	2lb 3oz
1.25kg	2lb 12oz
1.5kg	3lb 5oz
2kg	4lb 8oz
3kg	6lb 10oz
4kg	8lb 13oz
5kg	11lb

LIQUIDS

IMPERIAL TO METRIC

Conversion factors:

- fluid ounces (fl. oz) to millilitres (ml) x 28.4
- pints (pt) to litres (l) x 1.759

fl. oz	ml
1 tsp	5
1 dsp	10
1 tbsp	15
$1/2$ fl. oz	15
1	30
2	55
3	85
4	115
5 ($1/4$ pt)	140
6	170
8 ($1/2$ pt)	225
9	255
10	285
11	310
12	340
13	370
14	400
15 ($3/4$ pt)	425
16	455
20	565
30 ($1^1/2$pt)	850
35 ($1^3/4$ pt)	1l
40 (2 pt)	$1^1/4$l
$3^1/4$ pt	2l

METRIC TO IMPERIAL

Conversion factors:

- millilitres (ml) to fluid ounces (fl. oz) x 0.035
- litres (l) to pints (pt) x 0.4546

ml	fl. oz
1.25	$1/4$ tsp
2.5	$1/2$ tsp
5	1 tsp
10	2 tsp (1 dsp)
15	$1/2$ fl. oz (1 tbsp/3 tsp)
30	1 fl. oz (2 tbsp)
45	$1^1/2$ fl. oz
50	$1^3/4$
100	$3^1/2$
125	4
150	$5^1/4$
200	7
250	$8^3/4$
300	$10^1/2$
350	$12^1/4$
400	14
500	$17^1/2$
600	21
700	$24^1/2$
1l	35
2l	70
3l	90
5l	175

PRESENTATION

It's been said that if food looks delicious, people tend to find that it tastes delicious too. So, after spending a lot of time and energy producing the best breakfast you can, it would be daft not to go the extra mile and lay it out attractively.

If you're looking for the ideal canvas and frame for your culinary masterpiece then it ought to be a white plate. However, those of us with crockery plates needn't feel aesthetically disadvantaged – you can still make the dish look good. There are two methods of serving food. One is to present it on a large platter or oval dish from which you serve it, or the family helps themselves; the other is to serve it on individual plates. Either way, a little care 'n' flair will make both look extremely appetising.

HOT PLATES

An elderly restaurant tyrant once said, 'If my girls aren't squealing when they pick up the plates, I know they're not hot enough.' Whilst we don't suggest you use that as a bench-mark, it does indicate just how important hot plates are. If you've gone to a lot of bother to serve up an appetising hot meal then it makes sense to keep it at its optimum temperature for as long as possible. If you're serving breakfast from a platter, it's going to sit around on the table whilst the family decide whether or not they want seconds. Ideally, a hot platter should be kept that way on a simple candle-powered plate warmer – introduced to us decades ago by Chinese restaurants. If you don't have one then just ensure that the platter is as hot as possible. The same goes for individual plates whether you're serving from a platter or not.

SETTING THE PLATE

Symmetry It's a strange fact that, whilst we welcome symmetry in the human face and call it beauty, we don't like it on our plates. It's well documented that a meal laid out symmetrically on a plate looks strange and doesn't appeal, but the same food laid out asymmetrically does! That's why good chefs go to a lot of bother to treat the food on your plate as if it were a minor work of art. If you watch them on any of the TV shows, you'll see the precision with which they set out the individual elements of a meal. A possible exception to the rule is the fad for building the food up in the centre of the plate and surrounding it with jus (gravy, to you and me). Ignore the trend; it will pass!

Numbers Strange too is the fact that at the low end of the scale, food items laid out in even numbers don't look as good, or appeal as much, as if they were laid out in odd numbers. So three or five slices of tomato or black pudding on a platter look better than four.

Quantity Try not to load individual plates with too much food. It's difficult to make it look nice and it's off-putting, unless your family happen to all be trenchermen. The opposite is also to be avoided. Tiny portions laid out like a Picasso painting look pretentious and stingy.

Overlapping If you're serving slices of anything, whether on a serving dish or individual plates, always try and overlap them. You get more on the dish and it looks much better. Avoid laying any food on the rim of the plate. Keep that clear to set off what's in the centre.

Grease For health and aesthetic reasons you want as little grease or oil on the plate as possible. Even if you've grilled food rather than fried it, fat will still appear whilst you keep the food warm in an oven or under a grill. Kitchen paper is the answer – a dab here and there will soak up the excess. If you're really fussy about the oil on your fried eggs, dry them off on a piece of kitchen paper before transferring them to the plate.

GARNISHES

The standard green garnish tends to be parsley but there are lots more herbs and flowers out there that we can use. The main point to remember is that whatever you add to the plate or dish must complement the food and emphasise the artistry that's gone into producing it. Even a sprinkling of paprika on scrambled eggs works wonders. And if you've got the time and energy, viola or pansy petals on an omelette . . . a single yellow freesia on a kipper . . . a Venus flytrap in Mother-in-law's orange juice . . . you know the kind of thing!

Edible flowers and herbs Although there's no law that says we have to eat our garnish, if it's on the plate then as sure as eggs are eggs, someone is going to eat it. So make sure it's edible and, if you haven't grown it yourself, give it a good wash in cold water – you never know where it's been!

If using flowers, remove the stamens, pistils and the white portion at the base of the petal which has quite a bitter taste. Discretion and a light touch are the keynotes in using floral garnishes. For one thing, your dishes might end up looking like an entry in the Chelsea Flower Show, and more importantly, some flowers could be harmful if eaten in large quantities.

The simplest garnish for fruit juices is a thin slice of orange, lemon or lime. Together with a lump of ice, you can completely transform a mundane breakfast juice or even a glass of water. Herb flowers such as borage or lemon thyme look good, and other useful juice garnishes are lemon verbena, ginger mint, salad burnet and pineapple sage. And for that extravagant and romantic gesture on a special day, strip off the thorns and leaves from a long-stemmed rose, pop it into your beloved's glass and wait for them to send for the men in white coats.

GROWING HERBS

This section is aimed at cooks who don't have easy access to an established herb garden or who want their herbs – whether for flavouring or garnishing – within easy reach of the kitchen door.

Most culinary herbs can be grown in conventional pots, hanging baskets, window boxes, half barrels, strawberry pots, chimney pots . . . in fact, in a variety of containers whether indoors or out. Always ensure that whatever container you use has adequate drainage holes, however, and always crock well – placing a layer of stones or broken terracotta pieces in the base of the container to prevent the soil becoming water-logged. It's also a good idea to incorporate a 1cm ($^1/_2$in.) layer of horticultural sand one-third of the way up from the base. Like crocking, this will help with the drainage and stop the soil from compacting and harming the roots.

It's probably easiest if you visit your nearest nursery, buy your required herbs in small pots, replant them into their permanent home and follow the growing and care instructions provided. If keeping them in a pot of their own, then progressively pot each on into a larger container. Pot herbs from a supermarket are likely to be of poor growing quality, having been grown in warm greenhouses and in poor light. At best they will need hardening off before planting outside.

In simple terms, plants are like humans, they need to be kept out of draughts, fed, watered and talked to nicely at times. Just like us, some like full sun and lots to drink; others like partial shade and are more abstemious. Almost all herbs with aromatic foliage need lots of sun and well-drained soil to develop good flavour.

EDIBLE FLOWERS			
Anise hyssop	Gladiolus	Sage	Garden cress
Apple blossom	Grape hyacinth	Savory	Hyssop
Basil	Gypsophila	Scarlet runner	Lemon thyme
Bergamot	Hollyhock	bean	Lemon verbena
Borage	Honeysuckle	Squash	Loganberries
Burnet	Hyssop	Sweet pea	Marjoram
Chervil	Lavender	Sweet woodruff	Mint
Chive	Lemon blossom	Thyme	Nasturtium leaves
Chrysanthemum	(citrus)	Tulip	Oregano
Coriander	Lemon balm	Viola	Parsley
Cornflowers	Lilac	Wild roses	Raspberries
Daisy (English)	Lovage	Yucca	Red currants
Daisy, oxeye	Marigold		Rosemary
Dandelion	(calendula)	HERBS AND FRUITS	Sage
Daylily	Marjoram		Savoury, summer
(Hemerocallis)	Nasturtiums	Basil	Sorrel, common
Dill	Orange blossom	Black currants	Strawberries
Elderberry	Oregano	Borage	Strawberry, wild
Fennel	Pea (garden)	Brambles	Sweet cicely
Freesia	Pansies	Camomile	Tarragon
Geranium	Pinks	Chervil	Thymes
(Pelargonium)	Plum	Chives	Watercress
Geranium	Red clover	Citrus skins	White currants
(variegated)	Rocket	(julienne)	
	Rose	Coriander	
	Rosemary	Curry plant	

- Nasturtiums are a particularly useful plant in a window box or hanging basket. They're rich in vitamin C, keep neighbouring plants healthy and will survive – and indeed thrive – when you forget to water them. Their flowers and leaves can be eaten in salads and, after pickling, their seeds can be used instead of capers. Chopped nasturtium leaves can be added to scrambled eggs.
- Chives are another good mainstay plant and although they can be grown indoors, will become spindly and weak in flavour. They take a lot of nutrients out of the soil so need fairly frequent fertilising to encourage the growth of the green tops.
- Basil needs warmth and will survive on an indoor windowsill. Keep nipping off the top shoots to encourage bushy growth.
- Borage is easy to grow. Sow the seeds indoors in March.
- Coriander: if you can't get a coriander plant or commercially produced seeds, try soaking some coriander seeds from the spice cupboard and plant them up in a window box or garden bed. They're stragglier than the bought variety but still attractive.
- Marigold petals make a very colourful garnish.
- Dandelions: lift outdoor plants before the first frosts and replant them in pots indoors.
- Parsley: to grow indoors fill a pot half-full of potting compost, pour over some cold boiled water and then sprinkle some seeds on the surface. Cover with a thin layer of compost, stand in a saucer and keep moist. Can take up to six weeks to germinate. If growing out of doors you have to plant each spring. Keep cutting off parsley flower stalks to prevent the plant going to seed. Harvest the leaves frequently to encourage growth and bear in mind the old wives' tale: if parsley grows well, it's the woman who wears the trousers. So, depending on your gender, either fertilise it well or give it a good kick when you go past!
- Wild strawberries are particularly good for garnishing, being about the size of a pea. They have no runners, are evergreen, take up very little space and produce fruit right through until October. Garden centres should be able to supply them.

SEASONALITY

In the old days cooking was punctuated with foods coming into season. Our appreciation of the first early potatoes or the first raspberry was greatly increased by being deprived of them for a large part of the year. Seasonality gave culinary highlights to our menus and eagerly anticipated variety to our diets.

Modern life has all but wiped out those delights. Every conceivable type of produce is shipped by sea, air and land from all corners of the globe – brought to us by beneficent major multiple retailers on the excuse that it is by public demand – and frequently the cost is at the opposite end of the scale from the quality. It is only now, as we become more environmentally responsible, that the pollution penalty of flying strawberries in from the west coast of America or exotic vegetables from East Africa is being considered.

Whilst technology will certainly continue to extend the life of fresh produce, hopefully, global considerations may start to reduce the year-round availability of food items and we may get back to something akin to the 'good old days'. Certainly at the moment, most produce can be bought all year round but there are obviously times when it is of much higher quality. The following table is by no means comprehensive but gives the conventional availability of the major items (at their best) that have been discussed vis-à-vis breakfast.

Produce	Jan	Feb	Mar	Apr	May	Jun	Jul	Aug	Sep	Oct	Nov	Dec
Asparagus					•	•						
Bilberries					•	•	•	•	•	•	•	•
Blackberries					•	•	•	•	•	•	•	•
Blackcurrants					•	•	•	•	•	•	•	•
Fosters	•	•	•	•	•	•	•	•	•	•	•	•
Grapefruit	•	•	•	•	•					•	•	•
Grouse, red									•	•	•	•
Herring	•	•	•	•	•	•	•	•	•	•	•	•
Loganberries					•	•	•	•	•			
Mackerel	•	•	•	•	•	•	•	•	•	•	•	•
Mushrooms, field									•			
Parsley			•	•	•		•	•	•	•	•	
Pears	•	•	•	•	•	•			•	•	•	•
Pheasant	•									•	•	•
Quail	•	•	•	•	•	•	•	•	•	•	•	•
Raspberries					•	•	•	•	•	•		
Redcurrants					•	•	•	•	•	•	•	•
Rhubarb				•	•	•	•	•	•			
Rowan berries												
Salmon (wild)		•	•	•	•	•	•	•	•			
Salmon (farmed)	•	•	•	•	•	•	•	•	•	•	•	•
Strawberries					•	•	•	•	•	•		
Tomatoes (Scottish)			•	•	•	•	•	•	•	•		
Tomatoes	•	•	•	•	•	•	•	•	•	•	•	•
Trout, brown				•	•	•	•	•	•			
Trout, rainbow	•	•	•	•	•	•	•	•	•	•	•	•
Trout, sea			•	•	•	•	•					
Venison (red hinds)	•	15th								21st	•	•
Venison (red stags)					•	•	•	•	•	20th		

FOREIGN LANGUAGE BREAKFAST GLOSSARY

All too often we expect foreign visitors to speak English and, while most of them have a far better grasp of our language than we do of theirs, there will be times in the hospitality industry when gesticulations and fractured English in a very loud voice is not enough to explain some of the dishes that make up our famous British Breakfast.

This section is therefore aimed at all those in the 'breakfast business', be they B&B operators, hoteliers, restaurateurs, national catering chains or greasy-spoon proprietors. Even if your diners' English is passable, if you make the effort to speak their language, it's a great icebreaker and will make them feel very welcome.

If lack of pronunciation skills holds you back, then show guests this glossary and point to the relevant words. Similarly, if your guests have problems making themselves understood, then give them a copy.

English	French	German	Italian
BASICS			
bowl	le bol	die Schüssel	la scodella
cup	la tasse	die Tasse	la tazza
fork	la fourchette	die Gabel	la forchetta
glass	le verre	das Trinkglas	il bichiere
knife	le couteau	das Messer	il coltello
menu	le menu	die Speisekarte	il menù
napkin	la serviette	die Serviette	il tovagliolo
pepper	le poivre	der Pfeffer	il pepe
plate	l'assiette (f)	die Platte / der Teller	il piatto
salt	le sel	das Salz	il sale
sauce	la sauce	die Soße	la salsa
saucer	la soucoupe	die Untertasse	il piattino
spoon	la cuiller	der Löffel	il cucchiaio
sugar	le sucre	der Zucker	lo zucchero
table	la table	die Tafel / der Tisch	il tavolo
toothpick	le cure-dent	der Zahnstocher	lo stuzzicadenti
vinegar	le vinaigre	der Essig	l'aceto
DRINKS			
artificial sweeteners	les sucrettes	der Süßstoff	il dolcificante
coffee (black)	le café	der Kaffee schwarz	il caffè
coffee, white	le café au lait/crème	der Kaffee mit Milch	caffè americano con latte
coffee, espresso	l'express	der Expresso	l'espresso
coffee, cappuccino	le cappuccino	der Cappucino	il cappuccino
coffee, decaffeinated	le café décaféiné	der Kaffe koffeinfrei	il caffè decaffeinat
cream	la crème	die Sahne	la panna
hot chocolate	le chocolat chaud	die heiße Schokolade	la cioccolata calda

English	French	German	Italian
juice, fruit	le jus de fruits	der Fruchtsaft	il succo di frutta
juice, orange	le jus d'orange	der Orangensaft	il succo d'arancia
juice, fresh orange	orange pressée	der Orangensaft frischgepresst	la spremuta d'arancia
juice, grapefruit	le jus de pamplemousse	der Grapefruitsaft	il succo di pompelmo
juice, tomato	le jus de tomate	der Tomatensaft	il succo di pomodoro
juice, apple	le jus de pommes	der Apfelsaft	il succo di mela
juice, cranberry	le jus de canneberge	der Moosbeerensaft	il succo di mirtillo
juice, grape	le jus de raisin	der Traubensaft	il succo d'uva
juice, pineapple	le jus d'ananas	der Ananassaft	il succo d'ananas
milk	le lait	die Milch	il latte
tea (weak) (strong)	le thé (léger) (fort)	der Tee (schwach) (stark)	il tè leggero/forte
tea with milk	le thé au lait	der Tee mit Milch	il tè con latte
tea with lemon	le thé citron	Tee mit Zitrone	il tè con limone
tea with milk & sugar	le thé au lait, sucré	der Tee mit Milch und Zucker	il tè con latte e zucchero
tea, black	le thé noir	der Tee schwarz	il tè
tea, camomile	tisane de camomille	der Kamillentee	la camomilla
tea, China	le thé de Chine	chinesischer Tee	il tè cinese
tea, fruit	l'infusion aux fruits	der Fruchttee	il tè alla frutta
tea, herb	l'infusion / la tisane	der Kräutertee	il tè alle erbe
tea, Indian	le thé Indien	indischer Tee	il tè indiano
water	l'eau (f)	das Wasser	l'acqua
hot water	l'eau chaude	heißes Wasser	l'aqua calda
water, mineral still	l'eau non gazeuse	Mineralwasser ohne Kohlensäure	l'acqua minerale non gassata
water, mineral sparkling	l'eau gazeuse	Mineralwasser mit Kohlensäure	l'acqua minerale gassata
water, mineral	l'eau minérale	das Mineralwasser	l'acqua minerale

CEREALS

cornflakes	les cornflakes	die Cornflakes	i cornflakes
muesli	le muesli	das Müsli	il muesli
porridge	le porridge	die Haferflocken	il porridge (fiocchi d'avena e latte)

EGGS

egg, hard boiled	un oeuf dur	hart gekochtes Ei	l'uova sodo
egg, soft boiled	un oeuf à la coque	weich gekochtes Ei	l'uova alla coque
egg, poached	les oeuf poché	pochiertes Ei	l'uovao in camicia
egg, fried	un oeuf sur la plat	das Spiegelei	l'uova fritto
eggs, fried with bacon	des oeufs au bacon/jambon	Spiegelei mit Speck	uova e pancetta
eggs, scrambled	des oeufs brouillés	die Rühreier	le uova strapazzate
eggs, free range	ouefs de poules élevées en plein air	Eier aus artgerechter Haltung	le uova nostrane
omelette	l'omelette	das Omelette	la frittata
omelette, plain	omelette au naturel	Omelette natur	la frittatta semplice
omelette, ham	omelette au jambon	das Schinkenomelette	la frittata al prosciutto
omelette, cheese	omelette au fromage	das Käseomelette	la frittata al formaggio
omelette, mushroom	omelette aux champignons	Omelette mit Champignons	la frittata ai funghi
omelette, herb	omelette aux fines herbes	das, Kräuteromelette	la frittata alle erbe
quails	les cailles (f)	die Wachtel	le quaglie

PUDDINGS

cloutie dumpling	le pudding ecossais	der Fleischpudding	gnocchi giganti con sughetto di carne
pudding, black	boudin noir	Blutwurst	sangiunaccio nero
pudding, white	boudin blanc	Presssack	sangiunaccio bianco

English	French	German	Italian
pudding, fruit	pudding de fruit	Pudding mit Früchten	dolce con canditi e uvetta

FRUITS

apple	la pomme	der Apfel	la mela
baked apple	la pomme bonne femme	der Bratapfel	la mela co/al forno
banana	la banane	die Banane	la banana
blackberries	les mûres (f)	die Brombeeren	le more
figs	les figues (f)	die Feigen	i fichi
fruit	les fruits	die Frücht	la frutta
fruit salad	la salade de fruits	der Obstsalat	la macedonia di frutta
fruit, fresh	des fruits frais	frische Frücht	la frutta fresca
fruit, stewed (compote)	la compote	das Kompott	la frutta cotta con zucchero
grapefruit	le pamplemousse	die Pampelmuse	il pompelmo
grapes	le raisin	die Weintrauben	l'uva
melon	le melon	die Melone	il melone
plums	les prunes (f)	die Plaumen	le prugne
prunes	les pruneaux	die Backpflaumen	le prugna secshe
raspberries	les framboises (f)	die Himbeeren	i lamponi
strawberries	les fraises (f)	die Erdbeeren	le fragole

PRESERVES

honey (heather)	le miel (de bruyère)	der Honig	il miele
jam, strawberry	la confiture de fraises	die Erdbeermarmelade	la marmellata di fragole
jam, raspberry	la confiture de framboises	die Himbeermarmelade	la marmellata di lamponi
jam, blackcurrant	la confiture de cassis	schwarze Johannisbeerm armelade	la marmellata di ribes nero
jelly, redcurrant	la gelée de groseille rouge	rotes Johannisbeergelee	la marmellata di ribes rosso
marmalade	la confiture d'orange	die Orangenmarmelade	la marmellata d'arance

FISH

Arbroath smokies	le poisson fumé d'Arbroath	geräucherte Heringe	aringa affumicata di Arbroath
fish	le poisson	der Fisch	il pesce
fish cakes	les croquettes de poisson	die Fischfrikadelle	le croquettes di pesce
fish, grilled	le poisson grillé	Fisch gegrillt	il pesce alla griglia
fish, marinated	le poisson mariné	Fisch mariniert	il pesce marinato
gravadlax	le saumon à l'aneth	Gravadlachs	piatto a base di pesce
haddock, smoked	le haddock fumé	der Schellfisch geräuchert	il merluzzo affumicato
herring	le hareng	der Hering	l'aringa
kipper	le kipper	gesalzener Räucherhering	l'aringa affumicata
mackerel	le maquereau	die Makrele	lo sgombro
North Sea (haddock)	haddock de la Mer du Nord	Nordsee Schellfisch	il merrluzzo del Mare del Nord
salmon	le saumon	der Lachs	il salmone
salmon, smoked	le saumon fumé	Lachs geräuchert	il salmone affumicato
Tay salmon	le saumon peché dans la Tay	Tay lachs	il salmone del fiume Tay
trout	la truite	die Forelle	la trota
trout, smoked	la truite fumée	Forelle geräuchert	la trota affumicata
kedgeree	le pilaf de poisson	Reisgericht mit Fisch und gekochten Eiern	legumi e riso stile indiano
West coast	la Côte ouest	die Westküste	le costa Ovest

MEATS

bacon	le lard en tranches	der Speck	la pancetta
smoked	le lard fumé	der Speck geräuchert	affumicato/a

English	French	German	Italian
bacon, unsmoked	le lard non fumé	der Speck nichtgeräuchert	non affumicato/a
bacon, streaky	le lard gras	der Katenspeck	la pancetta striata
beef	le boeuf	das Rindfleisch	il manzo
duck	le canard	die Ente	l'anatra
ham	le jambon	der Schinken	il prosciutto
kidneys	les rognons (m)	die Nieren	i rognoni
lamb	l'agneau (m)	das Lammfleisch	l'agnello / la pecora
liver	le foie	die Leber	il fegato
meats, sliced cold	l'assiette anglaise	der Aufschnitt / kalte Platte	salumi cotti affettati
meats, smoked	la charcuterie fumée	Fleisch geräuchert / Geselchtes	la carne affumicata
pheasant	le faisan	der Fasan	il fagiano
pork	le porc	das Schweinefleisch	la carne di maiale
sausage, wild boar	la saucisse de sanglier	Wurst aus Wildschweinfleisch	la salsiccia di cinghiale
sausage, pork	la saucisse de porc	Wurst aus Schweinefleisch	la salsiccia di maiale
sausage, beef	la saucisse au bboeuf	Wurst aus Rindfleisch	la salsiccia
sausages	les saucisses (f)	die Würstchen	salsicce di carne e avena
venison	le chevreuil la venaison	das Wild / das Wildbrett	la carne di cervo
venison, smoked	le chevreuil fumé	Wild geräuchert	la selvaggina affumicata

COOKING METHODS

baked	au four	gebacken	al forno
boiled	bouilli	gekocht	lesso/a
fried	frit	gebraten	fritto/a
grilled	grillé	gegrillt	alla griglia
poached	poché	pochiert	bollito/a, in camicia
raw	cru	roh	crudo
smoked	fumé	geräuchert	affumicato/a
steamed	à l'étuvée	gedünstet	al vapore

VEGETABLES

beans	les haricots (m)	die Bohnen	i fagioli
baked beans	les haricots secs à las sauce tomate (m)	gebackene Bohnen	i fagioli in salsa di pomodoro
mushrooms	les champignons (m)	die Pilze / die Champignons	i funghi
potatoes	les pommes de terre (f)	die Kartoffeln	le patate
stuffed tomatoes	les tomates farcies	gefüllte Tomaten	i pomodori ripieni
tomatoes	les tomates (f)	die Tomaten	i pomodori

BREAD

Aberdeen butteries	petit pains d'Aberdeen	mit butter gebackene flache Brötchen	pasta sfoglia di Aberdeen
biscuits	les biscuits	die Kekse	i biscotti
bread	le pain	das Brot	il pane
bread, brown	le pain bis	das Graubrot	pane con farina integrale
bread, wholemeal	le pain complet	das Vollkornbrot	il pane integrale
oatcakes	les galettes d'avoine (f)	ungesüßte Haferkekse	le gallette di avena
pancakes with maple syrup	les crêpes au sirop d'érable	flache britische Pfannkuchen mit Ahornsirup	crepes con sciroppo d'acero
pastries	les pâtisseries (f)	die Teigwaren	paste
shortbread	le sablé	schottische Butterkekse	biscotto di pasta frolla
pancakes	les crêpes (f)	flache britische Eierkuchen	crepes
rolls	les petits pains (m)	die Brötchen	i panini
scone, potato	la galette de pomme de terre	kleine Kartoffelkuchen	panini rustici a base di patate

English	French	German	Italian
scones, soda	les scones	kleine Sodakuchen	panini rustici con bicarbonato di sodio
toast	le pain grillé	der Toast	il pane tostato
white		der Weißbrottoast	il pane tostato bianco
wholemeal		der Vollkornbrottoast	il pane tostato integrale
toast with butter	le pain grillé avec du beurre	Toast mit Butter	il pane tostato con burro
toast and marmalade	le pain grillé avec de la	Toast mit Orangenmarmelade	pane tostato e marmellata d'arance
waffles	les gaufres (f)	die Waffeln	cialde e base di purea di patate

MISCELLANEOUS

English	French	German	Italian
breakfast	le petit déjeuner	das Frühstück	la Prima Colazione
butter	le beurre	die Butter	il burro
cheese	le fromage	der Käse	il formaggio
children's portion	demi portion	die Kinderportion	una porzione per bambini
cinnamon	la cannelle	der Zimt	la cannella
cold	froid	kalt	freddo
good traditional home cooking	la bonne cuisine traditionelle	die Hausmannskost	cucina casalinga tradizionale
home-made	fait (à la) maison	hausgemacht	fatto in casa
hot	chaud	heiß	caldo
margarine	la margarine	die Margarine	la margarina
low fat spread	le beurre allégé à tartiner	fettarmer Brotaufstrich	margarina a basso contenuto di grassi
Scottish	Écossais	schottisch	Scozzese
variety of Scottish cheeses	plateau de fromages Ecossais	schottische Käseplatte	un misto di formaggi scozzesi
yoghurt	le yaourt	Yogurth	lo yogurt

USEFUL PHRASES

English	French	German	Italian
Come in	Entrez!	Kommen Sie herein!	Avanti!
Good morning	Bon jour	Guten Morgen	Buon giorno
Please sit down	Asseyez-vous	Bitte setzen Sie sich	Prego, si accomodi
Enjoy your meal	Bon appetit!	Guten Appetit!	Buon Appetito!
Is there anything else I can get you?	Est-ce que je peux vous apporter autre chose?	Kann ich noch etwas für Sie tun?	Desidera qualcos'altro?
Good night	Bonne nuit (only when going to bed)	Gute Nacht!	Buona notte!
Goodbye	Au revoir	Auf Wiedersehen!	Arrivederci!
Have a good journey	Bon voyage!	Gute Reise!	Buon viaggio!
Yes	Oui	Ja	Si
No	Non	Nein	No
Please	Si'l vous plait	Bitte	Prego
Thank you	Merci	Danke	Grazie
Sorry, I do not understand	Pardon! Je ne comprends pas	Verzeihung, ich verstehe Sie nicht	Scusi! Non capisco

BOOKS TO READ

The following publications may prove useful if you wish to read more about a given subject covered in this book. Many were used as information sources.

The Best of British Bacon Recipes, Mary Norwak and British Bacon,1979: out of print now but a very useful little book.

The Big Red Book of Tomatoes, Lindsey Bareham, 1999, ISBN 0-718-4204-7: a comprehensive book on all aspects of tomatoes and their use in cooking.

The Book of Ingredients, Philip Dowell and Adrian Bailey, 1995, ISBN 0-7181-3043-X: larger format (A4) version of Cook's Ingredients below.

Bread, Eric Treuille and Ursula Ferrigno, 1998, ISBN 0-7513-0607-X (hardback), 0-7513-2584-8 (paperback): a superbly illustrated guide to bread-making with over 100 recipes.

A Caledonian Feast, Annette Hope, 1987, ISBN 1-85158-077-8: a fascinating mix of social history and Scottish recipes.

The Complete Guide to Cookery. Anne Willan. 1995, Reader's Digest/Dorling Kindersley: no serious cook can be without this one. A classic.

The Complete Microwave Companion, Carol Bowen, 1997, ISBN 1-85967-694-4: lavishly illustrated and full of excellent microwave hints and recipes.

Cookery Corner, Morag Thompson,1992: selection of recipes from Thompson's column in *The Northern Scot*.

Cooking for Kids, Rosamund Richmond, 1981, ISBN 0-906908-40-X: very few breakfast recipes but good all the same if you want to get youngsters cooking.

Cooking with Flowers, Susan Belsinger, 1991, ISBN 0-7063-7050-3.

Cook's Ingredients, Dorling Kindersley, 1990, ISBN 0-86318-435-9: as always with Dorling Kindersley, this pocket encyclopaedia is stunningly illustrated.

Le Cordon Bleu, Breakfasts, 1998, ISBN 1-85391-720-6.

Farmhouse Cookery, Reader's Digest, 1980, ISBN 0-276-42086-1.

Favourite Derbyshire Recipes, Ann Wall, ISBN 1-898435-17-0: one of a series of very useful regional recipe booklets usually found in tourist outlets.

Flavour of Scotland, John Leese, 1992, ISBN 1-85217-0263-3.

The Food Lover's Companion, Sharon Tyler Herbst, 2001, ISBN 0-7641-1258-9: chef's bible for comprehensive definitions of almost 6,000 foods, drinks and culinary terms.

The Good Breakfast Book, Nikki and David Goldbeck,1992, ISBN 0-9606138-4-6: a useful and fascinating insight into American breakfasts.

Great Recipes for Good Health, Reader's Digest 1993, ISBN 0-276-42104-3.

Healing Foods, Miriam Polunin, ISBN 0-7513-0705-X: an incomparable book jam-packed with nutritional and health information.

Irish Heritage Cooking, Margaret M. Johnson, 1999, ISBN 0-86327-699-7: a rather schmaltzy view of Irish dishes but very good nevertheless.

Leisurely Breakfasts, Penny Farrell, 1995, ISBN 0-304-34755-8: 'Caviar with blinis' and 'Oysters with bacon and fish jelly' are just two of the OTT recipes in this luxury selection.

Loaf, Crust and Crumb, Silvija Davidson, 1995, ISBN 0-7181-3825-2: a guide to over 150 breads available in the UK and 200 recipes.

Miracle Foods, Anna Selby, 2001, ISBN 0-6006-0192-7: a must for anyone wishing to make the most of nature's functional foods.

Notes and Recipes from an Island Kitchen, Rosalind Burgess, 1993, ISBN 0-9465-3793-3: a selection of simple dishes using what the author grows and collects from her garden and foreshore on the Isle of Skye.

On Food and Cooking, Harold McGee,1984, ISBN 0-00-412657-2: the bible for serious students of the science of food and cooking.

Practical Food Smoking, Kate Walker,1995, ISBN 1-897784-45-7: an introduction to food smoking and smoking equipment.

Puddings and Desserts, Carol Bowen,1982, ISBN 0-600-32271-8: a superb all-colour book of desserts.

The Sainsbury Book of Quick Meals, Michell Berriedale Johnson, 1981, ISBN 0-86178-050-7.

Scottish Cookery, Catherine Brown, 1985, ISBN 0-86267-119-1: one of many books from Scotland's leading food historian and cookery expert.

Scottish Regional Recipes, Catherine Brown, 1981: another excellent work from the thoroughbred stable of Catherine Brown.

Teaching the Bairns to Cook, Liz Ashworth, 1996, ISBN 1-899827-23-4: traditional Scottish cooking for youngsters in an excellent simplified format.

Teaching the Bairns to Bake, Liz Ashworth,1996, ISBN 1-899827-24-2: same simplified treatment as the above.

The Tomato Cook Book, Victoria Lloyd-Davies, 1998, ISBN1-84065-0419.

Traditional Foods of Britain, Laura Mason with Catherine Brown, 1999, ISBN 0-9073-2587-4: an excellent textbook inventory funded by the European Commission and part of a programme to record and preserve European Culinary Heritage.

SELECTED SUPPLIERS

A small selection of specialist producers, most of whose products are available through mail order. If you know of other companies that you think should feature here or you are such a company, please provide brief details to the Publishers who will consider including you in any subsequent reprints. Details correct at time of going to press.

Locate the required product in this section and then turn to pp. 200–2 for details of the relevant producer.

PRODUCTS

Alligator, smoked
    Macdonald's Produce, Inverness
Arbroath Smokies
    Spink, Alex, Angus

Bacon
    Chatsworth Farm Shop, Derbyshire
    Denhay Farms, Dorset
    Dukeshill Ham Company, Shropshire
    Emmett's Stores, Suffolk
    Pickerings, Norwich
    Pirie & Son, James, Angus
    Sandbridge Farmhouse Bacon, Wilts
    Slack's, Cumbria
    Stephen Smith, Thetford
    Teesdale Trencherman, Co., Durham
    Tombuie Smokehouse, Perthshire
    Weald Smokery, East Sussex
  Ayrshire
    Ramsays of Carluke, Lanarkshire
  Sufolk sweet-cured
    Neave & Son, Suffolk
    Emmett's, Suffolk
    Rolfe, Suffolk
  Welsh
    Davies, Dyfed
    Edwards of Conwy
    Rees, Carmarthen
  Wiltshire
    Sandbridge, Wiltshire
    Eastbrook, Wiltshire
Black Puddings
    Brymer, Bruce, Angus
    Chatsworth Farm Shop, Derbyshire
    MacLeod of Macleod's, Stornoway
    Macleod, Charlie, Stornoway
    Morris, Jack, Manchester
    Pickerings, Norwich
    Ramsays of Carluke, Lanarkshire
    Scott & Son, John. Fife

    Slack's, Cumbria
Brasaola
Weald Smokery, East Sussex
Brosemeal, *see* Peasemeal

Cookware/kitchenware
    Lakeland, Cumbria
Cheese, smoked
    Galloway Smokehouse, Dumfries
    Macdonald's Smoked Produce
    Summer Isles Foods, Ross-shire
    Tombuie Smokehouse, Perthshire
Chicken, smoked
    Rannoch Smokery, Perthshire
    Summer Isles Foods, Ross-shire
    Tombuie Smokehouse, Perthshire
Clootie Dumplings
    Cloutie Dumpling Restaurant, Inverness
Cod, smoked
    Robson, Northumberland
Coffee mugs
    Infuser coffee mugs, *see* Infuser

Duck, smoked
    Keracher, Andrew, Perth
    Macdonald's Produce, Inverness
    Rannoch Smokery, Perthshire
    Summer Isles Foods, Ross-shire
    Tombuie Smokehouse, Perthshire
    Weald Smokery, East Sussex

Eel, smoked
    Weald Smokery, East Sussex
Eggs
  Quail
    Keracher, Andrew, Perth
  Smoked hens'
    Hickory House, Fife
  Smoked quail
    Keracher, Andrew, Perth
    Hickory House, Fife

Gravadlax
    Loch Fyne Oysters, Argyll
    Weald Smokery, East Sussex
Grouse, smoked
    Rannoch Smokery, Perthshire
Guinea fowl, smoked
    Tombuie Smokehouse, Perthshire

Haddock, smoked
    Bridfish Smokery, Dorset
    Robson, Northumberland
    Galloway Smokehouse, Dumfries
    Keracher, Andrew, Perth
    Spink, Alex, Angus
    Summer Isles Foods, Ross-shire
    Teesdale Trencherman, Co., Durham
    Weald Smokery, East Sussex
Haggis
    Brymer, Bruce, Angus
    Lindsay Grieve, Hawick
    MacSween of Edinburgh, Edinburgh
    Scott & Son, John. Fife
    Tombuie Smokehouse, Perthshire
  Smoked
    Macdonald's Produce, Inverness
  Vegetarian
    MacSween of Edinburgh
  Venison
    Fletchers of Auchtermuchty, Fife
Hams, cured/smoked
    Denhay Farms, Dorset
    Dukeshill Ham Company, Shropshire
    Emmett's Stores, Suffolk
    Ramsays of Carluke, Lanarkshire
    Sandbridge Farmhouse Bacon, Wilts
    Tombuie Smokehouse, Perthshire
    Weald Smokery, East Sussex
  Bradenham
    Sandbridge, Wiltshire
  Cumberland
    Woodall's, Cumbria

Suffolk
Emmett's Stores, Suffolk
Neave & Son, Suffolk
Rolfe, David, Suffolk
Welsh
Rees, Albert, Carmarthen
York
Radfords, Yorkshire
Scott, George, Yorkshire
Wild boar
Barrow Boar, Somerset
Herring, marinated
Daniel's Sweet Herring, Inverness
Keracher, Andrew, Perth
Loch Fyne Oysters, Argyll
Orkney Herring Co., Orkney
Spink, Alex, Angus
Herring, red
H. S. Fishing Ltd., Norfolk
Jones & Son, C. H., Suffolk
Honeys
Anderson, J. & E. Aberdeenshire
Blair Atholl Watermill, Perthshire
Chatsworth Farm Shop, Derbyshire
Denrosa Ltd, Perthshire
Galloway Honey Farm, Dumfries
Heatherhills Honey Farm. Perthshire
Nicoll's of Strathmore, Angus
Struan Apiaries, Ross-shire

Infuser coffee mugs
St George's Fine Bone China, Stoke-on-Trent

Kangaroo, smoked
Macdonald's Produce, Inverness
Kassela (smoked pork)
Weald Smokery, East Sussex
Kippers
Bridfish Smokery, Dorset
Devereaux, Isle of Man
Fjordling Smokehouses, Wilts
Fortunes, Yorkshire
Galloway Smokehouse, Dumfries
Loch Fyne Oysters, Argyll
Noble, Yorkshire
Richardson's Smokehouse, Suffolk
Robson, Northumberland
Spink, Alex, Angus
Summer Isles Foods, Ross-shire
Swallow Fish, Northumberland
Teesdale Trencherman, Co., Durham

Lamb, smoked
Tombuie Smokehouse, Perthshire

Mackerel, smoked
Bridfish Smokery, Dorset
Keracher, Andrew, Perth
Summer Isles Foods, Ross-shire

Muffins
Stanley's Crumpets, Lancashire
Mushrooms, wild
Mrs Tees Wild Mushrooms, Hampshire
Mussels, smoked
Loch Fyne Oysters, Argyll

Oatcakes
Scottish
MacGregor's Oatcakes, Wigtonshire
McKenzies Oatcakes, Turriff
Oatmeal of Alford, Kincardineshire
Tods of Orkney, Orkney
Wooleys Arran Oatcakes, Isle of Arran
Derbyshire
Chatsworth Farm Shop, Derbyshire
Staffordshire Oatcakes
High Lane Oatcakes, Staffs
Oatflakes, stoneground
Hogarth Ltd, John, Roxburghshire
Oatmeal, organic
Oatmeal of Alford, Kincardineshire
Oatmeal, stoneground
Aberfeldy Watermill, Perthshire
Golspie Mill, Sutherland
Lower City Mills, Perthshire
Oatmeal of Alford, Kincardineshire
Ostrich, smoked
Barrow Boar, Somerset
Macdonald's Produce, Inverness

Pastrami
Summer Isles Foods, Ross-shire
Peasemeal
Golspie Mill, Sutherland
Pheasant, smoked
Rannoch Smokery, Perthshire
Pigeon, smoked
Macdonald's Produce, Inverness
Partridge, smoked
Macdonald's Produce, Inverness
Pork, smoked
Tombuie Smokehouse, Perthshire
Weald Smokery, East Sussex
Preserves
Baxters of Speyside, Morayshire
Chatsworth Farm Shop, Derbyshire
Denrosa Ltd., Perthshire
Isabella's Relishes, Aberdeenshire
Wendy Brandon, Pembrokeshire

Quail, smoked
Macdonald's Produce, Inverness
Tombuie Smokehouse, Perthshire

Salmon, organic
Summer Isles Foods, Ross-shire
Salmon, smoked/cured
Dunkeld Smoked Salmon, Perthshire
Fjordling Smokehouses, Salisbury
Galloway Smokehouse, Dumfries

Keracher, Andrew, Perth
Macdonald's Produce, Inverness
Summer Isles Foods, Ross-shire
Weald Smokery, East Sussex
Salt, sea
Maldon, Essex
Sausage casings
Natural Casing Co. Ltd, Surrey
Sausages
Brymer, Bruce, Angus
Chatsworth Farm Shop, Derbyshire
Murdoch Brothers, Forres
Pickerings, Norwich
Pirie & Son, James, Angus
Slack's, Cumbria
Stephen Smith, Thetford
Cumberland
Woodall's, Cumbria
Gloucester
Cotswold Gourmet, Gloucestershire
Lincolnshire
Curtis, Lincoln
Newmarket
Musks, Suffolk
Powter's, Suffolk
Oxford
Stroff's, Oxfordshire
Game
Fletcher's, Fife
Galloway Smokehouse, Dumfries
Barrow Boar, Somerset
Smoked
Fjordling Smokehouses, Salisbury
Richardson's Smokehouse, Suffolk
Sandbridge Farmhouse Bacon, Wilts
Weald Smokery, East Sussex
Sausage seasonings (premixed)
Spiceblenders, Hull
Smokers
Brook's Home Smokers, Warwicks.
House of Hardy, Northumberland
Innes Walker, Ayrshire
Stamford Smokers, Lincs
West Country Stoves, Devon
Smokies, Arbroath
Keracher, Andrew, Perth
Spink, Alex. Angus

Tea, smoked
Macdonald's Produce, Inverness
Trout, smoked
Fjordling Smokehouses, Salisbury
Loch Fyne Oysters, Argyll
Macdonald's Produce, Inverness
Summer Isles Foods, Ross-shire

Venison, smoked
Fletchers of Auchtermuchty, Fife
Keracher, Andrew, Perth
Macdonald's Produce, Inverness
Rannoch Smokery, Perthshire

Summer Isles Foods, Ross-shire
Tombuie Smokehouse, Perthshire
Weald Smokery, East Sussex

White puddings
Brymer, Bruce, Angus
Scott & Son, John, Fife

CONTACT DETAILS

Aberfeldy Water Mill
Stone ground oatmeal
Mill St., Aberfeldy PH15 2BT
01887 820 803
www.aberfeldy-watermill.co.uk

Allinson
Bread recipe booklet
Allinson Baking Club, PO Box 695, Pewsey SN9 5QX
0870 240 2237
www.allinsonbaking.com

Anderson J. & E.
Honey
Luncarty Villa, Gladstone Terrace, Turriff
01888 562 705
www.theturrabee.com

Barrow Boar
Range of speciality sausages, and various exotic meats including smoked ostrich
Fosters Farm, South Barrow, Yeovil BA22 7LN
01963 440 315
www.barrowboar.co.uk

Baxters of Speyside
Preserves and marmalades
Fochabers IV32 7LD
01343 820 393
www.baxters.co.uk

British Sugar Plc
Sugar with pectin
Silver Spoon Creative Kitchen, PO Box 26, Oundle Road, Peterborough PE2 9QU
01733 563 171
www.silverspoon.co.uk

Bridfish Smokery
Kippers, smoked haddock and smoked mackerel fillets
Unit 1, The Old Laundry Industrial Estate, Sea Road North, Bridport DT6 3BD
01308 456 306
www.gypsy-gibb.com

Brooks Home Smokers
Home smokers
Unit 16, Ladbroke Park, Millers Road, Warwick CV34 5AE
01926 494 260

Chatsworth Farm Shop
Dry cured bacons, sausages, black pudding, oatcakes, marmalades, preserves
Stud Farm, Pilsley, Bakewell DE45 1UF
01246 583 392
www.gustum.com

Cloutie Dumpling Restaurant
Mail order cloutie dumplings
Skye of Curr, Dulnain Bridge, Inverness-shire PH26 3PA
0147985 1359
www.heathercentre.com

Cotswold Gourmet, The
Gloucester sausages
Butts Farm, South Cerney, Cirencester GL7 5QE
01285 862 224
www.cotswoldgourmet.com

Curtis, A. W.
Lincolnshire sausages
Long Leys Road, Lincoln LN1 1PL
01522 511 022

Daniel's Sweet Herring Ltd
Rollmop and sweet diced herring
14 Balmakeith Business Park, Nairn IV12 5QR
01667 451 155

Davies, D. I. J.
Welsh bacon
Newington Shop, Chapel St., Tregaron, Dfyed SY25 6HA
01974 298 565

Denhay Farms
Bacon, ham and farmhouse Cheddar
Broadoak, Bridport DT6 5NP
01308 458 963
www.denhay.co.uk

Denrosa Ltd
Top-quality Scottish honey, preserves, mustards and other products
Victoria St., Coupar Angus PH13 9AE
01828 627 721
www.denrosa.demon.co.uk.

Devereaux & Son., George
Manx kippers
33 Castle St., Douglas, Isle of Man IM1 2EX
01624 673 257
www.isleofmankippers.com

Dukeshill Ham Company
Traditional home cured hams and dry cured bacon
Deuxhill, Bridgnorth WV16 6AF
01746 789 519
www.dukeshillham.co.uk

Dunkeld Smoked Salmon Ltd
Springwells Smokehouse, Brae St., Dunkeld PH8 0BA
01350 727 639
www.dunkeldsmokedsalmon.com

Eastbrook Farm Organic Meats
Wiltshire sausages
Bishopstone, Swindon SN6 8PW
01793 791460
www.helenbrowningorganics.co.uk

Edwards of Conwy
Dry-cured bacon and Welsh sausages
18 High St., Conwy LL32 8DE
www.edwardsofconwy.co.uk

Emmett's Stores
Suffolk sweet pickled and mild cured ham and bacon
The Street, Peasenhall, Saxmundham IP17 2HJ
01728 660 250

H. S. Fishing Co. Ltd
Red herrings
Sutton Rd, Great Yarmouth NR30 3NA
01493 858 118

Fjordling Smokehouses
Smoked pork sausages, kippers, smoked salmon and trout
Dunstable Farm, Pitton Road, West Winterslow, Salisbury SP5 1SA
01980 862 689
www.fjordling.freeserve.co.uk

Fletchers of Auchtermuchty
Fresh and smoked venison and venison products
Reediehill, Auchtermuchty KY14 7HS
01337 828 369
www.fletchersscotland.co.uk

Fortunes
Whitby kippers
22 Henriettas St., Whitby YO22 4DW
01947 601 659

Galloway Smokehouse
Kippers, smoked haddock, game sausages, cheese, smoked salmon etc.
Carsmith, Newton Stewart DG8 7DN
01671 820 354
www.gallowaysmokehouse.co.uk

Golspie Mill
Stone-ground peasemeal; distribution through wholefood distributors
Dunrobin, Golspie KW10 6SF
01408 633 278

Grieve, Lindsay
Champion haggis-maker
29 High St., Hawick TD9 9BU
01450 372109.
www.angus.co.uk

Heather Hills Honey Farm
Own heather and blossom honey; Edradour whisky honey
Bridge of Cally, Blairgowrie PH10 7JG
01250 886 252
www.heather-hills.com

Hickory House
Smoked hens' and quail eggs
Nether Abbey, Newburgh KY14 6HA
01337 842 230

High Lane Oatcakes
Staffordshire oatcakes
597/599 High Lane, Burslem, Stoke on Trent ST6 7EP
01782 810 180
www.high-lane-oatcakes.co.uk

House of Hardy
Small food smokers
Willowburn, Alnwick NE66 2PF
01665 602 771
www.house-of-hardy.com

Inverawe Smokehouse
Smoked salmon
Lorne Fisheries Ltd, Inverawe House Taynuilt PA35 1HU
01866 822 446
www.smokedsalmon.co.uk

Inverloch Cheese Company
Gigha goats' cheese
Leim Farm, Isle of Gigha PA41 7AB
01586 552 692

Isabella's Preserves
Award-winning jams, jellies, marmalades, whisky marmalades, relishes and mustards
Lower Braikley, Methlick, Ellon AB41 7EY
01651 806 257
www.isabellaspreserves.co.uk

Jones and Son, C. H.
Red herrings
174 St Peters St., Lowestoft NR32 2LX
01502 573 863

Lakeland Ltd
Extensive range of innovative kitchen and cookware
Alexandra Buildings, Windermere LA23 1BQ
015394 88 100
www.lakelandlimited.co.uk

Loch Fyne Oysters, Argyll
Wide range of smoked fish and game
Clachan, Cairndow PA26 8BL
01499 600 264
www.loch-fyne.com

Macdonald's Smoked Produce
Smoked cheeses, exotic meats, fish, game and even haggis
Glenluig, Lochailort PH38 4NG
01687 470 266
www.smokedproduce.co.uk

MacGregor's Oatcakes
Oatcakes
22-24 Albert St., Newton Stewart DG8 6EJ
01671 402 678

MacLeod, Charles
Black puddings
Ropework Park, Matheson Rd, Stornoway HS1 2LB
01851 702 445
www.charlesmacleod.co.uk

MacLeod of MacLeod's
Black puddings
17 Church St., Stornoway HS1 2DH
01851 703 384

MacSween of Edinburgh
Haggis and other traditional Scottish products
Dryden Rd, Bilston Glen, Edinburgh EH20 9LZ
0131 440 2555
www.macsween.co.uk

Maldon Crystal Salt Co. Ltd
Sea salt
Wycke Hill Business park, Wycke Hill, Maldon CM9 6UZ
01621 853 315
www.maldonsalt.co.uk

Moniack Castle
Breakfast range of marmalades, jellies and jams
Moniack Castle, Kirkhill, Inverness IV5 7PQ
01463 831 283
www.the-tryst.co.uk

Morris, Jack
Gold medal black puddings
120 Market St., Farnworth, Bolton BL4 9AE
01204 577 727

Mrs Tees Wild Mushrooms
Probably the UK's leading specialist and mail order supplier of wild mushrooms
Gorse Meadow, Sway Rd, Lymington SO41 8LR
01590 673 354
www.wildmushrooms.co.uk

Murdoch Brothers
Sausages and dry-cured bacon
10 High St., Forres IV36 1DB
01309 672805

Musk's
Newmarket sausages
4 Goodwin Business Park, Newmarket CB8 7SQ
01638 662 626
www.musks.com

Natural Casing Co. Ltd
Sausage casings
PO Box 133, Farnham GU10 5HT
01252 850 454

Neave & Son, F. E.
Suffolk sweet-cured bacon
20 Cross Green, Debenham, Stowmarket IP14 6RW
01728 860 240

Nicoll's of Strathmore
Honeys, marmalades and jellies
Strathmore House, Douglastown, Forfar DD8 1TL
01307 463 732

Noble, R. J.
Whitby kippers
Kipper House, Henrietta St., Whitby YO22 4DW
01947 820 413

Oatmeal of Alford
Stone-ground oatmeal and organic oatmeal
Mains of Haulkerton, Laurencekirk AB30 1EL
01561 377 356
www.oatmealofalford.net

Orkney Herring Co. Ltd
Marinated herring in six flavours; marinated salmon and paté
Garson Industrial Estate, Stromness, Orkney KW16 3JU
01856 850 514
www.orkneyherring.com

Pettigrews of Kelso
Marmalades and preserves
Oven Wynd, Kelso TD5 7HS
01573 224 234
www.pettigrews.com

Pickerings
Dry-cured bacon, sausages and black puddings
30 The Street, Old Costessey, Norwich NR8 5DB
www.pickeringsofnorwich.co.uk

Pirie & Son, James
Traditionally cured bacon, sausages etc.
39 Church St., Newtyle PH12 8TZ
01828 650 301
www.localfamilybutcher.co.uk

Powter's
Newmarket sausages
The Pork Shop, Welllington St., Newmarket, Suffolk CB8 0HT
01638 662 418
www.powters.co.uk

Radford's Butchers
York hams
81 Coach Rd, Sleights, Whitby YO22 5EH
01947 810 229

Ramsay of Carluke Ltd
Traditional bacon curers for almost 150 years
22 Mount Stewart St., Carluke ML8 5ED.
01555 772 277
www.wellriggs.demon.co.uk

Rannoch Smokery
*Fresh and smoked venison; smoked chicken,
duck, grouse and pheasant*
Kinloch Rannoch, Pitlochry PH16 5QD
01882 632 344
www.rannochsmokery.co.uk

Rees, Albert
Welsh bacon and Welsh hams
Unit Hs 15, The Market, Carmarthen SA31
01267 231 204
www.carmarthenham.co.uk

Richardson's Smokehouse
Oak smoked kippers, bloaters, sausages
Bakers Lane, Orford IP12 2LH
01394 450 103

Robson & Sons, L.
*Craster kippers, smoked cod, haddock and
salmon*
Haven Hill, Craster, Alnwick NE66 3TR
01665 576 223
www.kipper.co.uk

Rolfe's of Walsham
Suffolk sweet-cured bacon
The Street, Walsham-le-Willows IP31 3AZ
01359 259 225

Sandbridge Farmhouse Bacon, Wilts
*Wiltshire and oak smoked, dry and sweet cured
bacon, hams and smoked pork sausages*
Sandbridge Farm, Bromham, Chippenham SN15
2JL
01380 850 304
www.sandridgefarmhousebacon.co.uk

Scott, George
York hams
81 Low Petergate, York YO1 2HY
01904 622 972
www.yorkham.co.uk

Scott, John & Son
*Haggis, black pudding, white pudding; gluten
free sausages*
25/27 High St., Dunfermline KY12 7DC
01383 724337

Slack's
*Dry-cured bacons, 10 varieties of sausages,
black pudding*
Newlands Farm, Raisbeck, Orton, Penrith CA10
3SG
01539 624 667
www.edirectory.co.uk/slacks

Stephen Smith
*Award-winning sausages and dry-cured and
Norfolk sweet-cured bacon*
23 High St., Watton, Thetford P25 6AB
01953 885 467
Steven.J.Smith@btinternet.com

Spiceblenders
*Premixed spices for most regional sausages plus
other speciality versions*
Malton St., Witham, Hull HU9 1BA
01482 324 103
www.spiceblenders.co.uk

Spink, Alex
Arbroath Smokies
24 Seagate, Arbroath DD1 1BJ
01241 879 056

Stamford Smokers
Small food smokers
Terracotta House, First Drift, Wothorpe, Stamford
PE9 3JL
01780 756 563

Stroff's Speciality Sausages
Oxford sausages
96 Covered Market, Oxford OX1 3DY
01865 200 922

Struan Apiaries
Own creamed honeys
Burnside Lane, Conon Bridge IV7 8EX
01349 861427

Summer Isle Foods
Smoked/cured fish, poultry, beef, cheese
Achiltibuie IV26 2YG
01854 622 353
www.summerislesfoods.co.uk

Swallow Fish
Caster kippers
2 South St., Seahouses NE68 7RP
01665 721 177

Tate & Lyle Sugars
Sugar with pectin
Fruitful Endeavours (Jam-making),
Consumer Advisory Service, Enterprise House,
45 Homesdale Road, Bromley BR2 9TE

Teesdale Trencherman
*Kippers, smoked haddock, dry-cured and smoked
bacon*
Startforth Hall, Barnard Castle DL12 9AG
01833 638 370
www.trencherman.com

Tods of Orkney
Scottish oatcakes
18 Bridge St., Kirkwall, Orkney KW15 1HR
01856 873 165
www.stockan-and-gardens.co.uk

Tombuie Smokehouse
*Smoked bacon, ham, lamb, guinea fowl, duck,
chicken, pork, quail, venison, cheeses*
Aberfeldy PH15 2JS
01887 820127
www.tombuie.com

Weald Smokery
*Very wide range of smoked fish, meats, cheese,
air-dried hams and beef*
Mount Farm, Flimwell TN5 7QL
01580 879 601
www.wealdsmokery.co.uk

Wendy Brandon Preserves
*Range of handmade marmalades, jams and
jellies*
Felin Wen, Boncath, Pembrokeshire, Wales
SA37 0JR
01239 841 568
www.wendybrandon.co.uk

West Country Stoves
Food smoking equipment
The Cobbles, Sandford, Rediton EX17 4NE
01363 772 027
www.coldsmoker.com

Wooleys of Arran
Oatcakes
Invercloy, Brodick, Isle of Arran KA27 8AJ
01770 302 280
www.wooleys.co.uk

INDEX